THE MENACE OF THE SUBLIME
to the
INDIVIDUAL SELF

THE MENACE OF THE SUBLIME
to the
INDIVIDUAL SELF

Kant, Schiller, Coleridge
and the
Disintegration of Romantic Identity

Linda Marie Brooks

The Edwin Mellen Press
Lewiston/Queenston/Lampeter

BH
301
.S7
B76
1995

Library of Congress Cataloging-in-Publication Data

Brooks, Linda Marie.
 The Menace of the sublime to the individual self in Kant,
Schiller, and Coleridge : the disintegration of identity in
romanticism / Linda M. Brooks.
   p.   cm.
 Includes bibliographical references and index.
 ISBN 0-7734-8752-2 (hardcover)
 1. Sublime, The. 2. Self (Philosophy) 3. Kant, Immanuel,
1724-1804. 4. Schiller, Friedrich, 1759-1805. 5. Coleridge, Samuel
Taylor, 1772-1834. I. Title.
BH301.S7B76   1996
141'.6--dc20   96-8613
                                                                              CIP

A CIP catalog record for this book is available from the British Library.

Copyright © 1995 Linda Marie Brooks

All rights reserved. For information contact

The Edwin Mellen Press	The Edwin Mellen Press
Box 450	Box 67
Lewiston, New York	Queenston, Ontario
USA 14092-0450	CANADA L0S 1L0

The Edwin Mellen Press, Ltd.
Lampeter, Dyfed, Wales
UNITED KINGDOM SA48 7DY

Printed in the United States of America

For Geoff, Chris, and Brenda

ACKNOWLEDGMENTS

The Andrew W. Mellon Foundation and the National Endowment for the Humanities provided grants and time needed to research the issues of this study. The generosity and patience of both institutions are due hearty thanks.

Sections of Chapter Three appeared in "Sublime Suicide: the End of Schiller's Aesthetics," *Friedrich von Schiller and the Drama of Human Existence*, edited by Alexej Ugrinski and Natalie Datlov, New York: Greenwood Press, 1988. It is an imprint of Greenwood Publishing Group, Inc. Westport, CT. I am grateful to Greenwood Press for permission to reprint the sections, and to Professors Ugrinski and Datlov for their outstanding Schiller Conference and for their many kindnesses.

The project has gathered too many friends to be listed here -- colleagues, acquaintances, and students whose comments or reactions have sifted into the final versions of this study. Those most involved, those who have done yeoman service, deserve mention. The entire study in its early stages benefited from Murray Krieger's continuous encouragement and numerous comments while reading the manuscript. This in the midst of tragedy. Murray, thank you.

Murray's, Fred Burwick's and David Hills's invaluable discussions of romantic aesthetics and the sublime provided the basis for whatever command I have of Schiller. George Rousseau helped me understand the sublime from the eighteenth-century perspective. Joseph Riddle's careful scrutiny of the chapters at an early stage also helped me clarify the sublime's relation to Kant and Schiller. Robert Leventhal taught me the true meaning of hyperbole in his own comments on the Schiller sections. Raimonda Modiano and Anthony Harding provided invaluable help with the Coleridge sections during readings of the manuscript's later stages. Joel Black, with his rage for order, has ironed out the more intricate sections more than once. And, as always, my student and old friend Jim Tyrell has guided me through the complexities of indexing and computer glitches.

My happiest and most lengthy debt is to my children, Geoff, Chris, and Brenda Brooks: to their unflagging interest despite the tortuous course of this study; to their keen reactions in reading or listening to the knottier sections; to their cheerful encouragement when all seemed lost; to their courage to follow, like Schiller, their own intuitions.

CONTENTS

Acknowledgments vii

INTRODUCTION 1
   Notes 7

1
SUBLIMITY AND THE ROMANTIC SELF 9
   The Problem of the Sublime 10
   Burke's Positive Sublime 14
   Kant's Negative Sublime 19
   Kantian Sublimity and Self-Conceit 24
   Kant and Romanticism's Negative Sublime 27
   The Self of the Negative Sublime 30
   Notes 37

2
KANT'S FRACTURED BRIDGE:
BREAKING THE LINK OF IDENTITY
   The End of the Line 49
   High Jumpers of the Sublime 53
   Sublime Leaps and Beautiful Flights 56
   Kant's Aesthetic Link 58
   Like a Bridge 60
   Sublime Ruptures 62
   Notes 69

3
SCHILLER'S FAILED *ÜBERGANG*: PRETENDING THE SELF
The Illusion of Identity 79
Schein and the Self 82
The Dissimulated *Ich* 86
The Divided Self 90
Sublimity and Self-Annihilation 97
Notes 105

4
COLERIDGE AND THE DISJUNCTIVE PERSONALITY 113
Self and the Sole True Something 114
The Bridge of Imagination 117
The Self as Mediator 121
Completing Schelling with Kant 123
Losing the Self 126
Ignore Thyself 129
Notes 135

5
THE EXTRAVAGANT SELF 141
The Posture of Excess 143
A Desperate Philosophy 146
Subliming the Self 149
A Death's Head Identity 152
Romanticism and a Sublimation Strange 154
Notes 165

Bibliography 169

Index 199

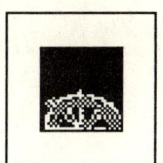

THE MENACE OF THE SUBLIME
to the
INDIVIDUAL SELF

> Deep Sky is of all visual impressions, the nearest akin to a feeling . . . or rather it is a melting away.
>
> -- Coleridge

INTRODUCTION

> The ascendance of the sublime is identical with the need for art to avoid 'playing down' its fundamental contradictions but to bring them out instead. No longer is reconciliation the result of conflict; the only aesthetic purpose is to articulate this conflict.[1]
>
> -- Theodor Adorno

Coleridge's description of his poem "Limbo" articulates the menace referred to in the title of this study: "A Specimen of the Sublime," he wrote of the poem, "dashed to pieces by cutting too close with her fiery Four in Hand round the corner of Nonsense." These hints of the poem's violence and irrationality, and Coleridge's own ambivalent response to the poem's style -- a style that he described elsewhere as containing "some of the most forceful . . . & with the most original imagery that my niggard Muse ever made me a present of" -- indicates the threat that Coleridge sensed in the poem's sublimity, a threat that goes to the heart of romantic arguments for man's ordering self.

The dilemma of the self is not new to romanticism. But the relation of that dilemma to certain types of the sublime is, despite fine recent studies, still unclear. The fundamental question underlying the sublime, a question prodding me since my earliest work on sublimity in 1975, is the impact of its radical incomprehensibility on the romantic idea of the self. Kant, whose account of the sublime is undoubtedly the most important for an understanding of this negative type of sublimity, argued that the sublime's unintelligibility provided the best way to remind us of the noumenal aspect of our selves, our "reason." But this reminder of our spiritual identity hinges on forgetting the rest of what constitutes us: our body, our desires, our relationships with others, our membership in communities -- our basic human understanding. For most of us, and surely for the romantics, the self turns on these connections, these building blocks of meaning supplied by the imagination. The basis of romantic aesthetics is a celebration of the imagination's "esemplastic" or linking force, of its power to spin out the self-other parallels that ground human identity and, particularly, that underwrite the overweening selfhood of the romantic poet.

Kant's sublime undermines these self-defining relationships supplied by the imagination. Despite grudging allowances of the creative genius's imaginative success, his definition of sublimity relies on the imagination's utter failure, on its inability to image forth any and all connections that, for the romantics, underpin a coherent idea of the self.[2] This concept of imaginative powerlessness in Kant's theory is underscored by the fact that art, ostensibly the zenith of the imagination's power, is not even a province of Kant's sublime. Art, Kant writes in the "Analytic of the Sublime," is a "mere appendix to aesthetical judging" (*"einen bloßen Anhang zur äesthetischen Beurteilung"*). Worse, the imagination -- the faculty that spins out the connections that underpin the self -- is, in the final analysis, a "mere nothing in comparison to reason."[3]

Introduction

What Kant's sublime meant for the concept of human identity was obvious to many of his contemporaries. Sublimity did not gird the romantic self, but as Kant wrote, did "violence" ("*Gewalt*") to it. It did not affirm the poet's identity, but undermined it with "pain" ("*Unlust*"), "dejection" and even "revulsion."[4] Of those who sensed the sublime's menace to the self and who attempted to counteract its implications with more positive constructs of identity, Schiller and Coleridge are among the most instructive. Both thinkers reveal the link between the negative sublimity Kant outlined and romantic projects of self-construction. Schiller's failed effort to establish a reconciling or linking aesthetics of the beautiful was the foundation for his concept of a new "sentimental" or "modern" identity; his project was repeatedly subverted by the implications underlying the divisiveness of Kant's sublime. Strongly influenced by Schiller, Coleridge envisioned a similarly "coadunative" or linking imagination that could underwrite the self, but also found this possibility subverted by the divisive implications underlying Kant's sublime. The two poets' ultimate abandonment of their linking theories in light of problems inherent in Kant's theory of sublimity is germinal to romantic poetics and to the modern sense of identity it produced. Given both writers' status as major theorists of the imagination, how, we seem obliged to ask, did such a subversion affect their theories? More important, what were the consequences for a romantic or, what is essentially the same, a modern concept of the self?

Part of the answer lies in Kant's own problems with the principles underlying the sublime. Kant valued unity much as Schiller and Coleridge, positing it not in empirical but in transcendental terms -- beyond phenomenal experience. Though noumenal, Kant's idea of unity constituted the basis of rational thought. By the time he finished his *Critique of Practical Reason*, however, he had discovered a considerable *dis*unity between the ideas of this second *Critique* and those of his earlier *Critique of Pure Reason*. The first *Critique* dealt with how we know things in the world; the second dealt with what is morally right. What he had left out, as he came to realize, was a link between the two. How does one get from the practical to the theoretical or, put another way, how does one make what is morally right part of what one knows about the world? Kant's third *Critique*, as he explained in its Introduction, was meant to bridge that divide.

This projected and, as will be shown, clearly unsuccessful role as link between the disjunctive provinces of his two earlier *Critiques* is fundamental to the sublimity that menaces, and drives, Coleridge's poem "Limbo." The irresolvable disjunction such a sublime imposes evokes an inevitable reconciling or bridging response. Each response is, by the nature of such sublimity, consigned to failure. Much as Schiller's and Coleridge's miscarried attempts to link phenonemal and noumenal, the third *Critique*'s proposed link between theoretical and practical succumbs to this divisiveness inherent in the sublime. What the failure of these bridging efforts shows is that the disjunctive nature of this type of sublimity subverts unity itself, both the logical unity that Kant intended and the self-defining imaginative unity sought by Schiller and Coleridge in their attempts to reknit the subject with external phenomena. With the subversion of such unity -- which effectively sunders noumenal and phenomenal, spirit and flesh, God and man, and all correlate metaphysical pairs -- comes the denial of any coherent sense of human identity.

Given the broad implications of this aspect of the sublime, the province of the present study is relatively narrow. Its purpose is to trace certain aspects of the sublime's subreptive character and the bridging theories they inspire, and to offer a preliminary account of the relation of such bridging projects to romantic ideas of the self. In chapter one, I present a general contrast between the fate of the self in positive versions of sublimity such as Burke's, and the self's less desirable fate in the negative type of the sublime developed by Kant. The second chapter traces the groundwork of romantic self-construction to an increasingly vertical sensibility in the late eighteenth and early nineteenth-century period, and then focuses on the spirit of that self-fashioning as it relates to the disjunction underpinning Kant's philosophy. Chapters three and four examine related phenomena in the works of Schiller and Coleridge -- the sublime's divisiveness, the consequent development of aesthetic theories intended to reconcile that divisiveness, and the self-constructive strategies underpinning these theories. The last chapter is a preliminary foray into the hyperbolic self-construction that accompanies the failure of romantic theories to bridge the sublime divide. The remarks of this chapter are intended not as conclusions but openings, ideally, into future studies of the sublime's relation to the romantic self.

NOTES

1. Theodor Adorno, *Aesthetic Theory* (London, 1986), 282.

2. Kant's claim that the imagination is creative in the case of genius does not lessen the basic role played by the imagination's failure in his theory of the sublime. The creativity of genius occurs in the production of beautiful art, not in the feeling of the sublime. Immanuel Kant, *The Critique of Judgment*, trans. J. C. Meredith (Rpt. 1952; Oxford, 1957). All translations are taken from the Meredith edition, unless otherwise noted, and are cited as *CofJ*. *Kritik der Urteilskraft*, hrsg. Gerhard Lehmann (Stuttgart, 1976). Quotations in German are taken from the Lehmann Reclam edition, unless otherwise noted, and appear as *KdU*. See *CofJ*, "Analytic of the Sublime," "Of the Faculties of the Mind that Constitute Genius," §49, p. 158; "*Von der Vermögen des Gemüts, welche das Genie ausmachen*," §49, pp. 247-48.

3. *CofJ* "Analytic of the Sublime": "a mere appendix," §23, pp. 84-5: "*einen bloßen Anhang zur äesthetischen Beurteilung*," "*Analytik des Erhabenen*," §23, p. 136; "a mere nothing," §26, p. 95: ". . . *unsere Einbildungskraft in ihrer ganzen Grenzlosigkeit, und mit ihr die Natur als gegen die Ideen der Vernunft, wenn sie eine ihnen angemessene Darstellung verschaffen soll, verschwindend vorstellt*," §26, p. 153.

4. "Thus the very violence which is done to the subject through the imagination is judged as purposive *in reference to the whole determination of the mind*. The *quality* of the feeling of the sublime is that it is a feeling of pain in reference to the faculty by which we judge aesthetically." *CofJ*, "Analytic of the

Sublime," §27, p. 98: ". . .*wobei aber doch eben dieselbe Gewalt, die dem Subjekte durch die Einbildungskraft widerfährt, für die ganze Bestimmung des Gemüts als zweckmäßig beurteilt wird. Die Qualität des Gefühls des Erhabenen ist: das sie ein Gefühl der Unlust über das äesthetische Beurteilungsvermögen an einem Gegenstande ist, die darin doch zugleich als zweckmäßig vorgestellt wird,"* §27, p. 157. Elsewhere, the sublime "does violence to the imagination," (*CofJ*, §23, p. 83): "*das . . . Erhabene . . . [ist] gleichsam gewalttätig für die Einbildskraft*" (§23, p. 135).

1

SUBLIMITY AND THE ROMANTIC SELF

> Amid all these fine flights concerning the Soul, the Intellect, and the One, what becomes of poor 'I,' -- of the *Self* of each person? [1]
>
> -- Coleridge

The paradox of what Coleridge called "boundless or endless allness -- the sublime" underpins the romantic quest for "self" -- for unity with the external world. Although numerous studies have added extensively to our knowledge of the sublime,[2] few have dealt systematically with sublimity's relation to the self. This study explores that relation. The work central to this project is the now classic treatment of sublimity -- Thomas Weiskel's *The Romantic Sublime* (1978).[3] Weiskel focuses systematically on what most studies assume, the sublime's reliance on transcendence. Taking Weiskel's outline of sublime transcendence as a starting point, I turn in the opposite direction, examining the nontranscendent character of the sublime -- what Harold Bloom and Weiskel call the "negative sublime," and its implications for romanticism's view of the self.

The Problem of the Sublime

> The transcendent . . . is for the imagination like an abyss in which it fears to lose itself.[4]
>
> -- Kant

> The *one* Object is *most* often the Self or proximate existence -- but sometimes it is not so, as in sublimity . . . ex.gr. -- . . . *'I lost myself*.[5]
>
> -- Coleridge

The term "sublime" is clouded in vagueness, both as a phenomenon and as a critical term. Dismissed regularly as a "loosely descriptive adjective,"[6] its history is checkered by responses ranging from grudging acceptance to wholehearted rejection. Benedetto Croce[7] writes "that it belongs not to the aesthetic but to psychology." E. F. Carritt throws it out of aesthetics because of its "hostile relation to the human will."[8] F. E. Sparshott vacillates between half-hearted interest -- "it takes up a lot of room in this book simply because it has taken up more room in others"[9] -- and serious consideration of its place in aesthetic theory. "Discreditable or not," he writes,

> people do find things sublime, whether or not they use that word to express their finding; and, to them, the sublimity they find is the most important aspect of their most outstanding encounters with the arts . . . Just that is the

justification of giving the sublime a special place in aesthetics (Sparshott 80).

Ironically, charges leveled against the sublime's vagueness indicate both its own obscurity and the possibly consequent obscurity of attempts to deal with it. Despite its problematic nature, however, "sublimity" remains valuable not only because it describes our encounters with the arts, but because of its integral role in romantic and modern ideas of the self.[10]

Put simply, the sublime is an aesthetic concept based on objects that defy conceptualization. The phenomena of sublimity's characteristic tropes -- the endless sky, the boundless sea, a mountain whose peak is concealed by clouds -- demonstrate the sublime's resistance to attempts to bring it within the province of the understanding. Unlike the conventional aesthetics of the beautiful, whose familiar forms please by their correspondence to intellectual constructs, the formless sublime appeals through the terror of the incomprehensible or the overwhelming. Attributed to the third-century philosopher Longinus,[11] the concept of the sublime, following Boileau's translation of the Greek thinker, reemerged in early eighteenth-century England in the theories of Dennis and Addison.[12] Its disconcerting characteristics provided an appropriate aesthetic expression of the increasing skepticism, provoked by scientific and philosophical theories, toward traditional sources of certainty.

Although useful, most discussions of the sublime fail to emphasize sufficiently the distinction between positive, eighteenth-century versions of sublimity and what became romanticism's negative interpretation. To be sure, the sublime is a negative aesthetics *par excellence*, questioning art's representational function. But what distinguishes the romantic forms of sublimity is their incapacity to come to terms with this negativity. Eighteenth-century theorists of sublimity, such as Dennis, Addison, Beattie, and particularly Edmund Burke in his *Philosophical Enquiry into the Origin of Our Ideas of the Sublime and the Beautiful*, overcome the impasse through an appeal to the godhead and to the efficacy of the human imagination. According to Burke, while we cannot understand the sublime, we can trust that its incomprehensibility gives evidence of an ordering, if awesome, divinity. We can also, through an imaginative response to the sublime object, "expand" or "rise" to meet and even *participate* in its overwhelming power. Hence, though eighteenth-century theories reflect the doubt of the era, they contain a built-in resolution given by a faith in the divine order behind the sublime, and in the power of the imagination that deals with it. Romantic accounts of sublimity frequently lack such solutions, a lack that darkens romantic poetics and that casts doubt on its concepts of the self.

Kant's romantic type of sublimity is sharply illustrated in the writings of Schiller and Coleridge, especially in relation to their view of human identity. Strongly influenced by Kant, the two writers encounter similar problems with, and respond in similar ways to the implications of Kant's theory. Both poets are celebrated for having presented imposing arguments for a recuperative or imaginatively triumphant aesthetics of the beautiful (in Coleridge, of the "imagination") that underwrites the self. However, the gradual subversion of their theories by principles outlined in the Kantian sublime demonstrates the affect of this type of sublimity within the romantic project.

Central to the sublime is the subject's notion of self and its relation to the sublime object. Without this relation -- if the self disappears in an experience of the sublime, as Raimonda Modiano observes accurately -- the sublime ceases to have meaning.[13] The self's relation to the sublime can vary, however, and this variation dictates the type of sublimity manifested. In its more positive forms, the sublime affirms and heightens the subject's sense of identity. Schiller, who was to encounter the darkest aspect of sublimity produced in the preromantic era, still maintained a belief in the sublime's capacity to elevate the onlooker. "This consciousness of ourselves," he wrote, "must always dominate in order that the great and the horrible may have for us an aesthetic value. It is because the soul before such sights as these feels itself inspired and *lifted above itself* that they are designated under the name . . . sublime."[14] Schiller's words express the positive version of sublimity mentioned earlier. But they also reveal an important departure from the sublime's more sanguine theorists, such as Burke, Beattie, and others. To such eighteenth-century thinkers, while the sublime elevates, it leaves the observer intact. There is no *ecstasis* in eighteenth-century sublimity; we do not "*lose ourselves*," as Coleridge describes above. Similarly, with Schiller's sublime, even in its positive manifestation, we are taken *beyond* ourselves (*sich . . . über sich selbst gehoben*).[15] This early sign of the self's disintegration in such an experience is what comes to define Kant's darker, negative sublime.

Just as Burke's *Enquiry* represents the eighteenth-century version of the sublime, Kant's *Critique of Judgment* marks the shift to its romantic counterpart. Kant's "Analytic of the Sublime" presents a model for a type of sublimity that has become irresolvable. Unlike the theological and imaginative certainties of Burke's account, Kantian sublimity both denies a teleology and presupposes a failure of the imagination. On the whole, as Meyer Abrams has noted, Kant's philosophy rests on a theological construct.[16] His theory of the sublime thus plays a minor role in his critical system in which intellect (*Verstand*) and imagination (*Einbildungskraft*) are subordinated to pure reason (*Vernunft*). However, the negative implications of this theory become a major feature in romantic aesthetics. The questioning of the self inherent in the sublime's unrepresentability foreshadows what Hegel would characterize in his *Aesthetic Lectures* as the waning of romantic art, and what both Schiller and Coleridge would call "sentimental," or romantic, art's "empty play of representation."

Burke's Positive Sublime

> I began to ask myself; is a system of philosophy, as different from mere history and historic classification, possible? . . . I was for a while disposed to answer the first question in the negative, and to admit that the sole practicable employment for the human mind was to observe, to collect, and to classify. But I soon felt, that human nature itself fought up against this willful resignation of intellect: and as soon did I find, that the scheme taken with all its consequences and cleared of all its inconsistencies, was not less impracticable, than contra-natural.[17]
>
> -- Coleridge

Compared to Burke,[18] Kant's account of the sublime[19] is markedly negative. Burke's is a thrilling idea of the sublime. It is terror, darkness, overwhelming size, formlessness, and the like. But it is always scintillating, a "delightful" horror, as he calls it. We come away from Burke's sublimity exhilarated. Though Kant builds on Burke's idea of the sublime's terror, obscurity, overwhelming dimensions, and power, the necessary effect of Kant's theory of the sublime is dejection, a feeling of disheartened malaise rather than exhilaration. By rejecting the eighteenth-century emphasis on taste, Kant refocuses the sublime on an epistemological concern. The question of sublimity becomes that of what we can and cannot know, essentially the question of the limits of human knowledge. What Kant's sublime tells us, ultimately, is that we cannot *know* anything. Certainly, Kant assures us, we can have a negative idea (that is, the idea that we cannot get a sensible idea) of the absolute concepts of our sublime human reason. And that, says Kant, should console, indeed, exalt us, because that faculty, or "reason," is ours. But something is amiss with this purely rational exaltation of Kant's. The Kantian sublime, our awesome reason, even though it is ours, does not seem part of us. In Kant's descriptions it is chastising, even alien: it is a "foreign will," a "secret power."[20] It does not seem part of our self, or our personal identity. Thus, while our sublime reason grasps the concept of totality, the "merely" corporeal remainder of our being -- and that involves not only our sensory but our emotional, imaginative, and cognitive features -- is left, in Kant's words, "humiliated."

The negative character of Kant's sublime is thrown into sharp relief when compared more closely with Burke's. The technical distinction, itself significant, is the difference between an argument based on faculty psychology and one grounded on transcendental principles. Burke's is an empirical theory of aesthetic taste, based on sensations and our physiological and psychological responses to them. Kant's is a transcendental theory of aesthetic judgment, based on a formal or *a priori* system of non-sensory principles of morality, out of which aesthetic judgment forms an integral component. Burke's is a physical theory of the sublime. It rests on the distinction between the positive "pleasure" of the beautiful, and the painful "delight" of sublimity. "Terror," arising from "passions related to self-preservation which turn mostly on pain and danger," is the "ruling principle" of Burke's sublime (*Enquiry* 84).

Whether Burke cites "vast cataracts," "raging storms," architectural structures of great magnitude, or simply the "starry heaven" as objects that excite a feeling of sublimity, each of his examples provide a source of terror which is *external*, that is, phenomenally objective, and which is essentially vast and powerful (*Enquiry*, 103, 104, 109). Even the sublime's celebrated "obscurity" becomes a component of vastness, since its fearfulness lies in "the eye not being able to perceive the bounds" (*Enquiry* 101). Vastness, in turn, proves tantamount to power: "I know of nothing sublime," Burke remarks with finality, "which is not some modification of power" (*Enquiry* 94). But neither vastness nor power can evoke the sublime without also arousing a sense of danger. For instance, the "terror" and hence the sublimity of "power" would utterly disappear if one could "strip a degree of strength of its ability to hurt" (*Enquiry* 94-5). As in most eighteenth-century theories, Burke requires a necessary relation of power to vastness, and a characterization of both as a clear, if controlled, threat. In a word, the Burkeian sublime is a boundless force which terrifies because of its inherent associations with destruction. The sublime is "sublime" because of its intrinsic superiority, indeed hostility, to human physical and cognitive capacity.

Eighteenth-century writers draw from the sense of an external, hostile force to create the sublime in their poetry. As artistic representation, the sublime assumes the form of external objects which are either physically or psychologically overwhelming. The physically terrifying is usually posed by natural phenomena -- precipitous chasms, raging seas, and clashing storms emerging as a trademark of eighteenth-century sublimity. The psychologically overwhelming in external phenomena, that which defies human cognition, assumes both natural and man-made form. The infinite sky, endless horizons, boundless bodies of water, enormous mountains whose peaks are undiscernible, become poetic representations of the sublime's psychological devastation. Man-made objects are equally awesome; ancient ruins, crumbled by time, defy understanding through their temporal remoteness; architectural structures presenting a repetitive series of shapes, such as arches which seem to recede infinitely, undermine human perception of their limits in space.

Though initially overwhelmed by such phenomena, however, eighteenth-century and pre-romantic writers draw from such experience a marked sense of exaltation, connected with the idea of the hidden presence of an infinite deity. Burke clearly links the sublime to the divine, the awe of sublimity being nothing less than "the inseparable union of a sacred and reverential awe, with our ideas of divinity" (*Enquiry* 70). Nothing, Burke observes, can "strike the mind with its greatness which does not make some sort of approach to infinity" (*Enquiry*, Boulton, 63). To Burke, infinity is ultimately the divine, the awesome spirit of God in *The Book of Job*, which Burke quotes as an "amazingly sublime" example of an obscure and infinite "presence" (*Enquiry*, Boulton, 63). In our experience of the sublime, he writes, "everything terrible in nature is called up to heighten the awe and solemnity of the divine presence" (*Enquiry*, Boulton, 69). We aspire to this ultimate sublimity, for "whilst we consider the Godhead, we are bound to ascend to these pure and intellectual ideas."[21] Burke's theory epitomizes the "dilating" exaltation of eighteenth-century sublimity: "Infinity fills the mind with delightful horror" because the sublimity of God is the ultimate infinity, and the contemplation of this ultimate "dilates and elevates the soul" (*Enquiry*, Boulton, liv, 73).

It is true that this sense of a boundless force provokes an initial "terror" in the subject, an "astonishment" in which "all motions are suspended" in a state of an "unnatural tension of the nerves."[22] Yet, though painful, such horror is "tinged with tranquility" and "delight" (*Enquiry* 88, 149). Within these positive notions of "tranquility" and "delight" -- notions stemming ultimately from a sense of union with God -- Burke outlines the major element of eighteenth-century sublimity that will dissolve in Kant's account. In the face of terrible objects, Burke writes, we experience a type of mental "swelling," expanding as it were, to meet and embrace a part of the object's power. We thus establish an affinity with the sublime object and, ultimately, with the divine presence behind it. The subject's equality and participation produces the "delight" that dispels our terror:

> Whatever . . . tends to raise a man in his own opinion produces a sort of swelling and triumph, that is extremely

> grateful to the human mind; and this swelling is never more perceived, nor operates with more force, than when without danger we are conversant with terrible objects; the mind always claiming to itself some part of the dignity and importance of the things which it contemplates (*Enquiry* 84).

Burke senses the vagueness of Longinus's metaphor that the subject participates in sublimity through her heightened response to it, essentially that she partakes of greatness simply by being thrilled by it. Attempting to clarify the manner in which this delightful elevation occurs, he offers other, equally nebulous images of sublime "ascent," such as the claim that "Terror . . . raises the emotions of the body" (*Enquiry* 147). He manages to articulate his idea of the self's exaltation, however, in his consideration of infinity and the imagination.

Burke's focus on the imagination is important, since it shows the main distinction between Burke's sublimity and Kant's, a distinction that accounts for much of what occurs to the idea of self in the romantic sublime. Infinity, which belongs to vastness or magnitude,[23] Burke explains, "offers a situation in which the imagination meets no check" (*Enquiry* 101). Magnitude is therefore requisite to sublimity, as is the avoidance of "small" objects, in response to which "the imagination cannot rise to any idea of infinity" (*Enquiry* 103). But this magnitude, and the imagination's response to it, is where Burke's sublimity differs from Kant's. Unchecked by any phenomenal limitation in the sublime moment, the Burkeian imagination assumes command. In face of a boundless object, the subject's imagination responds by rising to and embracing -- if not containing in sensible image -- the idea of infinity that magnitude embodies. This, then, is the self's exaltation in Burke's sublime -- the terror followed by the subject's "tranquility" and "delight" in the sense of its own expansion and participation in the sublime object. The self's exaltation is brought about almost exclusively by the imagination, through whose boundless activity we seem to ascend or expand to meet the sublime object, and to embrace, ultimately, the divine.

Burke's account of the subject's fate in the sublime is clear. Confronted with the sublime object, the subject's imagination responds actively, positively, and effectively, producing a "triumph that is extremely grateful to the human mind." Though the imagination cannot produce a sensible image, or cannot ground a rational cognition of the sublime force that confounds our empirical perception, it nevertheless "lifts" us through its labor and creates a process of transcendence by which we meet and participate in the overwhelming object, rest, "under the arm, as it were, of almighty power" (*Enquiry*, Boulton, 68). Though initially terrifying, the Burkeian sublime allows the subject, *as* mutable being, to succeed, to claim for herself some part of the dignity and importance of the sublime force that she contemplates. If we "tremble" with the sublime, Burke writes, we also "rejoice" (*Enquiry*, Boulton, 68).

Kant's Negative Sublime

> '[S]elf-conceit' . . . is something which determination by the moral law 'strikes down' and 'humiliates' altogether.[24]
> -- Paul Crowther

Crowther's characterization of Kant's moral law, of its stringency toward anything that smacks of self-aggrandizement, is accurate. It also bodes ill for Burke's sublime exaltation of the self when such exaltation is transferred to Kant's version of sublimity. Kant's sublime initially seems a reflection of Burke's.[25] But while Kant is clearly struck by the elevating implications of eighteenth-century or Burkeian sublimity, his account reveals a distinctly moral resonance,[26] one in keeping with his concepts of the moral law. As a result, Kant's view of sublime loftiness proves inimical to Burke's idea of the subject's exaltation as an affective representation in art. In the elevation of Kantian sublimity, the subject's imagination plays no positive, or creative role. And although Kant borrows Burke's distinction between beauty's "pleasure" and sublimity's delightful "pain," Kant's ground for this delight rests on noumenal or non-sensory principles. Kant is influenced by Burke's use of fear as the turning point between beauty and sublimity. And he will at times acknowledge a possible delight in sublime fear.[27] But he is adamantly against the physiological emphasis of Burkeian "terror," and the consequently physical character of Burke's "pleasant pleasure" and "delightful pain." This physicality precludes the properly noumenal grounding of an aesthetic, Kant argues, since both "*gratification* and *pain*, though preceding from the imagination or even from representations of the understanding, are always in the last resort corporeal." Judgments based on "terror," "pain," and the consequent "pleasure" or "delight" which attend them are "egoistic." They deny the necessary "*pluralistic* validity" (universality) of aesthetic judgments which, if they are pure, rest upon an *a priori* principle (*CofJ* 32). They smack of self-conceit.

Grounded in the transcendental, Kant's theory of sublimity necessarily requires that the imagination, since it deals with both noumenal and phenomenal provinces,[28] fail. This is the point at which the self's exaltation, *as* affective response, disappears. The phenomenal sense of elevation, of a delightful affinity with powers beyond the subject's ken, is supplanted in Kantian sublimity by a sense of deprivation and sacrifice.[29]

Like Burke, Kant distinguishes the two main features of sublimity as vastness and power, naming them, respectively, the "Mathematical" and "Dynamic" sublime (*Mathematisch-Erhabenen, Dynamisch-Erhabenen*).[30] It is in that object, Kant observes, "provided it gives signs of magnitude and power, that nature chiefly excites the ideas of the sublime" (*CofJ*, §23,

84). Unlike Burke's theory, however, which argues for an external source of terror, the force that evokes awe in Kantian sublimity is an internal one. More important, while Burke's account rests on an imaginative triumph, Kant's is grounded on the imagination's inadequacy: "No sensible form," Kant writes,

> can contain the sublime properly so-called. This concerns ideas of the reason which, although no adequate presentation is possible for them, *by this inadequateness* . . . are aroused and summoned into the mind.[31]

The subject's sense of imaginative inadequacy is central to the Kantian response to sublimity. Kant repeatedly insists on the necessity of the imagination's failure and the unnerving implications of that failure:

> The feeling of our incapacity to attain to an idea *which is a law for us* is *respect*. Now the idea of the comprehension of every phenomenon . . . in a whole of intuition, is an idea imposed upon us by the law of reason, which recognizes no . . . measure except the absolute whole. But our imagination, even in its greatest efforts, in respect of that comprehension, . . .[and] with reference to the presentation of the idea . . . exhibits its own limits and inadequacy[.][32]

As a boundless external force which, according to Burke, could be overcome by the imagination, Kantian sublimity permits the imagination merely a futile attempt before its collapse.[33] The failure, more significantly, produces not exaltation in the subject but obedient "respect" ("*Achtung*").

To Kant, the source of such sublime fear or awe is an internal one. In a sublime experience, the external object only "excites" a process by which we then discover that our fear and displeasure have their source within ourselves. "The object," says Kant, only "lends itself to a presentation of a sublimity discoverable in the mind" (*CofJ*, §23, p. 84). Such internal sublimity, the "Reason," is a vast and supersensible power within us, which not only comprehends infinity, but actually contains it as a unit beneath its standard of absolute totality. According to Kant,

> ... if we enlarge our empirical faculty of representation (mathematical or dynamical) with a view to the intuition of nature, reason inevitably steps forward, as the faculty concerned with the independence of the absolute totality, and calls forth the effort of the mind, unavailing though it might be, to make the representation of sense adequate to this totality. This effort, and the feeling of the unattainability of the idea by means of the imagination is itself a presentation of the subjective finality of our mind . . . the mind's supersensible province.[34]

Imagine the Kantian observer. She looks at the sky which, say, rolls with turbulent gray clouds and stretches endlessly into an infinite horizon. Her reason immediately contains it and calls upon the representational faculty, the imagination, to embody this contained infinity in terms of a sensible image. Although the imagination, with the understanding, can create units of measure vast as the earth's dimensions, it is still bound to images of measurable, sensible form (*CofJ*, §26, p. 95). In the face of this boundless sky, therefore, the imagination falls back, resoundingly inadequate. Here is Kant's switch. Not only does the imagination fall back, but when it does, it is not the boundless sky that appears awesome but the reason itself, the vast and supersensible power within our minds, which can contain the sky, indeed the universe, as a grain of sand.

It is frequently argued that Kant's sublime produces a type of pleasurable satisfaction, as in Burke, precisely through this imaginative failure. This is a serious misconception. It is not "pleasure" but a voluntary self-abnegation, rather like the Carthusian "pleasure" of wearing a hair-shirt. It is derived from the idea that if one, as a sensible being, cannot fully participate in such autonomous reason, he can at least be in willing accordance with it by eschewing all connection with his corporeal existence. This voluntary resignation is scarcely what Burke meant by "painful delight." Throughout Kant's philosophy, reason is equivalent to and substitute for God. But since we must not think of it as a "being" in any way, we might call it a supersensible "power," which rather than existing beyond or above us, is within us.³⁵ One's accordance with the universal and unconditional laws of such power has nothing to do with "pleasure" or even painful delight, as it is ordinarily conceived. Described by Kant, it is rather a kind of intellectual self-sacrifice, the reason for which must always remain mysterious. As Kant explains,

> the satisfaction in the sublime . . . is then only *negative* . . . a feeling that the imagination is depriving itself of its freedom by receiving a final determination in accordance with a law other than its empirical employment. It thus acquires an extension and a might greater than it sacrifices -- the ground of which, however, is concealed from itself -- while yet it *feels the sacrifice or deprivation, and, at the same time, the cause to which it is subjected.*³⁶

The imagination, the faculty that deals with our phenomenal as well as noumenal existence, presents only a sense of sacrifice and deprivation. One wonders what the imagination's "employment," other than its "empirical" one, might be in the sublime, since at this absolute level it must remain inactive and inadequate. Equally puzzling is the "might and extension" which the imagination supposedly gains, since the "ground" of such extension or elevation is "concealed" from us as sensible, indeed, as cognitive beings. As Kant observes, "a pure judgment upon the sublime must . . . have no end belonging to the Object as its determining ground, if it is to be aesthetic and not to be tainted with any judgment of understanding or reason."³⁷ In the last analysis, Kant implies, neither reason (our noumenal element) nor understanding (our cognitive faculty), can enter into the actual aesthetic judgment of the sublime. We are thus not even aided by reason, for in such a judgment the imagination is left to fend for itself without the support of either rational or cognitive powers.

Kantian Sublimity and Self-Conceit

> I am = Verb active sui generis, causative but not transitive.[38]
>
> -- Coleridge

In terms of the subject's understanding, Kantian sublimity is meaningless. This is not surprising if we consider that the thrust of Kant's three *Critiques* is an examination of the limits of human knowledge. In the *Critique of Pure Reason*, Kant argues that ultimate knowledge can only be transcendentally assumed. True knowledge is not sensible but "intelligible;" its truths are of a synthetic *a priori* (i.e., non-sensory) character, and thus are inaccessible through any concepts which draw upon the sensible province of human existence. "Man," says Kant, "is a mere trifle in relation to the omnipotence of nature, or rather to its inaccessible highest cause."[39]

Whatever knowledge we *are* able to attain is at best negative knowledge, since "insofar as human beings can accomplish anything," he writes, "it can only be through their negative wisdom" (*Contest* 189). This negative wisdom is precisely the awareness that we *can not know*. True knowledge, says Kant, is constituted by the fundamental ideas of reason: "What reason actually demands," he writes,

> is that all knowledge obtained by the understanding should be in the last resort dependent on certain highest Principles,

> for only if this is so can Reason's fundamental Idea, the
> Idea of a complete system of all knowledge, be regarded as
> capable of being realized.[40]

And yet, even if we subjugate all our information obtained as sensible beings (those sensory intuitions filtered through the imagination and the understanding) we still cannot attain to a true, a complete system of knowledge. While "what we are expected to do," H. W. Cassirer writes, "is to try to discover the totality of conditions, . . . this does not mean that they are ever given to us, nor even that we shall ever be able to fulfill Reason's demand. The Idea of a totality is an ideal maximum which can never be attained in the sensible world" (Cassirer 42). As phenomenal beings, in other words, we can know nothing. This works well for Kant's ideas of morality, which rest on a complete abnegation of the self. The ultimate truths, human knowledge *per se*, should be as immaterial as the moral principles by which humanity is guided. But it is a questionable aesthetics.[41]

It is not accidental that the subversiveness of Kant's sublime to human cognition would also render it a paradigm of self-denial. As an aesthetics, it rests on an inherent hostility to the sensuousness of human being. All the subject's material elements fall away in Kant's sublime, even the understanding which, again, participates in the senses. The subject is devastated, yet only in this devastation does she get a fleeting reflection, as through a glass darkly, of pure, noumenal truth. Cognition or understanding and imaginative representation of this "knowledge" is precluded, however. There is nothing, on these levels, that she can "know". (Indeed, it is difficult to understand on what level Kant would claim we, as human creatures, *do* know something.)

Two problems lead to the unmeaning which characterizes Kant's sublime. First, Kant has already asserted in the *Critique of Pure Reason* that human knowledge is grounded in the subject's imagination. All synthesis of external phenomena, including the sense of the linear succession of events -- the certainty of a cause/effect relationship without which all knowledge becomes dubious -- rests, according to Kant, upon the imagination: "Synthesis in general," he tells us, "is the mere result of the power of imagination, a blind but indispensable function of the soul, without which we should have no knowledge whatsoever."[42] Second, Kant claims that knowledge rests as well on self-conscious or "transcendental apperception:"[43]

> There can be in us no modes of knowledge, no connection or unity of one mode of knowledge with another, without that unity of consciousness which precedes all data of intuitions, and by relation to which representation of objects is alone possible. This pure original unchangeable consciousness I shall name *transcendental apperception* . . . this unity of consciousness would be impossible if the mind in knowledge of the manifold could not become conscious of the identity of function whereby it synthetically combines it in one knowledge. The original and necessary consciousness of the identity of the self is thus at the same time a consciousness of an equally necessary unity of the synthesis of all appearances according to concepts, that is, according to rules.[44]

Both of these fundamental grounds of knowledge, however, are subverted in the "Analytic of the Sublime." By making the imagination's inadequacy the definitive feature of sublimity, Kant avers that the sublime determines a certain impossibility of knowledge. By confining apperception or self-consciousness to the purely subjective arena, giving it only "subjective validity,"[45] Kant reduces it to the same "merely regulative" (hypothetical) rather than "constitutive" (genetic) function as that *a priori* principle by which we give ourselves a rule of formal unity for our aesthetic judgments. On Kant's definition, *apperception*, a fundamental element of human knowledge and of human identity, has nothing to do with objective phenomena -- no constitutive relation to the external world.[46] In Kant's sublime, the grounds of objective knowledge are denied. The remaining "knowledge," a purely subjective one, throws us back upon a self which possesses no comprehensible relation to the world.[47]

Kant and Romanticism's Negative Sublime

> . . . absorbed by some unknown gulf into some unknown abyss.[48]
> -- Coleridge

Given its antagonistic stance toward the self, Kant's theory of sublimity sets the stage for romanticism's peculiarly autobiographical version of the negative sublime. Romantic negative sublimity is the aesthetic theory and praxis of an autobiographical aesthetics -- a skeptical process of self-construction that occurs in response to such antagonism. This view of negative sublimity differs from its usual meaning. The term "negative sublime" is not new. Harold Bloom has used it to characterize Coleridge's unfinished poems fragments "Limbo" and "Ne Plus Ultra." However, though Bloom suggests the term's relation to his "revisionary ratio" "*Apophrades*" -- the "return of the dead" or ultimate phase in the development of the "strong" poet -- he tells us neither what the negative sublime actually is, or what features of the two poems would indicate negative sublimity. We are left with the tantalizing if somewhat cryptically expressed idea that had Coleridge continued in this vein, he "could have become, at last, the poet of the Miltonic abyss," and that these two fragments "enable Coleridge to claim a corner of Milton's Chaos as his own."[49]

Thomas Weiskel took the negative sublime more seriously. Nearly all its features are assembled in his book, though he neither contrasts it to Burke's positive account nor examines Kant's third *Critique* in any detail. Weiskel argues that the negative sublime, unlike the "egotistical" or "Wordsworthian" sublime, reflects Kant's theory of sublimity. The purpose of negative sublimity, Weiskel observes accurately, is to expose and thus subvert the illusory or "subreptive" character of beauty's reconciling function, its intrinsic affinity, one might add, with human meaning. As an inherently subversive, indeed, "defeatist" aesthetic (Weiskel 44), or rather as an inherently subversive or defeatist "ethic" (Weiskel 46), the negative sublime characteristically leads to "existential alienation," in fact to "alienation in all its forms" (Weiskel 43, 46). Taken too far, to the extreme lengths that Schiller takes Kant's theory of sublimity, the negative sublime becomes a "transcendent dead-end," "the sublime as suicide" (Weiskel 48).

Weiskel, in short, had nearly assembled the puzzle of negative sublimity. The negative sublime is indeed a clear expression of Kant's theory. Its purpose is precisely the subversion of any recuperative notion of aesthetics. And, though Weiskel did not pursue it, the literature which it characterizes not only assumes the inevitable tone of existential resignation, but often slips toward the idea of suicide. Both tendencies are patent in Schiller and Coleridge. But Weiskel focused on the "structure and psychology of *transcendence*," which led him to dismiss the possibility of its existence as a poetic phenomenon: "Fortunately," he writes, "there were many ways of eliding, attacking or subverting the central paradox of the negative sublime, and its pure expression is to be encountered only in theory or in the Germans" (Weiskel 48). The pure expression of the negative sublime, however, not only pervades English as well as German literature (theory and otherwise), but becomes a defining characteristic of a large part of its poetry.

If Weiskel did not actually take up the negative sublime as critical apparatus, he described a process occurring in all sublimity which elucidates the sublime's relation to the self. The sublime moment, he wrote, consists of a three-phase "progress"[50] which 1) begins with a state of equilibrium, 2) moves into the terror and confusion brought about by the unsettling eruption of a sublime object or idea, and 3) ends with the mind's reappropriation of equilibrium, though on a higher or transcendent level. Phase three is characterized by the mind's recovering its balance by "constituting a fresh relation between itself and the object such that the very indeterminacy which erupted in phase two is taken as symbolizing the mind's relation to a transcendent order" (Weiskel 24). What occurs to the third step in Kant's sublime illuminates sublimity's role in romantic self-construction.

Weiskel's third phase, the reassuring idea of the mind's "relation to a transcendent order," is missing in Kant's sublime, and in the art that reflects it. As we have seen, the attempt at "transcendence" in Kantian, or negative, sublimity -- the task of following the Königsberg philosopher up the Carthusian ladder of rational asceticism -- is, in terms of an aesthetics, dubious at best.[51] Were the sublime anything but Kantian, the transcendence which Weiskel claims for it might be operative. It cannot be, however, under Kant's negative emphasis. With such sublimity, what confronts us is not an "aesthetics of transcendence," as the title of Weiskel's book would imply -- "transcendence" describes Burke's *positive*, eighteenth-century sublime -- but an aesthetics of inadequacy. By "inadequacy" I mean the subject's inability to give an anthropomorphic order to the external phenomena that surrounds her -- the relational order, supplied by the imagination, that constitutes conventional concepts of the self. As Weiskel remarks, but unfortunately does not develop: "The defeat of the imagination accomplishes subjectively the end of the natural order" (Weiskel 42). It is with the absence of such order that the subject, as "natural" self, disappears.

The focus on Kant in this discussion does not mean that Kant "caused" or initiated negative sublimity. However, because of the problem of locating a starting point of negative sublimity, either in terms of what Edward Said calls the "active" sense of "beginning" ("The beginning A leads to B") or the "passive" one ("X is the origin of Y"), let us simply consider Kant as an early symptom rather than the origination of the negative sublime.[52] It could be argued that Kant's particularly negative interpretation of an already subversive aesthetic, could not have appeared as anything *but* negative sublimity in the third *Critique*. To take an aesthetic whose subject matter inherently defies human comprehension, and to turn it on the question of human knowledge, is to ensure the production of the negative sublime. But, again, Kant is only a very early symptom. This theoretical symptom, however, contains the germ of every aesthetic expression of negative sublimity in romanticism.

The Self of the Negative Sublime

The world a tomb is . . .[53]

-- Schiller

The consequences of the Kantian negative sublime are both psychological and representational. In view of the character of sublimity, the two are in fact inseparable. For the sake of clarity, we may divide them into two distinct categories: the effect on the identity of the poet, and the effect on the representational mode in which the poet attempts to express meaning. With regard to the poet's identity, the negative sublime always occurs at the expense of the empirical, the personal "self." We have seen Kant's dismissal of the sensuous, the cognitive, and the imaginative elements of humanity in his description of the proper, the dutiful, response to the sublime. In Kant's sublime, these synthesizing faculties by which one conventionally orders reality -- their reassuring discoveries of similarities in the dissimilar, of identity in difference, both of which, incidentally, are ensured in the reconciling aesthetics of the beautiful -- are swept away. The negative sublime is an aesthetics not of identity but of difference, of the gap that opens between the empirical subject and the world she perceives. As Weiskel observes, by subverting the reconciliation intimated by the beautiful, "the sublime splits consciousness into alienated halves" (Weiskel 48). The tenuous ground of such duality leads the poet away from the concerns of phenomenal existence -- now rendered insignificant -- to an increasing interest in the other-worldly. Confronted with the notion of the sublime, Kant himself reaches for the supersensible concept of the *Ding an sich* or "thing in itself" in an attempt to ground his unstable *a priori* principle for judging sublimity. Schiller and Coleridge turn to the supersensible as well in their response to sublimity -- through an appeal to the divine or, if the difficulty of vision overwhelms, to thoughts of mortality. Either way, negative sublimity inevitably occurs at the expense of the poet's sensible, or empirical, existence.

At such a cost, the question of identity or, essentially, the question of the self becomes a central concern. This is a distinctly alienating aesthetic, throwing the poet deep within herself. Praising its isolating tendency, Frances Ferguson remarks that "the sublime elevates one's individual relations with that mountain (or whatever natural object one perceives as sublime) above one's relationship to other human beings."[54] Ferguson's idea that the sublime removes the poet from society is important, for it underscores the intrinsically solitary character of sublimity. However, the negative sublime does not "elevate" the poet either above or beyond society in any hierarchical sense of her having become superior to the madding crowd. On the contrary, it tears the poet from a communal existence simply because she has lost her comprehension of, and her affinity with, its conventional systems. The negative sublime throws the poet back upon herself, not as a positive and deliberate anodyne against society's ills, but as a negative response of stark confusion at society's normative structures. Society's order has become alien, incomprehensible.

The "fear" instilled by the negative sublime is an intensely private one, a sense of inadequacy which the poet has little desire to submit to public scrutiny. It is a conceptual incapacity before Kant's "mathematical" sublime, a conceptual and physical inadequacy before his "dynamic" sublime, both of which Schiller will find epitomized in sublimity's ultimate province, death. The state induced by this negative sublimity reminds the poet that she is indeed alone, even in a crowd; as she enters the world, so shall she leave it. It is this solitude, this self-centeredness that characterizes the negative sublime. It is not the isolated superiority that Ferguson describes, but Burke's "darkness," "silence," "vacuity," and "privation," raised by Kant's theory to metaphysical proportion. Schiller will speak of the "living death" of solitude. Coleridge will call its self-imprisonment a "lifeless, dull privation," and will summarize its vacuous insularity in the Ancient Mariner's words: "Alone, alone, all, all alone."

The centrality of self is not merely an alienating proposition, however, but a virtually maddening one, in which the possibility of reappropriating meaning is constantly disrupted. In throwing the poet back upon himself, the negative sublime locks him within a self-reflexive circle in which he is constantly brought up short by the sudden awareness of the fictitiousness of his own attempts at signification. The aesthetics characteristic of such a state comes to reflect a fundamental ambiguity, which embraces both the poet's conscious attempt to escape the parabastic or illusion-breaking specularity of his self-consciousness, and the self-reflexive questioning of such attempts. Such an aesthetics of negative sublimity produces a radically self-reflexive discourse, a literature which calls into question its own authenticity. On the one hand, Schiller complains of the disruptive effects of his specular nature upon his ability to create; and Coleridge repeatedly calls for "outness," for "externality" in order to escape the imaginative paralysis of his own specular predicament, the "viper thoughts" that coil around his mind. On the other hand, Schiller will cast off the "veil" of meaning promised by a reconciling beauty as a mere "counterfeit," and Coleridge will admit his own bad faith, his conscious adherence to "falsehood," and his awareness that his *Notebook*, his fictive existence, is his "only friend."

A striking literary tendency thus emerges, a double gesture which manifests both the poet's demystified or sentimental/modern state (his despair of meaning), and his willed projection of a mystified or naive/classic state (his belief in meaning). With this double gesture, the poet consciously *forgets* his fragmented empirical identity, replacing it with a fictive self in which some significance, however illusory, might inhere. This autobiographical endeavor becomes a central feature of the aesthetics of negative sublimity. Schiller prescribes it in *Naive and Sentimental Poetry*; Coleridge attempts it in the *Biographia* and immortalizes its futility in the fate of the Ancient Mariner, who is doomed to retell his story of self throughout eternity.

Construction of the self under such circumstances is impossible, however, using only conventional modes of representation -- the representational modes of an aesthetics of the beautiful. Reflecting the tenuousness of the self in the sublime, the poet's representational process itself becomes problematic. Negative sublimity is sheer indeterminacy. Even on a philosophical level, the sublime remains an inherently indeterminate concept, precisely because of the uncertainty of any predication with regard to it. Its indeterminacy strikes Kant himself, who must reach for an ontological concept simply to ground the sublime's epistemologically grounding principle. Such indeterminacy is only exacerbated by the sublime's inherent obscurity. Because Kant draws liberally, too liberally, from what Burke and other eighteenth-century writers defined as sublime formlessness, even he succumbs to its abyssal incoherence. Its formlessness leads Kant to neglect to provide the sublime with a transcendental deduction -- a deduction which would ensure its universality -- and thus seriously weaken his argument for judgments of the sublime as pure aesthetic judgments.

More significantly, if the sublime's indeterminacy troubles Kant on a philosophical plane, its unrepresentability proves even more serious for the poet guided by such an aesthetics. Limiting himself to transcendental considerations, Kant could at least adhere to the concept of the moral law -- the demand of pure reason -- as an ultimately ordering or organizing principle. (In fact, very much according to Kant's design, it is the surrounding chaos of sublimity that causes the adamantine character of that law to stand out in clear relief.) On a phenomenal level, however (the province of the poet), the negative sublime is a sheer representational "lawlessness," which the poet can only attempt to control. Coleridge, for instance, will confront and futilely attempt to contain what he considers the philosophical counterpart of sublimity, associationist philosophy, whose stark materiality intrinsically undermines the self. Schiller, struck with the same "infinite heterogeneity" of the sublime in *Naive and Sentimental Poetry*, will ultimately invoke Kant's moral law, simply to avoid "an infinite fall into a bottomless abyss."

In so far as the poet's autobiographical project relies on beauty's synthesizing function, therefore, it must necessarily prove inadequate. Again, the negative sublime is an aesthetic not of identity but of difference; it subverts the unifying approach of traditional aesthetics, the connections needed for conventional notions of personal identity. Walter Hipple notes a telling omission in eighteenth-century aesthetic theory which suggests that the sublime's tendency to undermine the beautiful -- and along with the beautiful, the morality underpinning traditional selfhood -- was suspected long before Schiller and Coleridge confronted it. The suspicion motivated strategies intended to avoid rather than confront the question:

> The real question of Hutcheson's use of Addison is: Why, in supplementing Addison's simple notion of beauty with his own more philosophical conception, did Hutcheson leave Addison's grandeur and novelty untransformed? . . . The explanation presumably is, that grandeur and novelty do not share with beauty that particularly intimate connection with morality . . . Beauty emerges [in Hutcheson] from the relation of part and part, part and whole, and so . . . does morality; the senses appropriated to beauty and morality are concerned, therefore, with analogous relationships. Grandeur, however, is not susceptible of this kind of analysis . . . Construction of an aesthetics of sublimity alongside that of beauty might well have meant dissolution of the exclusive benevolism of Hutchesonian ethics.[55]

"Construction" of this subversive aesthetics is precisely what has occurred by the time Schiller and Coleridge begin to write. Unlike the eighteenth-century poet, Schiller and Coleridge can no longer draw on the linear relation of part to part and part to whole that beauty supplies. The sublime has exposed its unifying function as illusion.

Confronted with an aesthetics which is not susceptible to linear or conventional representation, the poet of the negative sublime devises what becomes a characteristic conceptual vocabulary. "Duality," "conflict," and "division" become common ideas. Explaining his failed poems, Coleridge notes the destructive tension between the infinite character of his philosophical concepts and their representation in poetic form. Schiller crystallizes the unresolved divisiveness of the representation of the sublime, observing that the "sentimental" or "modern" poet, essentially the romantic poet, "is always involved with two conflicting representations . . . actuality as a limit and his ideas as infinitude." The very material of the sentimental or romantic poet is the incomprehensibility of the sublime; he must craft his poetry and, more importantly, his alternative identity, from "whatever is insusceptible of representation."

The conflict between the representation of actuality and the idea of infinitude disturbs sequentiality and *telos*, precluding the ideal of a linear work informed by closure. Kant himself had admitted that while the goal of reason was a complete system of knowledge, such totality was unachievable in the sensible world. With the aesthetics of sublimity, the poet's work thus necessarily lacks entelechy, and the poet's shift to a hyperbolic level in order to craft a closure becomes a major characteristic of this subversive aesthetics. Following Kant's example, Schiller and Coleridge attempt to ensure entelechy through their own "bridging" models. In Schiller it becomes the play drive, in Coleridge, the poetic imagination, both of which, working through their projected ability to span the gap between sense and reason, or subject and object, may reestablish the possibility of a self, or "life," telically and eschatologically directed toward a purposeful end.

NOTES

1. In *Inquiring Spirit: A Coleridge Reader* (New York, 1968), 15.

2. Samuel Monk's *The Sublime* (1935) has been joined by Walter Hipple's *The Beautiful, The Sublime, and the Picturesque* (1957) and Marjorie Hope Nicolson's *Mountain Gloom and Mountain Glory* (1959) in charting the role of sublimity in the neoclassical period. Albert Wlecke's *Wordsworth and the Sublime* (1973), Stuart Ende's *Keats and the Sublime* (1976) and more recently, Steven Knapp's *Personification and the Sublime* (1985), Suzanne Guerlac's *Impersonal Sublime* (1990), Vincent De Luca's *Words of Eternity* (1991) and Frances Ferguson's *Solitude and the Sublime* (1992) have examined the vagaries of sublimity in romanticism. Ferguson's "Burke and the Bathos of Experience" (1981) and Jean-François Lyotard's "Philosophy of Phrases" (1981) have extended the concept of sublimity beyond the romantic time frame, interpreting its anti-social character as a model of postmodernism. Lyotard's "What is Postmodernism?" (1984) praises the sublime's "lawlessness" and Ferguson its linguistic "obscurity" as countermeasures to contemporary instrumental reasoning. In similar focuses on language, Neil Hertz's "A Reading of Longinus" (1984) relates the Longinian sublimity to the problems of quotation and representation, and Jerome Christensen (*Coleridge's Blessed Machine of Language* (1981) uses Coleridge to argue that an "obscure" style is tantamount to a "sublime" style. Hertz's *The End of the Line* (1985) and Henry Sussman's *Psyche and Text* (1993) explore the role of psychoanalysis in the sublime, Hugh Silverman's and Gary Aylsworth's edition *The Textual Sublime* (1990) relates sublimity to poststructuralism, as does Jeffrey Librett's collection *Of the Sublime: Presence in Question* (1993), and Patricia Yaeger's "Toward a Female Sublime" (1989) posits a specifically "female" version of sublime aesthetics. Other useful sources on the sublime are the special issues of *New Literary History* 2 (Winter 1985) and *Studies in Romanticism* 2

(Summer 1987).

3. Thomas Weiskel, *The Romantic Sublime: Studies in the Structure and Psychology of Transcendence* (Baltimore, 1976). Hereafter, Weiskel.

4. *CofJ*, "Of the Quality of the Satisfaction in our Judgments upon the Sublime," §27, p. 97: "*Das Überschwengliche für die Einbildungskraft . . . ist gleichsam ein Abgrund, worin sie sich selbst zu verlieren fürchtet,*" *KdU*, "*Von der Qualität des Wohlgefallens in der Beurteilen des Erhabenen,*" 27, pp. 155-56.

5. *The Notebooks of Samuel Taylor Coleridge*, ed. Kathleen Coburn (New York, 1957-), IV, 4540, f36 T. Hereafter *CN*.

6. Malcome Ware, *Sublimity in the Novels of Ann Radcliffe* (Upsala, 1963), 60.

7. Benedetto Croce, *Aesthetic* (New York, 1929). Croce treats the sublime under the heading of "the aesthetic of the sympathetic" in which it is grouped with other "Pseudo-aesthetic concepts" (87). Such concepts are "completely foreign to Aesthetic," he writes, since "Aesthetic does not recognize the sympathetic" (88). Not only is the sublime "excluded from Aesthetic," but it is cast from philosophy altogether, being with its sister concepts "without philosophic value." The sublime, then, "belongs to Psychology" and shares with its fellow "psychological constructions" the "impossibility of rigorous definition" (89).

8. E. F. Carritt, *The Theory of Beauty* (Rpt. 1914; London, 1962), 160. Hereafter, Carritt.

9. F. E. Sparshott, *The Structure of Aesthetics* (Toronto, 1963), 79. Hereafter, Sparshott.

10. To Jean-François Lyotard, for instance, the "*Begebenheit*" (event or occurrence) of the sublime "marks what has been called 'postmodernity' to designate our time" ("Philosophy of Phrases," 25); in Lyotard's "What is

Postmodernism?" the unrepresentability of the sublime indicates postmodernism's refusal of the modernist nostalgia for form. See Lyotard, "Answering the Question: What is Postmodernism?" in *The Postmodern Condition*; Linda M. Brooks, "Sublimity and Theatricality: Romantic Pre-Postmodernism" *Modern Language Notes*, 105, no. 5 (Winter, 1990): 939-64.

11. Longinus, "On the Sublime," *Critical Theory Since Plato* (New York, 1981); 76-102. The concept of the "sublime" first appears in a work entitled "On the Sublime." The author and date of composition are unknown, though estimates place it in the first century A.D. Mistakenly attributed over the centuries to the third-century Greek philosopher Cassius Longinus because of its length, his authorship of the piece has been retained. Hereafter, Longinus.

12. Though unaware of the critical significance of his discovery, Addison was the first to establish the sublime as a distinct aesthetic category. See Monk, *The Sublime* (Ann Arbor, 1960); 21, 46, 54.

13. Raimonda Modiano, "Humanism and the Comic Sublime," *SiR* 2 (Summer, 1987); 231-245.

14. Schiller, "Detached Reflections on Different Questions of Aesthetics," *Complete Works of Friedrich von Schiller*, ed. Dole (Boston, 1910), V 277. All translations of Schiller are taken from the Dole edition unless otherwise noted, and cited as Dole. "Zerstreute Betrachtungen über verschiedene äesthetische Gegenstände." *Schiller's Werke, Nationalausgabe* (Weimar, 1962), XX; 229. Citations of Schiller in German are taken from the *Nationalausgabe* edition unless otherwise noted, and appear as *Werke*. Hereafter, "Detached Reflections."

15. Schiller, "*Zerstreute Betrachtungen über verschiedene äesthetische Gegenstände,*" *Werke*, XX; 229.

16. See Meyer Abrams, "Kant and the Theology of Art," *Notre Dame English Journal*, XIII (1981); 75-106.

17. *CN*, Text, III, 281-82.

[18.] Edmund Burke, *A Philosophical Enquiry into the Origins of Our Ideas of the Sublime and the Beautiful*, *Works* (London, 1964), I, 49-178. References to Burke's *Enquiry* are taken from the Bohn edition unless otherwise noted, and appear as *Enquiry*.

[19.] See *The Critique of Judgment*. Though published in 1790, Kant's outline of the sublime in the third *Critique* was little known in England until Coleridge's introduction of it in the early decades of the nineteenth century (Monk 6). Kant's earlier work *Observations on the Feeling of the Beautiful and the Sublime* (1763) primarily mirrored Burke's *Enquiry*, and consequently had little effect on Burke's influence. The seeds, however, of his particularly stringent view of the sublime may be found in this early work, especially his distinction between the "splendid" and the "noble" sublime, the latter becoming the sublimity of the third *Critique*.

[20.] See Kant's description of reason in *Dreams of a Spirit-Seer*: "When we consider our needs in relation to our environment," he writes, "we cannot do it without experiencing a certain sensation of restraint and limitation which lets us know that a foreign will, as it were, is active in us, and that our liking is subject to the condition of *external* consent. A *secret power* compels us to adapt our intentions to the will of others, or to this *foreign will*, although this is often done unwillingly, and conflicts strongly with our selfish inclination." Kant, *Dreams of a Spirit-Seer, Illustrated by Dreams of Metaphysics* (London, 1900), 63, my italics.

[21.] *Enquiry*, 97; *Enquiry*, Boulton, 68.

[22.] *Enquiry*, 88, 145. For a discussion of the significance of physical pain in Burke's theory, see G. S. Rousseau, "Quotation Marks: Burke's Enquiry and the Aesthetics of Pain," *Journal for the History of the Behavioral Sciences* (April, 1985).

[23.] *Enquiry* 100-101. In section eight, which he entitles "Infinity," Burke writes: "Another source of the sublime is infinity; if it does not rather belong to the last." By "the last," he means section seven, entitled "Vastness."

24. Paul Crowther, *The Kantian Sublime: From Morality to Art* (Oxford, 1989), 23. Hereafter, Crowther.

25. In the earlier, less systematic work on the subject, *Observation on the Feeling of the Beautiful and the Sublime* (1763) which succeeds Burke's *Enquiry* by six years and which clearly echoes its predecessor, Kant makes no mention of Burke. He does acknowledge the *Enquiry* in his 1790 *Critique of Judgment*, though, referring to it as an instance of the "merely empirical" and "physiological" approaches to the problem which, compared to his own "transcendental" treatment, are narrow and unsuccessful (*CofJ*, "Of the Problem of a Deduction of Judgments of Taste," §36 p. 130; "*Einem solchen, wenn es nicht bloßes Empfindungs-, sondern ein formales Reflexions-Urteil ist. . . ,*" "*Von der Aufgabe einer Deduktion der Geschmacksurteile,*" §36, p. 204.

26. Kant writes: ". . . a feeling for the sublime in nature cannot well be thought without combining therewith a mental disposition which is akin to the moral" (*CofJ*, "General Remark upon the Exposition of the Aesthetical Reflective Judgment," §29, p. 109: "*In der Tat läßt sich ein Gefühl für das Erhabene der Natur nicht wohl denken, ohne ein Stimmung des Gemüts, die der zum moralischen ähnlich ist, damit zu verbinden,*" "*Allgemeine Anmerkung zur Exposition der äesthetischen reflecktierenden Urteil,*" §29, p. 173. Such statements run through the aesthetic half of his *Critique*.

27. "Bold, overhanging . . . threatening rocks; clouds piled up the vault of the sky, moving with lightening flashes and thunder peals; volcanoes in all their violence of destruction; hurricanes with their track of devastation; the boundless ocean in a state of tumult . . . [are] the more attractive the more fearful they are, provided only that we are in security, "*CofJ*, "Of Nature Regarded as Might," "Analytic of the Sublime," §28, p. 100: "*Kühne überhangende gleichsam drohende Felsen, am Himmel sich auftürmende Donnerwolken, mit Blitzen und Krachen einherziehend, Vulkane in ihrer ganzen zerstörenden Gewalt, Orkane mit ihrer zurückgelassenen Verwüstung, der grenzenlose Ozean, in Empörung gesetzt . . . machen unser Vermögen zu wiederstehen, in Vergleichung mit ihrer Macht, zur unbedeutenden Kleinigkeit. Aber ihr Anblick nur um desto anziehender, je furchtbarer er ist, wenn wir uns nur in Sicherheit befinden,*" "*Von der Natur als einer Macht,*" §28, p. 160. This and a few similar statements are the closest Kant comes to the feeling Burke speaks of -- those coinages such as "tranquility tinged with terror" -- which mark the sensuous nature of his theory. In Kant, fear is necessary to "excite" the ideas of sublimity. But he means by this only

to set them in motion. This reveals an important difference in the two theories. Not only is sublime fear not sensuously relished as it is in Burke, even the "negative pleasure" of sublimity is scarcely emphasized.

28. Kant explains that the "imagination, in accordance with laws of association, makes our state of contentment depend upon physical conditions" (*CofJ*, "The Deduction of Aesthetical Judgments on the Objects of Nature Must not be Directed to What We Call Sublime in Nature but Only to the Beautiful," §30, p. 121: "*Die Deduktion der äesthetische Urteil über die Gegenstände der Natur darf nicht auf das, was wir in dieser erhaben nennen, sondern nur auf das Schöne, gerichten werden,*" §30, p. 190.

29. I am aware that in Kant this feeling of deprivation and sacrifice is for a higher cause which ultimately allows the dejected viewer of terrifying natural objects to become aware of a supersensible faculty within himself which surpasses all that appears sublime in the phenomenal or natural world. But this awareness occurs only on a noumenal level (that of our supersensible reason), and not at all on the level of emotional response (that of the imagination) on which the poet operates.

30. Though the imagination proves inadequate to the comprehension of both the Mathematical and Dynamic sublime, there exist, according to Kant, faculties in the mind which are adequate to comprehend and surmount them. Kant does distinguish the reason as the supersensible faculty adequate to the Mathematical sublime, since it comprehends even infinity. Reason, recognizing only totality or "the whole" as its standard, contains infinity itself as a mere "unit" under that standard (*CofJ*, §26, 92-93). But in regard to the Dynamic sublime, though a faculty ideally exists which is adequate to comprehend and surpass it, Kant fails to distinguish precisely what that faculty is. Since we are dealing with the type of sublimity in Kant in which the imagination falls back and we then look with awe at this super-sensible faculty within us, we must deal with the type of Kant's sublime which provides us with such a faculty.

31. *CofJ*, "Transition from the Faculty Which Judges of the Beautiful to That Which Judges of the Sublime,"§23, p. 84, italics mine: "*das eigentliche Erhabene kann in keiner sinnlichen Form enthalten sein, sondern trifft nur Ideen der Vernunft: welche, obgleich keine ihnen angemessene Darstellung möglich ist, eben durch diese Unangemessenheit, welche sich sinnlich darstellen läßt, rege gemacht und ins Gemüt gerufen werden,*" "*Übergang von dem Beurteilungsvermögen des*

Schönen zu dem des Erhabenen," §23, p. 136

[32.] *CofJ*, "Of the Quality of the Satisfaction in Our Judgments of the Sublime," §27, p: 96: *"Das Gefühl der Unangemessenheit unseres Vermögens zur Erreichung einer Idee, die für uns Gesetzt ist, ist ACHTUNG. Nun ist die Idee zur Zusammenfassung einer jeden Erscheinung, die uns gegeben werden mag, in die Anschauung eines Ganzen, eine solche welche uns durch ein Gesetz der Vernunft auferlegt ist, die kein anderes bestimmtes für jedermann gültiges und unveränderliches Maß erkennt, als die Absolut-Ganze. Unsere Einbildungskraft aber beweiset, selbst in ihrer größten Anstrengung, in Ansehung der von ihr verlangten Zusammenfassung eines gegebenen Gegenstandes in ein Ganzes der Anschauung . . . ihre Schranken und Unangemessenheit . . . ,* "Von der Qualität des Wohlgefallens in der Beurteilung des Erhabenen," §27, p. 154

[33.] I conflate the "fear" of the dynamic sublime (power) with the "respect" of the mathematical sublime (magnitude). Kant himself uses them interchangeably, speaking of fear in his discussion of magnitude. Indeed, he cannot maintain a rigorous difference, since for the purposes of his system or moral philosophy, he never completes his theory of the sublime (see Carritt 153).

[34.] *CofJ*, "General Remark upon the Exposition of the Aesthetical Reflective Judgment," § 29, p. 108: *"wenn wir unser empirisches Vorstellungsvermögen (mathematisch, oder dynamisch) für die Anschauung der Natur erweitern; so tritt unausbleiblich die Vernunft hinzu, als Vermögen der Independenz der absoluten Totalität, und bringt die, obzwar vergebliche, Bestrebung des Gemüts hervor, die Vorstellung der Sinne dieser angemessen zu machen. Diese Bestrebung, und das Gefühl der Unerreichbarkeit der Idee durch die Einbildungskraft, ist selbst eine Darstellung der subjecktiven Zweckmäßigkeit unseres Gemüts im Gebrauche der Einbildungskraft für dessen übersinnliche Bestimmung,"* "Allgemeine Anmerkung zur Exposition der ästhetischen reflecktierenden Urteil," §29, pp. 171-72.

[35.] It is significant that to Kant, the most apt expression of sublimity is the Jewish commandment: "Thou shalt make unto thyself no graven images," *CofJ*, "General Remark upon the Exposition of the Aesthetical Reflective Judgment," §29, p. 115: *"Vielleicht gibt es keine erhabenere Stelle im Gesetzbuche der Juden, als das Gebot: Du sollst dir kein Bildnis machen,"* "Allgemeine Anmerkung zur Exposition der ästhetischen reflecktierenden Urteil," §29, p. 182.

36. *CofJ*, "*General Remark upon the Exposition of the Aesthetical Judgment,*" §29, p. 109: "*Das Wohlgefallen am Erhabenen . . . ist daher auch nur negativ . . . nämlich ein Gefühl der Beraubung der Freiheit der Einbildungskraft durch die selbst, indem die nach einem andern Gesetze, als dem des empirischen Gebrauchs, zweckmäßig bestimmt wird. Dadurch bekommt sie eine Erweiterung und Macht, welche großer ist, als die, welche sie aufopfert, deren Grund aber ihr selbst verborgen ist, statt dessen sie die Aufopferung oder die Beraubung, und zugleich die Ursache fühlt, der sie unterworfen wird,*" "*Allgemeine Anmerkung zur Exposition der äesthetischen reflecktierenden Urteil,*" §29, p. 173.

37. *CofJ*, "Of That Estimation of the Magnitude of Natural Things Which is Requisite for the Idea of the Sublime," §26, p. 91: "*Ein reines Urteil über das Erhabene aber muß gar keinen Zweck des Objeckts zum Bestimmungsgrunde haben, wenn es äesthetisch und nicht mit irgendeinem Verstandes- oder Vernunft-urteile vermengt sein soll,*" "*Von der Größenschätzung der Naturdinge, die zur Idee des Erhabenen erforderlich ist,*" §26, pp. 147-8.

38. Coleridge, *CN*, IV, 4523, T.

39. Kant, *The Contest of the Faculties*, in *Kant's Political Writings* (London, 1977), 185. Hereafter, *Contest*.

40. H. W. Cassirer, "The Critique of Pure Reason," in *A Commentary on Kant's Critique of Judgment* (London, 1938), 32. Hereafter, Cassirer.

41. Crowther argues that Kant does nod toward art in his "Analytic of the Sublime." See Crowther, "Sublimity, Art, and Beyond," in *The Kantian Sublime* (Oxford, 1989), 152-74.

42. Kant, *Critique of Pure Reason*, trans. Norman Kemp Smith (New York, 1965), b103, p. 112. Hereafter, *CofPR*.

43. Kant's unity of apperception or self-consciousness is admirably clarified by Orsini:

> ... we could not reach even an empirical generalization if the representations involved were not brought together as the objects of one and the same consciousness. If all the representations of red belonged to one consciousness, and those of heat to another, neither could reach the conclusion that red things are hot. So all consciousness involves self-consciousness, and the identity of consciousness in the various acts of thought presupposes the unity of consciousness with itself. If I were not aware of myself, I could not recognize myself in successive acts of perception and unify them in a generalization.

Elsewhere, Orsini explains:

> The transcendental unity of apperception upon which everything else is shown to depend, is the act of self-consciousness, or as Kant designated it 'the I think.' ... self-consciousness constitutes the Transcendental Unity of Apperception. It is Transcendental, because it is the a priori condition of all experience: without awareness of self there can be no awareness of anything else.

See G. N. G. Orsini, *Coleridge and German Idealism* (Carbondale, 1969), 120, 117. Hereafter, Orsini.

44. *CofPR*, A107-108, p. 136.

45. See Paul Guyer, *Kant and the Claims of Taste* (Cambridge, MA: 1979), 42, 290. Hereafter, Guyer. See also Guyer's remark that, cut off from empirical intuitions (phenomenal experience), Kant's notion of transcendental apperception entails "the absence of any means for verifying claims of knowledge," 98.

46. Kant does not even make the unity of apperception an act of the will, which would at least give it a higher, that is, a transcendental reality, as Coleridge, and Schelling, tried vainly to do. See Coleridge, *Biographia Literaria*, eds. Engell and Bate (Princeton, NJ: 1983), I, 153, 155n3. References

to Coleridge's *Biographia* will be taken from this edition unless otherwise noted and will appear as *BL*.

[47.] Part of Kant's stringency regarding what we can know would seem to lie in his own ambivalent position. On the one hand, as Kemp Smith has pointed out, is Kant's

> 'critical' view, according to which all statements that transcend experience are delusive: man cannot possibly acquire knowledge of an unconditioned whole of which only a conditioned part is accessible to him. But the other trend leads strongly toward philosophic Idealism: ideas of the whole provide knowledge of the unconditional (in Orsini, 134).

Kant wants knowledge of the unconditional but eschews mystical claims to such knowledge. Thus, in order to assert the possibility of such knowledge, he must create rules ever more restrictive of the corporeal subject, whose claim to absolute knowledge must, of necessity, be impossible. Only in this way can Kant move toward synthetic *a priori* truths, knowledge attained by the pure reason, which has long since abandoned any connection to the sensible world.

[48.] *BL*, II, 139.

[49.] In a somewhat contradictory remark, Bloom claims that Coleridge's poems, for the most part, "are not the poems of a strong poet, that is, of a man vaulting into the Sublime." This becomes puzzling in view of Bloom's almost immediately preceding characterization of Coleridge as a "high-jumper of the Sublime" (255). I would suggest that this earlier characterization is what Bloom is actually struggling with, and indeed clearly senses in Coleridge's poems, "Limbo" and "Ne Plus Ultra." Bloom briefly considers the conversation poems and then the several "supernatural" poems in which, to Bloom, Coleridge "refuses the full exercise of a strong poet's misprisions" (256-64). "After that, sadly enough," he writes,

> we have only a very few occasional poems of any quality by Coleridge, and they are mostly not the poems of a strong poet, that is, of a man vaulting into the Sublime . . . But there is a significant exception, the late manuscript fragment

"Limbo" and the evidently still later fragment "Ne Plus Ultra." Here, and I think here only, Coleridge experiences the particular reward of the strong poet in his last phase, what I have called the apophrades or return of the dead, not a Counter-Sublime but a negative Sublime, like the Last Poems of Yeats or The Rock of Stevens. Indeed, negative sublimity is the mode of these Coleridgeian fragments, and indicates to us what Coleridge might have become had he permitted himself enough of the perverse zeal that the great poet must exhibit in malforming his great precursor. "Limbo" and "Ne Plus Ultra" show that Coleridge could have become, at last, the poet of the Miltonic abyss, the bard of Demogorgon. Even as they stand, these fragments make us read Book II of *Paradise Lost* a little differently; they enable Coleridge to claim a corner of Milton's Chaos as his own (264).

One can see why Bloom must deny Coleridge the status of "sublime" or "strong" poet. Bloom does not consider the fact that much of Coleridge's prose is itself a clear wrestle with the negative sublime. Confined to the idea that a "strong" poet is only one who defiantly misreads and rewrites a precursor's poem, Bloom restricts his thoughts to Coleridge's "poetic" works, and hence misses the "strength" of this "ostrich" poet, as Coleridge calls himself, a strength which when clarified in the prose, in turn reveals the intensely "sublime" character of Coleridge's poetry. Of course, a great deal depends on what one means by "strength." Nevertheless, in spite of his own critical paradigm, Bloom struggles toward an acknowledgement of the "negative sublimity" of Coleridge's writing, particularly as it is evidenced in Coleridge's two fragment poems. He can do little with the insight, however, simply because it does not fit a critical model which though brilliant and highly useful, calls for the "strength," the courage of an Oedipal revolt, rather than the same qualities inherent in an existential resignation. See Harold Bloom, "Coleridge: The Anxiety of Influence," in *New Perspectives on Coleridge and Wordsworth* (New York, 1972), 247-69.

[50.] Weiskel is aware of the fictive "temporality" of this construct. See p. 24.

[51.] The irrelevant and even unfavorable character of Kant's theory of sublimity to an actual aesthetics is underscored not only by his own admission that the "sublime" is "a mere appendix to the analytical judging" (*CofJ*, "Analytic of the Sublime," §23, pp. 84-5), but also in a remark made by J. H. Bernard in the "Introduction" to his translation of the third *Critique*. "And it is not a little remarkable," Bernard writes,

> that the man who could write thus feelingly about the emotions inspired by grand and savage scenery [in his writings on the sublime] had never seen a mountain in his life. The power and insight of his observations here are in marked contrast to the poverty of some of his remarks about the characteristics of beauty (*CofJ*, trans. J. H. Bernard, editor's Introduction, xxi).

Bernard's focus on Kant's treatment of sublimity without the benefit of the natural models is useful. However, one should note that Kant's inclination to the negative aspects of sublimity was inherent, while his attitude toward what Schiller called beauty's harmonious or reconciling features was an uncomfortable one. Though aided by the beautiful (versus sublime) environs of Königsberg, Kant faltered tellingly in his depictions of beauty.

[52.] Edward Said, *Beginnings: Intention and Method* (Baltimore, 1975), 6. Hereafter, *Beginnings*.

[53.] Schiller, "The Poetry of Life," 1. 152.

[54.] Ferguson, *Solitude and the Sublime* (1992), 32, 45-46; Ferguson, "Bathos," *Glyph* 8, p. 73.

[55.] Walter John Hipple, Jr., *The Beautiful, the Sublime and the Picturesque in Eighteenth-Century British Aesthetic Theory* (Carbondale, IL: 1957), 34-5. Hereafter, Hipple.

2

KANT'S FRACTURED BRIDGE: BREAKING THE LINK OF IDENTITY

> Spanning, as with a bridge sublime,
> That awful lapse of human time,
> That gulph unfathomably spread
> Between the living and the dead.[1]
>
> -- Thomas Love Peacock

The End of the Line

An end to the road is reached in romantic music, which presents a future neither determined by the past, as in Bach, nor summoned by the past, as in Mozart, but a sequence of peaks of intensity undirected to an end.[2]

-- Wilfred Mellers

Romantic art relinquishes closure. Its paintings reflect the blurs of Constable or the ruins of Piranesi, its music the surges of Schumann and the gaps of Chopin. Peaks of undirected intensity, such art identifies with a "freedom intuited from the 'deepest self,'" Mellers writes. Its music changes not through rational laws as in baroque temporality, or through the conscious decisions of a moral agent, as in classical temporality, but from "a revelation of the 'incongruence between . . . concrete actuality . . . and the self's struggles to shape it.'" "Struggle, failure, and renewed struggle" become romantic ends in themselves, Mellers writes of Brahms, whose movements "begin in major affirmation and end with minor reversal." The tendency reverses Bach's harmonic counterpoint -- a technique aimed at "the pinnacle of the rational: a reflection of Leibnitz's 'mirror of the mind of God.'"

The tendency that Mellers discerns in romantic art is epistemological. Constricted by the implications underlying the sublime, romantic thought is random, desultory, abortive. Like the force that erupts between Wordsworth and his goal in the Simplon Pass, the sublime blocks the romantic observer's path, opening an abyss between the subject and her desire for a meaning beyond the certainty of death. This characteristic disruption produces a waning of linear progression in romantic art, a disappearance of what Karl Kroeber calls romanticism's "movement or flow in time."[3] In *The Sense of An Ending*, Frank Kermode traces the process -- already full-blown in the romantic period -- by which thought's traditionally "rectilinear" progress toward its "end," and narratives whose meanings are informed by endings, give way to stories lacking a *telos*. Not infrequently, such art becomes a bizarre remedy for telic absence. In such cases, artistic expressions of sublimity's apocalyptic experience become substitutes for, or foreshadowings of, that "end." If romantic writers could not in good faith reach back to origins and beginnings, in other words, they could verify existence by fictional confrontations with endings, often with death itself. Romantic attempts at narrative, a genre associated with plot and linear movement, produced instead formless so-so tales bereft of conclusion.[4] Most remained beginnings in Said's sense of the word, implying return and repetition rather than simple linear accomplishment.[5]

A corresponding transformation of biblical narrative suggests the epistemological depth of the subversion of linearity in romanticism. According to Hans Frei, the precritical realistic reading of biblical narrative was grounded in the belief held that "if the real historical world described by the several biblical stories is a single world of one temporal sequence, there must in principle be one cumulative story to depict it. Consequently, the several biblical stories narrating sequential elements in time must fit together into one narrative."[6] As the eighteenth century progressed, this mode of interpretation and the *Weltanschauung*, or world view, it represented broke down. As a result, traditional biblical narrative, in which meaning could unfold only within a causal or linear sequence of actual or historical events, events further strengthened by typological and figurative accretion, gave way to an emphasis upon allegorical and proleptic readings of single events (Frei 4-6). These latter are removed from their position within historical sequence, remaining isolated fragments rather than sequential moments of a narrative.

The sublime's arrest of movement is the aesthetic expression, and the theoretical equivalent, of this transformation of linearity.[7] The effects of such a shift assume a telling appearance throughout romantic literature, issuing in forms, or anti-forms, which themselves are expressions of the negative sublime. De Quincey's abandonment of logical progression for a type of farrago-like association is exemplary. Rejecting linear continuity for his own metaphor of "'chasms'" to describe his writing, De Quincey attempts to occupy space rather than follow a straight line from one place to another. This desire, J. Hillis Miller writes, is the real cause of De Quincey's digressiveness. Characterizing the circumlocutions of De Quincey's style, Hillis Miller writes,

> De Quincey's thought is not merely sinuous; the word is not strong enough: it is naturally spiral. . . . [T]he image of this spiral movement is the thyrsus. The nominal subject is the dry peeled stick at the center which holds things

> together and gives them a linear direction. The stick is only there for the sake of the flowers, leaves, and blossoms, the digressive meanderings which go about and about the shaft, and give it a three-dimensional volume. Only if De Quincey's style is digressive can it fill up space and avoid shrinking to a dessicated line and paradigm of death.

Marking De Quincey's reluctance or incapacity to move toward logical conclusion, Hillis Miller likens this absence of linearity to a spiral of complex arabesques or "parasitic" vines, woven and rewoven vainly about a thyrsus in order to forestall the approach of De Quincey's language towards its end, its mortal conclusion.[8]

Pre-romantic satire evinces a similar arrest of linearity. Alvin Kernan notes the tendency in the last book of Pope's *Dunciad* -- the book which departed from Enlightenment unity -- whose "lack of tight cause and effect linking" forms "a crucial part of the definition of the action." Lacking an absolute ideal, a corrective stance on which to base improvement of social ills, the linear progression of Pope's satire comes to a halt, curling back on itself in "pools" of invective.[9] Wordsworth's *Prelude*, with its constant doubling back, contains the same repetition. Paul Jay demonstrates convincingly that Wordsworth's repeated recounting of the same event is because the event is, at a fundamental level, the story of the problem of representation. It is a story which in essence cannot be told, except in a series of futile gestures, particularly in light of what Wordsworth and, indeed, all romantics wish to present. Origins, beginnings, the logos of authority are unrepresentable, inexpressible. Their presentation is always a representation, a repetition and not the originary word. As Wordsworth wrote: "if [*The Prelude*] appears to have redundancies, this defect . . . I have always found incurable. The fault lies too deep, and is in the first conception."[10] Shelley's "The Triumph of Life," in which the same tale is told three times, as if it could not be told, could not reach its end, even had Shelley lived, reveals the same tendency.

These are all responses, however, that with the disruption of linearity come, in however varying a manner, to a virtual halt. Brought up short by the negation of the sublime, the writing displays little in the way of evasive tactics, little or nothing in the way of action or movement. One quintessential "action" remains in romanticism's response to the negative sublime, however: a vertical one. At the brink of the abyss, one can leap, or one can fall.

High Jumpers of the Sublime

> Here pause, Reader! Imagine yourself seated in some cloud-scaling swing, oscillating under the impulse of lunatic hands; . . Seated in such a swing, fast as you reach the lowest point of depression, may you rely on racing up to a starry altitude of corresponding ascent. Ups and downs you will see, heights and depths, in our fiery course together.[11]
> -- De Quincey

Romantics writers replace the linearity of biblical narrative with what has been called "verticality." They become what Harold Bloom calls "high-jumpers of the Sublime."[12] Critical awareness of romantic verticality is not new. Northrop Frye has noted the "profound change" in the post-Newtonian romantics' "spatial projection of reality," a change dictated in part by the concepts of gravitation and the solar system.[13] But though Frye correctly noted romanticism's falling movement, he neglected its frequent soarings -- leaps which in Schiller and Coleridge occur as direct responses to the sublime. Bloom and Paul de Man extend Frye's idea with a view of romanticism's "spatial antinomies" of "high and low."[14] In developing his six revisionary ratios, Bloom observes that the four master tropes which Burke claimed governed post-enlightenment poetry (irony, metonymy, metaphor and synecdoche) cannot account for the representations characteristic of romanticism.[15] New tropes, *Daemonization* (hyperbole/litotes) and *Apophrades* (metalepsis) must be added, both of which are "strong" enough for the task of the more consciously "belated" romantic poet (*Map* 35).

Apophrades, the trope by which the poet passes from "origins" to "repetition and continuity," and from there to discontinuity and a willful "raising of the dead," explains certain tendencies in Schiller and Coleridge, and in the romantic self (*Map* 47). The discontinuity of *Apophrades* illuminates the fragmentary character of Coleridge's work. Its psychology of a "return of the dead" parallels both Schiller's and Coleridge's encounters with the negative sublime, and the morbidity of their literary response to those encounters. Bloom's general psychology of *Daemonization*, the "romance of trespass," explains both poets as well. With *Daemonization*, the defiantly belated poet refuses (like Milton's Satan) his latecomer status, returns to his origin, and deliberately violating its sacred or daemonic ground, begets there his own perverse "counter-sublime" (*Map* 35, 37). Schiller "trespasses" on such ground but stops short, turning the violation on himself in his interpretation of the sublime as suicide. Coleridge, however, contrary to Bloom's estimation (*Figures* 14), not only trespasses on such ground but, becoming *daemonic* or "strong" poet *par excellence*, clearly produces his own "counter-sublime." "Limbo" is such a product.

Bloom's notion of romantic verticality illuminates the excess of the romantic self. Though *Apophrades* accounts for the fragmentation of romantic identity, *Daemonization* describes the poet's vertical extravagance in an experience of the sublime. The major trope of *Daemonization* is hyperbole/litotes and its spatial antinomies are high and low (*Map* 84), both qualities intrinsic to the sublime. *Daemonization* is also the only trope in Bloom's scheme with sufficient hyperbolic power to enable the poet to produce her or his own counter-sublime.

De Man's concept of "demystification," on the other hand, illuminates the ironic duality of the romantic self. Though de Man drew on the metaphor of verticality to describe romanticism, he interpreted its ambivalence not as a shortcoming, as Bloom does, but as a characteristic strength. Romantic sensibility is constituted by two simultaneous impulses, de man argued -- mystification or "*falling* into the myth of an organic totality" and demystification, or "*falling (or rising)*" into awareness of the myth's fictive character. De Man's idea that the painful ambivalence of demystification constitutes the "true voice of early romantic literature"[16] illustrates the bifurcated character of romantic identity under the influence of the negative sublime. Demystification, de Man argued, is like Baudelaire's *dédoublement* (the subject's doubling of itself), in which the artistic or philosophical person laughs at herself falling -- she laughs at a mistaken assumption she was making about herself and about the myth of totality or meaning that she had believed possible. She must continue to make the assumption, however, knowing that she will relinquish and take up the myth of totality *ad infinitum*.[17]

Most striking in its relevance to the sublime's link to romantic identity is the dejection such duality creates. This ironic two-fold self -- a type of Baudelaireian "*folie lucide*," de Man notes -- comes into being "*only at the expense of [the subject's] empirical self*, falling (or rising) from a stage of mystified adjustment into the knowledge of his mystification" ("Temporality" 214, my italics). Thus, despite the apparent gains won for the romantic self by such verticality, the response is, in the last analysis, rationally untenable. The poet's only recourse, bereft of the linear progress of logic, becomes ultimately a leap of faith (*hypsous*), or an uncanny fall (*buthos*) -- the Greek βυΘσs, a bottom or bed, as of the sea or of an abyss.

Sublime Leaps and Beautiful Flights

> O man, thou half-dead Angel.[18]
>
> -- Coleridge

The leap of the romantic sublime differs from the ascents of eighteenth-century sublimity, those soarings described by Weiskel as an "aesthetics of transcendence." The vertical character of sublime landscape -- its endless skies, precipitous crags, and the like -- complements Burke's notion of the soul's upward "expansion" in response to the sublime. Such notions, however, are informed by the idea of transcendence, and represent what Marjorie Hope Nicolson calls an "aesthetics of infinity," in which "infinity" is not the emptiness faced by the romantics, but the boundless province of the divine.[19] Though the romantic leap grew out of these traditional notions of sublimity, two major differences distinguished the eighteenth-century ascent from its romantic counterpart in the negative sublime. Romantic flight did not reflect a transcendence or "expansion" of the phenomenal self into the divine, but a self-annihilative vaulting born of a wish for the divine rather than a certainty of its existence. In addition, while eighteenth-century response to sublimity was limited to ascents -- sinkings were non-existent and despair, if it occurred, was only a momentary preface to exaltation -- romantic response to sublimity could take two possible directions: "up" in a vague wish for the divine, and "down," in a plunge into the depths of an alienated self.

A comparison of the poetic composition and the projection of the self in an aesthetics of the beautiful reveals the implications of the sublime's vertical dynamics. Beauty's movement is always forward and horizontal, or linear, since teleological meaning is assured by the fact that Beauty is grounded in the mimetic tradition. It is "founded on a Conformity," Hutcheson writes, "or a kind of Unity between the Original and the Copy."[20] Similarly, in the aesthetics of the beautiful, the projection of the self is outward and social, and characterized by security, since beauty rests on cultural certainties. Beauty is characterized by "proportion, order, regularity, and rules" (Nicolson 288), a notion echoed in Burke's remark: "I call Beauty a social quality," and in Kant's observation that "the beautiful interests us only in society."[21] While a poetry defined by beauty exhibits a telic, linear progression, the movement of poetic composition in the "lawless" sublime -- whose only rule is what Lyotard aptly describes as "the rule of non-regulation"[22] -- is either "up" into some godless void, or "down" into the "night-like mine or pit," as Hegel calls it, of a disenfranchised self.[23]

Kant's Aesthetic Link

> The path is broken, *fracta*, breached.[24]
>
> -- Derrida

If, in the last analysis, such verticality became the only viable response to the sublime's abyss, earlier, more hopeful strategies focused on the attempt to bridge the aporia of sublimity with a new aesthetics. Romanticism had typically imbued art and the imagination with a mediational function, a capacity to breach the chasm opened in the romantic period by the "disappearance of God."[25] Kant, Schiller, and Coleridge are no exceptions. Each attempted to recover the possibility of humanistic meaning -- meaning interchangeable to varying degrees, depending on the writer, with the godhead -- through a linear process. The telic endeavor was to be managed by way of a bridge-like aesthetic response that might synthesize the heterogeneity of external phenomena. Although some commentators have noted the reconciling projects of each writer, and others have discussed the failure of one or another of the projects, none, to my knowledge, has presented the three projects together as roughly one single effort. More important, no commentator appears to have noted the identical nature of each of their failures, or to have identified the nature of each as the consequence of the sublime.[26] Despite the similar projects of all three writers, none of their respective bridges reached its opposite shore. The collapse of each, and the related nature of the problems that Kant, Schiller and Coleridge encounter, illustrate the multiplicity of fronts on which the sublime subverts a unifying or reconciliatory aesthetics.

The concept of art as a mode of bridging the self's sensuous and rational faculties finds its most celebrated proponent in Kant, who, with the *Critique of Judgment*, attempts to establish a view of aesthetic judgment as a mediating link between the disparate realms of his two former *Critiques*. Kant is usually seen as a champion of the schism between man's phenomenal and noumenal identity; Schiller and Coleridge are presented as attempting to bridge the gap. Much as the two poets, however, Kant was troubled by the rift, which he saw manifested in the gap between finite man and his supersensible destiny. Kant's *Critique of Pure Reason* is, as Paul Wolff writes, primarily "a philosophy of the self,"[27] fusing an absolute self with absolute reason. By the time he composed his third *Critique*, however, Kant had come to realize that what he had *not* fused were the disparate realms of his two former *Critiques* -- the realms of what one knows through rational principles (*The Critique of Pure Reason*) and of what one ought morally to do in the practical world (*The Critique of Practical Reason*). *The Critique of Judgment* (1790) was designed to connect the human activity implied by these two realms, using man's aesthetic judgment as a mediating principle.

Although Kant approved of the distinction between what he called theoretical or *Natural Philosophy* (*theoretische als Naturphilosophie*) and practical or *Moral Philosophy*" (*praktische als Moralphilosophie*),[28] he sensed an incompleteness in the disparity between them: "A critique of pure reason," he wrote,

> of our faculty of judging *a priori* according to principles, would be incomplete if the judgment, which as a cognitive faculty also makes claim to such principles, were not treated as a particular part of it . . . For if such system is one day to be completed under the general name of metaphysic . . . the soil of the edifice must be explored by critique as deep down as the faculty of the principles independent of experience, in order that it may sink in no part, for this would inevitably bring about the downfall of the whole.[29]

In order to rescue a system that had somehow fallen into halves, Kant reached for the judgment as a *cognitive* faculty (as opposed to the reason's judgment according to *a priori* principles) in order to reconnect them.

Like a Bridge

Extremes meet.[30]

-- Coleridge

As numerous commentators have noted, Kant's project was unsteady from the start,[31] revealing its tenuousness even in the tone he used to present it:[32]

> Now even if an immeasurable gulf is fixed between the sensible realm of the concept of nature and the supersensible realm of the concept of freedom, so that no transition is possible from the first to the second . . . just as if they were two different worlds . . . yet the second is *meant* to have an influence upon the first. The concept of freedom is meant to actualize in the world of sense the purpose proposed by its laws. There must, therefore, be a ground of the *unity* of the supersensible, which lies at the basis of nature, . . ; and the concept of this ground, . . . makes possible the transition from one mode of thought according to the principles of one to that according to the principles of the other.[33]

The gap between the two provinces of pure and practical reason may be profound, he writes, but they are nevertheless "meant" to be connected and thus "must" be connected -- as if desire, expressed with sufficient intensity could make something so.

The unsteadiness of his mediating argument lies not only in his reliance on authorial fiat, and or on his use of mystical oxymorons -- the bridge rests on a "supersensible substrate" ("*übersinnliches Substrat*")[34] -- but in his dependence on analogical method, which, as Guyer notes, is still "held to undermine his whole argument in the Critique of Judgment" (Guyer 35). In Kant's Introduction, whose title itself reveals the *Critique*'s mediating strategy -- "Of the Critique of Judgment as a Means of Combining the Two Parts of Philosophy into a Whole" -- he admits that his method is not logical but analogical, the strategy that Schiller would later take up for his own mediating project in his optimistic *Kallias Letters*, and then discard in "On the Sublime" as "counterfeit." Kant's explanation is worth following closely:

> . . . the division of philosophy into theoretical and practical is justified. But in the family of the supreme cognitive faculties there is a middle term between the understanding and the reason. This is the *judgment*, of which we may have cause for supposing according to analogy that it may contain in itself . . . a special principle of its own to be sought according to laws, although merely subjective *a priori* . . .
> But besides (to judge by analogy), there is a new ground for bringing the judgment into connection with another arrangement of our representative faculties, which seems to be of even greater importance . . . For all faculties or capacities of the soul can be reduced to three . . .: the *faculty of knowledge*, the *feeling of pleasure and pain*, and the *faculty of desire*. For the faculty of knowledge the understanding is alone legislative . . . For the faculty of desire . . . the reason . . . is alone *a priori* legislative. Now between the faculties of knowledge and desire there is the feeling of pleasure, just as the judgment mediates between the understanding and the reason. We may therefore suppose provisionally that the judgment likewise

> contains in itself an *a priori* principle. And . . . we may also suppose that the judgment will bring about a transition from the pure faculty of knowledge, the realm of natural concepts, to the realm of the concept of freedom, just as in its logical use it makes possible the transition from understanding to reason.[35]

Juggling his characteristic tripartite structures (reason, understanding, judgment; desire, knowledge, pleasure), Kant admits that he is 1) reasoning by "provisional supposition" and "analogy" that in matters of pleasure and pain, the judgment will perform just as it does in logical matters, that is, as mediator, and 2) that he is positing analogically the judgment's possession of an *a priori* "principle" (albeit *subjective*[36]), without which any faculty lacks authority.

Sublime Ruptures

> [T]he strength of lunacy may belong to human dreams . . . even as a bridge gathers cohesion and strength from the increasing resistance into which it is forced by increasing pressure.[37]
>
> -- De Quincey

Kant's admission of the "immeasurable gulf" between theoretical and practical knowledge, his dependence on the mere wish that they be bridged (they are "meant" to be, they "must"), and his tenuous analogical methods[38] to show that they are, comprise only part of his problems, however. Hastily written in his advancing years, the *Critique of Judgment* as a sense/reason "link" fails most crucially through Kant's peculiarly moral interpretation of the sublime. Kant, as Paul Crowther notes accurately, connects sublimity so closely with morality that he reduces the sublime to "a kind of indirect moral experience."[39] As a result, the sublime undermines the *Critique*'s most plausible argument for aesthetic judgment's mediating function -- its "disinterestedness." Kant needs to show that what we know by pure and practical reason is connected to the finite world -- that the transcendent aspect of our identity is related to the aspect that acts in the physical world. The beautiful, he argues, the object of aesthetic judgment, can provide the connection, since the observer's perception of and pleasure in an object involves her sensible faculties (her imagination and understanding) and her supersensible faculty (her reason) in judging a beautiful object "disinterestedly" -- independent of any purpose. Combining reason (apprehension of the form of purposiveness) with the senses (perception of the object), the subject's aesthetic judgment of the beautiful seems to ensure the desired mediation between reason and understanding. But Kant forgets that the disinterestedness of our judgments of beauty, what he calls "*Zweckmässigkeit ohne Zweck*" or "purposiveness without purpose," must exclude the representation of *any* purpose, including a moral one (*CofJ*, §18, 73). Hence, when later in the "Dialectic of Aesthetic Judgment" Kant declares beauty the symbol of morality, he undermines the disinterestedness, that is to say, the purely rational component of aesthetic judgment, and thus subverts the possibility of such judgment standing as a sense/reason mediator between the theoretical and the practical (*CofJ*, §59, 196).

The problems of the "Dialectic" stem in large part from the character of the sublime in the preceding *Critique*, since the emphasis on stringent self-abnegation, the hallmark of Kantian sublimity, necessarily undermines the concept of a sense/reason harmony or aesthetic bridge. Kant's idea of such harmony, here between imagination and understanding, has already become unsteady, since he cannot clarify harmony as the central explanatory concept he wishes it to be, even in judgments of the beautiful (Guyer, 11, 248-55). Kant's main task in the *Critique of Judgment*"[40] is to find out

> [w]hether now the judgment, which in the order of our

> cognitive faculties *forms a mediating link* between understanding and reason, also has principles *a priori* for itself; whether these are constitutive or merely regulative . . .; and whether they give a rule *a priori* to the feeling of pleasure and pain, as the *mediating link* between the cognitive faculty [understanding] and the faculty of desire [reason] . . . -- these are the questions with which the present *Critique of Judgment* is concerned.[41]

Kant decides that the judgment *does* have "in itself a principle *a priori* of the possibility of nature, but only in a subjective aspect, by which it prescribes not to nature (autonomy), but to itself (heautonomy) a law for its reflection upon nature" (*CofJ*, Introduction, V, p. 22). It is, in other words, a transcendental principle (regulative and not constitutive) of the "unity," "design" or "purposiveness" of nature, a purposiveness not cognizable by our senses but thinkable.

By "subjective" and "heautonomous," Kant means that the *a priori* principle and rule of judgment "ascribe nothing to the object (of nature) but only represent the peculiar way in which we must proceed in reflection upon the objects of nature" (*CofJ*, Introduction, V, p. 20). However, the rule that the judgment gives, a rule which is "to form a mediating link between the cognitive faculty [understanding] and the faculty of desire [reason]" (Crawford 18) *does not obtain in the sublime*. This is because the rule rests on the "purposive *harmony* of an object (whether a product of nature or of art) with the mutual relations of the cognitive faculties (the imagination and the understanding)." The sublime, dealing only with the reason, rests on the *dis*harmony of these faculties. As Guyer explains, "Kant's fundamental explanation of aesthetic response as a harmony between imagination and understanding leaves no room for the feeling of the sublime" (Guyer 399).

The universality of aesthetic judgment which is so crucial to Kant's argument loses its ground in the sublime as well. Kant cannot claim a universality for the "negative pleasure" of the sublime since, again, the rule for aesthetic pleasure (positive or negative) rests on a *harmony* of the faculties. In fact, it is not only the sublime's preclusion by the idea of harmony, but the lack of universality in sublimity that leads Guyer to exclude the sublime from his study altogether. To Guyer, the sublime "seem[s] something of an afterthought" in Kant's system (Guyer 399), since Kant even dismisses its need for a transcendental deduction (needed in the case of beauty) on the rather questionable grounds that it is based on all men's morality, and that it is a response to formlessness and not to a form. Guyer writes:

> The universal imputation of the judgment of sublimity presupposes that all persons have the same limits on their imagination, and that this faculty will interact with reason in the same way in the case of any given subject. If a transcendental deduction is needed [a deduction, indeed, which Crawford characterizes as "the key to the Critique of Taste"] to justify such an assumption about the imagination and its harmony with another faculty of cognition in the case of beauty, then it is also needed for the judgment of sublimity, which likewise assumes the fundamental similarity of faculties among human subjects. That the feeling of sublimity is a response to formlessness rather than to form does not affect this requirement.[42]

The negative sublime has subverted Kant's bridge of aesthetic judgment on a variety of fronts. First, the basic moral thrust of the sublime,[43] which is designed *only* to put us in mind of that self-abnegative supersensible aspect of our being, leads Kant to make beauty a symbol of morality and thereby destroy the disinterestedness of our judgment of the beautiful, a disinterestedness which is Kant's only plausible concept of a linking of sensuous perception (the realm of understanding) and a purely rational response (the realm of reason). Second, the divisiveness of the sublime subverts the two logical components essential to the idea of establishing aesthetic judgment as a sense/reason bridge. Kant needs both an *a priori* principle *and* an *a priori* rule as mediating links. He must have an *a priori* principle for aesthetic judgment in order to bring judgment in as a bridge which can span the gulf between the theoretical and the practical. (Significantly, it is aesthetic judgment *alone*, and not teleological judgment, which contains this *a priori* principle of the formal purposiveness of nature.)[44] However, he cannot establish this principle logically but only "suppose" one analogically.[45] The use of analogy forces Kant into a tenuous dependence on metaphor (having abandoned the mathematical "accuracy" of logical syllogisms), and into implications of identity, sameness, and unity -- the stuff of analogy. He is thus attempting to make a principle grounded in identity fit the sublime, which is clearly an aesthetics of difference. Third, the same sublime divisiveness subverts the *a priori* rule as well. This is because the "rule," given by the *a priori* principle is not only necessary to "complete" the *Critique of Pure Reason* (*CofJ*, Preface, p. 4), but is it*self* the sense/reason mediator. It is grounded, in other words, in a "harmony" of the faculties, and the sublime precludes such a harmony. Finally, it is the formlessness of the sublime that subverts the universality, and hence the linking character, of aesthetic judgment. Due to its lack of form, Kant neglects to give sublimity a transcendental deduction, and without such a deduction, universality is impossible. Yet, universality is necessary to the notion of a sense/reason bridge, since it is demanded by reason, which commands that an aesthetic judgment be true for all men. Without universality, an important part of the rational component of the sense/reason link is omitted.

Kant wrote that in order to "complete" the system, to forestall "the downfall of the whole," he needed to explore deep beneath the structure. But he had probed too deeply. He had apparently sensed the structure's unsteadiness, and that at some profound level, the sublime was inimical to any attempt to use aesthetic judgment to mediate between the theoretical and practical. Kant would indeed seem to have found the "ground" of "the supersensible, the "*übersinnliches Substrat*" that lies at the basis of nature"; but it was nothing like "harmony." It is not by chance that Kant dismissed the sublime as "a mere appendix to the analytical judging" (*CofJ*, II, §23;

85), nor is it by chance that the section on the "Dynamic Sublime" remains unfinished.[46] Yet, though already revealing the fissures that hint at its own collapse, the fragmentary bridge of the third *Critique* was re-adopted as a system of aesthetic mediation by Schiller, and applied directly to the concept of human identity.

NOTES

1. Thomas Love Peacock, "Newark Abbey, August, 1842: With a Reminiscence of 1807," 11. 15-18.

2. David Greene's study of Beethoven's modernity offers suggestive implications for the strangely abortive movement of romantic art. "As philosophical parallel" to the concept of romantic music as a "sequence of peaks of intensity undirected toward an end,"

> Greene educes Schelling, with his identification of necessity with a freedom intuited from the 'deepest self'; and cites nineteenth-century examples in which what for the late eighteenth century would have been failure is considered success, albeit in a private rather than a public context. Change in romantic music is the consequence not of laws which can be rationally understood, as in baroque temporality, nor of the conscious decisions of a moral agent, as in classical temporality; it is rather a revelation of the 'incongruence between the concrete actuality that transpires and the self's struggles to shape it'. Struggle, failure, and renewed struggle become ends in themselves: as in many of Brahms' movements which, beginning in major affirmation, end with minor reversal. This is the opposite pole to Bach's harmonic counterpoint which . . . Greene describes as a demonstratio of Leibnitz's 'mirror of the mind of God'.

Wilfred Mellers, "The Influence of the Future," review of David B. Greene,

Temporal Processes in Beethoven's Music (New York: Gordon & Breach 1983.) In *TLS*, June 29, 1984, p. 723.

[3] Karl Kroeber, *Romantic Narrative Art* (Madison 1966), 6. Hereafter, Kroeber.

[4] For a useful discussion of the disappearance of endings in romantic narrative see Frank Kermode, *The Sense of an Ending: Studies in the Theory of Fiction* (Rpt. 1966; London, 1970), 127. See "The Modern Apocalypse," 67-, *passim*.

[5] Said, *Beginnings*, xiii.

[6] Hans W. Frei, *The Eclipse of Biblical Narrative: A Study in Eighteenth and Nineteenth Century Hermeneutics* (New Haven, 1974), 2. Hereafter, Frei.

[7] It is not by chance that this arrest of linear narrative is related to Jakobson's distinction between the disruption of romantic crisis literature, which is expressed in metaphor, and the metonymic dominance of linear history. Closely aligned as well is Bloom's interpretation of Jakobson in his revisionary ratios, particularly *kenosis*, which as de Man observed, "breaks up a totality into discontinuous fragments [,] substitut[ing] a contiguity (in temporal terms, a repetition) for an analogy or resemblance (in temporal terms a genesis) and thus rediscover[ing], in its turn, the familiar metaphor-metonymy opposition, though with an epistemological twist that was lacking in Jakobson's version." See Paul de Man, "Review of Harold Bloom's Anxiety of Influence," in *Blindness* (Minneapolis, 1983), 187-229, 225.

[8] J. Hillis Miller, *The Disappearance of God: Five Nineteenth-Century Writers* (Cambridge, 1963), 39-40. Hereafter, Hillis Miller.

[9] Alvin B. Kernan, *The Plot of Satire* (Rpt. 1965; New Haven, 1974), 112-113. Hereafter, Kernan.

10. See Paul Jay, *Being in the Text: Self-Representation from Wordsworth to Roland Barthes* (Ithaca, 1984), 77. Hereafter, Jay.

11. Thomas De Quincey, "Dreaming," *Suspiria de Profundis, Works*, ed., Masson, XIII, 339.

12. Harold Bloom, *Figures of Capable Imagination* (New York, 1976), 7. Hereafter *Figures*.

13. Northrop Frye, "The Drunken Boat: The Revolutionary Element in Romanticism," in *Romanticism: Points of View*, (Englewood Cliffs, 1970), 299-314: 301. Hereafter, Frye. Frye, however, limited romantic verticality to a descent, omitting the correlate ascending metaphor, simply "because," as he argued, "there is nothing up there." Downward or "'within' metaphors are more reassuring than 'up there' metaphors" (303). As Frye would have it, "The metaphorical structure of romantic imagery tends to move inside and downward instead of outside and upward, hence the creative world is deep within" (308).

14. de Man, "Review of Anxiety," in *Blindness*, 275.

15. Harold Bloom, *Map of Misreading* (New York, 1975), 94. Hereafter, Bloom, *Map*.

16. "Rhetoric of Temporality," in *Blindness*, 187-229: 207, 223. Hereafter, "Temporality."

17. Likening the falling and rising movement of romantic sensibility to Baudelaire's process of *dédoublement*, de Man writes:

> At the moment that the artistic or philosophical, that is, the language-determined, man laughs at himself falling, he is laughing at a mistaken, mystified assumption he was making about himself . . . The Fall, in the literal as well as the theological sense, reminds him of the purely instrumental, reified character of his relationship to nature . . . In the

idea of the fall thus conceived, a progression in self-knowledge is certainly implicit: the man who has fallen is somewhat wiser than the fool who walks around oblivious of the crack in the pavement about to trip him up. And the fallen philosopher reflecting on the discrepancy between the two successive stages is wiser still, but this does not in the least prevent him from stumbling in his turn. It seems instead that his wisdom can be gained only at the cost of such a fall. The mere falling of others does not suffice; he has to go down himself. The ironic two-fold self that the writer or philosopher constitutes by his language seems able to come into being only at the expense of his empirical self, falling (or rising) from a stage of mystified adjustment into the knowledge of his mystification ("Temporality" 214).

[18.] *CN*, I, 273; III, 4088, f156.

[19.] It was not only Burke who characterized the response to sublimity as an ascent or upward expansion to notions of divinity; the eighteenth century reveled in such flight. As Addison remarked: "Of all objects that I have ever seen, there is none which affects my imagination so much as the sea or ocean . . . Such an object naturally raises in my thought the idea of an Almighty Being, and convinces me of his existence as much as a metaphysical demonstration." (Addison, *Spectator* 489, quoted in Nicolson, *Mountain Gloom*, 306). Eighteenth-century observers of the sublime were "finding that their 'elastical souls' expanded with the vastness and expansiveness of nature" to participate in the divine (Nicolson 270), an ascent shared by the "intellect [which] *rises* with the feeling" (Nicolson 287, italics mine). To Shaftesbury -- who, tellingly, did not distinguish the sublime from the beautiful -- "the Sublime was a higher and more majestic Beauty. It was a power 'which naturally . . . *raises* the imagination to an opinion . . . of something majestic and divine. . . .We cannot help being transported with the thought of it . . . [for it] *raises* us above ourselves'" (Nicolson, 300, italics mine.) Assuredly, the eighteenth century prefigured the rising movement of the romantic negative sublime. However, those "soaring souls" of the eighteenth century, "who found liberation for the imagination in the 'vast'" (Nicolson 303), found that liberation in the province of the divine.

20. Francis Hutcheson, "An Inquiry into the Original of our Ideas of Beauty and Virtue," in Hipple, 27.

21. Burke, *Enquiry*, part I, x. 42-3; Kant, *CofJ*, "Analytic of the Sublime," §41, p. 139.

22. Lyotard, "Philosophy of Phrases," 20.

23. Hegel, *Philosophy of Mind, Part III of the Encyclopedia of the Philosophical Sciences*, trans. William Wallace (Rpt. 1830; Oxford, 1978), 453, p. 204.

24. Derrida, "Freud and the Scene of Writing," in *Writing and Difference*, trans. Alan Bass (Chicago, 1978), 196-278, 200.

25. See Hillis Miller, *The Disappearance of God* (Cambridge, 1963).

26. One exception to this critical neglect is Derrida, at least regarding Kant, who clearly illustrates the inefficacy of Kant's aesthetic system to bridge the gulf between the theoretical and the practical. See "Parergon," in *October*, IX (*La Verité en Peinture*).

27. See Paul Wolff, *Autonomy and Reason* (New York, 1973), 9, *passim*.

28. *CofJ*, Introduction, "Of the Division of Philosophy," I, p. 7. "*So wird die Philosophie in zwei, de Prinzipien nach ganz verschiedene, Teile in die theoretische als Naturphilosophie, und die praktische als Moralphilosophie . . . mit Recht eingeteilt.*" Einteilung, "*Von der Eintelung der Philosophie,*" I, p. 22.

29. *CofJ*, Preface, p. 4: "*Eine Kritik der reinen Vernunft, d.i. unseres Vermögens nach Prinzipien a priori zu urteilen, würde unvollständig sein, wenn die der Urteilskraft, welche für sich as Erkenntnisvermögen darauf auch Anspruch macht, nicht als ein besonderer Teil derselben abgehandelt würde; . . . Denn,*

wenn ein solches System unter dem allgemeinen Namen der Metaphysik einmal zustande kommen soll . . . so muß die Kritik den Boden zu diesem Gebäude vorher so tief, als die erste Grundlage des Vermögens von der Erfahrung unabhänginger Prinzipien liegt, erforscht haben, damit es nicht an irgendeinem Teile sinke, welches den Einsturz des Ganzen unvermeidlich nach sich ziehen würde," Vorrede, p. 17. Kant's metaphors continually suggest the abyssal terrain of sublimity. He writes of "territories," "realms," "dwelling places" belonging to the "unbounded but also inaccessible field . . . of the supersensible." See *CofJ*, Intro. II; 11, and Guyer, *Kant and the Claims of Taste*, 36.

30. Coleridge, *CN*, III, T, 3400, 3405.

31. See R. W. Bretall, "Kant's Theory of the Sublime," *Heritage of Kant* (Princeton, NJ: 1962); Donald Crawford, *Kant's Aesthetic Theory* (Madison, 1974); Paul Crowther, *The Kantian Sublime* (Oxford: 1989); Jacques Derrida, *Parergon*, in *October* IX; Paul Guyer, *Kant and the Claims of Taste* (Cambridge, MA: 1979); and Robert Paul Wolff, *Kant's Theory of Mental Activity* (Cambridge, MA: 1963), 224 n2.

32. For a discussion of the apocalyptic tone of Kant's later writing, see Jacques Derrida, *Raising the Tone of Philosophy: Late Essays by Immanuel Kant* (Baltimore, 1994).

33. *CofJ*, "Of the Realm of Philosophy in General," Introduction, II, p. 12: "*Ob nun zwar eine unübersehbare Kuft zwischen dem Gebiete des Naturbegriffs, als dem Sinnlichen, und dem Gebiete des Freiheitsbegriffs, als dem Übersinnlichen, befestigt ist, so daß von dem ersteren zum anderen . . . kein Übergang möglich ist, gleich als ob es so viel verschiedene Welten wären, . . . so soll doch diese auf jene einen Einfluß haben, nämlich der Freiheitsbegriff soll den durch seine Gesetze aufgegebenen Zweck in der Sinnenwelt wirklich machen; . . . Also muß es doch einen Grund der Einheit des Übersinnlichen, welches der Natur zum Grunde liegt, . . . wovon der Begriff . . . den Übergang von der Denkungsart nach den Prinzipien der einen, zu der nach Prinzipien der anderen, möglich macht.*" "*Vom Gebiete der Philosophie überhaupt*," *Einleitung*, II, pp. 28-29. Repeated metaphors of "mediation" and "transition" underscore the projected bridging role. See *CofJ*, Intro, IX; p. 33.

34. Kant writes: "[T]hat magnitude of a natural object on which the imagination fruitlessly spends its whole faculty of comprehension must carry our concept of nature to a *supersensible substrate* (*übersinnliches Substrat*) (which lies at its basis and also at the basis of our faculty of thought)' (*CofJ*, "Analytic of the Sublime," §26, p. 94: "*so muß diejenige Größe eines Naturobjeckts an welcher die Einbildungskraft ihr ganzes Vermögen der Zuzammenfassung fruchtlos verwendet, den Begriff der Natur auf ein übersinnliches Substrat (welches ihr und zugleich unserm Vermögen zu denken zum Grund liegt) fuhren,*" §26, p. 152). Robert Paul Wolff rightly calls Kant's phrase "supersensible substrate," "the last word in mixed metaphors," a vagueness which remains unresolved by Rudolf Makkreel's claim that Kant's "expression 'supersensible substrate of nature' points both above sense and below nature." See Robert Wolff, *Kant's Theory of Mental Activity* (Cambridge, MA: 1963), 224, n2; Rudolf Makkreel, "Imagination and Temporality in Kant's Theory of the Sublime," *The Journal of Aesthetics and Art Criticism*, XLII/3, Spring 1984, 303-315; Makkreel, *Imagination and Interpretation in Kant: The Hermeneutical Import of the Critique of Judgment* (Chicago, 1990), 81; Linda Marie Brooks, "Sublimity and Theatricality," *MLN*; 105; 5 (Winter, 1990): 939-64: 942.

35. *CofJ*, "Of the Critique of Judgment as a Means of Combining the Two Parts of Philosophy into a Whole," Introduction, III, 13-15: ". . . *die Einteilung der Philosophie in die theoretische und praktische rechtfertigt [ist]. Allein in der Familie der oberen Erkenntnisvermögen gibt es doch ein Mittelglied zwischen dem Verstande und der Vernunft. Dieses ist die Urteilskraft, von welcher man Ursache hat, nach der Analogie zu vermuten, daß sie ebensowohl . . ., doch ein ihr eigenes Prinzip nach Gesetzen zu suchen, allenfalls ein Bloß subjektives a priori . . . Hierzu kommt aber noch (nach der anologie zu urteilen) ein neuer Grund, die Urteilskraft mit einer anderen Ordnung unserer Vorstellungskräfte in der Verknüpfung zu bringen, welche von noch großerer Wichtigkeit zu sein scheint . . . Denn alle Seelenvermögen, oder Fähigkeiten, können auf die drei zurückgefürt werden, . . .: das Erkenntnisvermögen, das Gefühlderlust und Unlust, und das Begehrungsvermögen. Für das Erkenntnisvermögen ist allein der Verstand gesetzgebend . . . Für das Begehrungsvermögen . . . ist allein die Vernunft . . . a priori gesetzgebend. Nun ist zwischen dem Erkenntnis- und dem Begehrungsvermögen das Gefühl der Lust, so wie zwischen dem Verstande und der Vernunft die Urteilskraft, enthalten. Es ist also wenigstens vorläufig zu vermuten, daß die Urteilskraft eben so wohl für sich ein Prinzip a priori enthalte, und, . . . ebensowohl einen Übergang vom reinen Erkenntnisvermögen, d.i. vom Gebiete der Naturbegriffe zum Gebiete des Freiheitsbegriff, bewirken werde, als sie in logischen Gebrauche den Übergang vom Verstande zur Vernunft möglich macht*," "*Von der Kritik der Urteilskraft, als einem Verbindungsmittel der zwei*

Teile der Philosophie zu einem Ganzen," Einleitung, III, 30-33.

36. As opposed to an objective principle, a subjective principle cannot offer determinate concepts of objects.

37. Thomas De Quincey, "Dreaming," 339.

38. On the analogical method and "mere architectonic isomorphism" of Kant's supposition that judgment has any *a priori* principles, see Guyer, *Kant and the Claims of Taste* (Cambridge, 1979), 37.

39. See Paul Crowther, *The Kantian Sublime* (Oxford, 1992), 166. Lacking even an "object" to "judge," Kant's sublime aesthetics is not actually an aesthetic, and belongs rather as an appendix to the *Critique of Practical Reason*.

40. See Crawford, *Kant's Aesthetic Theory* (Madison, 1974), 18.

41. *CofJ*, Preface 4, italics mine. "*Ob nun die Urteilskraft, die in der Ordnung unserer Erkenntnisvermögen zwischen dem Verstande und der Vernunft ein Mittleglied ausmacht, auch für sich Prinzipien a priori habe; ob diese konsitutiv oder bloß regulativ sind . . . und ob sie den Gefühle der Lust und Unlust, als dem Mittegliede zwischen dem Erkenntnisvermögen und Begehrungsvermögen . . . a priori die Regel gebe: das ist es, womit sich gegenwärtige Kritik der Urteilskraft beschäftigt, Vorrede*, 16-17.

42. See Guyer, 266; Crawford, 69.

43. The intrinsically moral nature of Kant's aesthetics is underscored by Guyer's questioning of Kant's methods: "Although his consideration of such a moral foundation for taste seems out of place at this point in his argument," Guyer writes, Kant nevertheless introduces the view "that the universal validity of aesthetic judgment requires a moral as well as an epistemological foundation." Guyer, 254.

44. See *CofJ*, Introduction, VIII, p. 30.

45. See *CofJ*, Introduction, 3-15.

46. See Carritt, *Theory of Beauty*, 160.

3

SCHILLER'S FAILED *ÜBERGANG*: PRETENDING THE SELF

> How will I now find a bridge from this sensuous dependency to moral freedom?[1]
> -- Schiller

The Illusion of Identity

Less systematic than Kant's, Schiller's theory of bridging the subject's conflicting impulses into one unified identity succumbed easily to the sublime. His celebrated concept of an aesthetic impulse that harmonized man's sensuous and rational faculties rested squarely on sublime principles that, by definition, subvert unity. Schiller writes that "art is a free citizen that calls to us 'be free like me.'" But his definition of beauty as "freedom in appearance" is drawn from the most serious limitations of Kant's aesthetic theory: analogical argumentation, indeterminate concepts, and Kant's wisely undeveloped notion of "*Heautonomie*," or the "appearance" of freedom. Kant himself was troubled by all three aspects, and with good reason. We have seen the problematic analogical method by which he initially establishes the necessary *a priori* principle for aesthetic judgment, a method that has been held to undermine his whole argument in the *Critique of Judgment*.[2] Kant had little choice, however, since his tenuous analogical approach stemmed largely from the related problem of grounding his system on the indeterminate concept of a harmony of the faculties. Lacking a predicate of sensible intuition like that supporting a determinate concept, the indeterminate concept of a harmony of the faculties rested on uncertain evidence. In both Kant and Schiller, the basis for aesthetic response is precisely this indeterminate concept (Guyer 136, 337). The fact that its indeterminacy worried Kant is clear in his sudden and otherwise inexplicable substitution of an ontological grounding in the supersensible for the concept's purely epistemological or psychological ground. "We should look for Kant to argue that aesthetic judgments do not admit of dispute because they are not based on determinate concepts," Guyer explains,

> but that they do admit of contention and rational claims to intersubjective validity because they are based in the indeterminate concept of the harmony of the higher cognitive faculties, which provides a rational ground for expectation of intersubjective agreement without any proofs. But the concept of the harmony of the faculties is not what Kant now adduces as the indeterminate and undeterminable concept which founds aesthetic judgment. Instead, what he introduces into his argument is 'the transcendental rational concept of the supersensible which lies at the basis of all intuition . . .'
> Nothing has prepared us for the connection of Kant's aesthetic theory to the metaphysical distinction between appearance and the thing in itself . . . Kant . . . proceeds as if the concept of the supersensible or noumenal ground of both subjects and objects of knowledge and taste were the *only* indeterminate concept available, and infers that it must be this concept which is the ground of the judgments of taste. . . . The indeterminate concept of the harmony of the faculties . . . either is a purely epistemological concept . . .

> or is a psychological concept. The concept of the supersensible, by contrast, is . . . an ontological concept . . . and, it must be noted . . . an ontology, which did not have to be invoked earlier in Kant's argument. It now seems to be invoked either because a transcendental dialectic requires transcendental idealism, or because the suggestion that those who make judgments of taste share a common supersensible ground not only with the objects of their judgments but also with one another may be expected somehow to silence the skeptic. It appears, then, that there is . . . an unintended equivocation in [Kant's] solution . . .

As Guyer shows, it is the indeterminacy of the concept that bothers Kant, the province of the sublime "wherein," Lacoue-Labarthe writes, "the process of the *unsure* initiates."[3] The idea that his theory of aesthetic judgment rests on such ground sends Kant into the supersensible, a tactic which in invalidating his argument, strongly underscores the subversive aspects of the sublime in his system (Guyer 338-40).

For the same reasons, Kant was equally suspicious of his notion of heautonomy, restricting the "freedom" it offered in his *a priori* principle of aesthetic judgment to a merely subjective status. The principle of heautonomy enables us to give the law of nature's "formal purposiveness" to our*selves*, to our *reflection* upon nature and thus to the way we view things in order to facilitate cognition of external phenomena. But we certainly may not prescribe it to the external objects of nature, a nature to which such a law would be mere "contingency." There is no heautonomy in external reality, Kant cautioned; only in ourselves. Kant's dismissal of sublimity as a "mere appendix" to his third *Critique* is a tactical response against these troublesome features of his argument. His need for analogical demonstration, for indeterminate rather than determinate concepts, and for the displacement of reason's autonomy (*Autonomie*) by a subjective *h*eautonomy (*Heautonomie*) -- needs generated by implications underlying the sublime -- signalled the tenuousness of his system in the third *Critique*. To the older philosopher, the "world of truth" could be transcendental; it could be merely regulative and not constitutive; but it could not be so whimsical that it slipped into enthusiasm or "monomania." Not so for Schiller, however. With typical bravado but clearly less philosophical insight, Schiller took up Kant's troublesome methods and erected an aesthetic theory that promised to harmonize man's divided self through sheer illusion.

Schein and the Self

> Man, neither altogether satisfied with the senses, nor forever capable of thought, wanted a middle state, a bridge between the two states, bringing them into harmony.[4]
> -- Schiller

With the intention of restoring man's "humanity" or autonomous self, Schiller refashioned Kant's idea of heautonomy as the "*appearance* of autonomy" -- a mode by which man's divided sensuous and rational faculties could be reunited. With his warring impulses finally harmonized, man's humanity and his autonomous identity as "the being who wills" would be restored. Although Schiller had toyed with the idea of a harmony of the faculties in his earliest philosophical essays,[5] his first real efforts to develop a theory appeared in the *Kallias* Letters (1793).[6] Challenging Kant's divorce of sense and reason in moral matters, Schiller's goal was to re-wed man's sensible and rational faculties through a state of "aesthetic freedom." In the Feb. 8 Letter, Schiller appropriated Kant's notion of "heautonomy," making it the core of his aesthetic theory. Schiller's well-known definition of beauty rests on this interpretation of heautonomy:

> Beauty, in the widest sense, is an appearance which is analogous to the form of pure will or freedom. Beauty, therefore, is nothing else than freedom in appearance.[7]

Schiller's idea of "Freedom in appearance" (*Freiheit in der Erscheinung* and occasionally, *Autonomie in der Erscheinung*") is Kant's he*autonomy with a twist. Unlike Kant, Schiller focused on the illusion of freedom, its *appearance* or *Schein*. In Schiller's version, heautonomy specifically means not the actuality or reality of freedom, or autonomy (*nicht Freiheit in der Tat*), but the "appearance" of freedom (*sondern bloss . . . Autonomie in der Erscheinung*). Similarly, the "freedom" created by the sense/reason harmony that we achieve through our aesthetic response to the beautiful is not Kant's autonomy, but *he*autonomy, illusory.

Schiller carefully underscored the illusory nature of the freedom offered by his notion of heautonomy, and the fact that its connection to beauty was purely analogical.[8] In the February 18 Letter in which he outlines an analogical basis for the positing of freedom, he insists that he is dealing with a "representation" of freedom (*Darstellung der Freiheit*.)[9] Appearance, he explains, is nothing more than the analogical process (*Vorstellungsart der Dinge*) or the mind's habit of making analogical relationships. By analogical process, he means in particular the mind's representation of things as being free (*Kallias*, Feb. 23, p. 174). By the "appearance of freedom" (*Freiheit in der Erscheinung*), he means the aesthetic *representation* of freedom, the *he*autonomy achieved by art and the imagination.

Schiller deliberately compounds his theory's fictiveness, enlisting his illusory concept of heautonomy as the ground for Kant's already indeterminate concept of the harmony of the faculties (which even *Kant* thought required a supersensible ground). The double-indeterminacy of Schiller's strategy dramatizes what Lacoue-Labarthe calls an "originary power or *art of dissimulation*." In the face of this basic uncertainty, Lacoue-Labarthe observes,

> There does exist a 'solution': the idea . . . of a power or an *original* art of *dissimulation* (*Verstellung*, a perversion of *Vorstellung* or representation) by which man supplements his feebleness, his fragility, his brevity of existence, by which in other words he compensates for his finitude. Dissimulation defines itself as a force of illusion, but such that it can deceive itself, up to the point of taking itself for the force of truth (as if there were a force of truth . . .). It is thus not something other than the unconscious, the artistic instinct, but rather considered here as an original *forgetting* that inevitably implies an aesthetic response to terror (the weakness of the intellect, the absolute indifference of nature, its infinite repetitive mortal flux), the inadmissible of art, this negative crumpling and absence of certification which is already a nihilism wherein the 'lie' passes itself off for 'truth', the metaphor for the concept, myth for science, etc., and wherein the process of *unsure* initiates. ("Detour" 51-2).

"Worn away" by increasing age and by the potential breakdown in his own system, Kant himself had practiced a philosophical sleight of hand in passing off the "ground of the unity of the supersensible" as the basis of his formless concept of the harmony of the faculties.[10] Schiller, that "Bard tremendous in sublimity,"[11] as Coleridge described him, pushed Kant's dissimulation further, constructing a sublime figure of man's heautonomous "pure will" (*Reiner Wille*), which in its unfallen unity could fuse the beautiful and the morally good.

"'Reiner Wille' and the correlate 'Freiheit' exist in Schiller's mind *prior to either aesthetic or ethical differentiation*," Kerry observes, "and so provide a radical analogy of form between these areas." This prelapsarian *Reiner Wille* is founded on nothing but Schiller's nostalgic interpretation of "heautonomy." For Schiller, this is no longer Kant's merely subjective self-legislation in an act of reflective judgment, but an original, almost mystical inner will that can bestow autonomy not simply on human judgment and cognition but on external objects as well. Surpassing Kant's "unity of the supersensible" to ground his indeterminate harmony of the faculties, Schiller rests such harmony -- and, indeed, "*Die Schöne Seele*" and "*Moralische Schönheit*" (the Beautiful Soul and Moral Beauty), the basic components of his entire system -- on a "prime abstraction," in essence a primal fiction, of the heautonomous "*Reiner Wille*" (Kerry 43).

Outstripping Kant's system as a philosophy of the self, Schiller's figure of the *Reiner Wille* foreshadows the counter-identity of the romantic sublime. Like Wallace Stevens' absolute Angel[12] who could close the schism between fiction and reality, the *Reiner Wille* becomes a presence, a "'thing' [*Person, Wesen, Ding*]" in Schiller's system. It "takes on a curious metaphysical existence, suspiciously like the prohibited 'Thing in itself,'" Kerry writes (Kerry 60). For Schiller, heautonomy is no longer Kant's merely subjective self-legislation in an act of reflective judgment, but a primordial aspect of our objective identity that can bestow autonomy on man and world alike. Well beyond Kant's uncanny "unity of the supersensible" or "supersensible substrate," Schiller rests his own idea of a harmony of the faculties[13] on the autofigurational abstraction of a prelapsarian inner being, a being he calls elsewhere "the beautiful soul" (*Die Schöne Seele*).

"Reflecting or producing oneself is a *heauton*," Lacoue-Labarthe writes, [14] and Schiller's freedom in appearance is, indeed, Kant's wisely undeveloped *heautonomy* -- pushed to Schiller's positive reading of what he elsewhere decries as the "phantastic." Schiller consciously emphasizes the illusory aspect of such freedom, resting it on the free play of the imagination in its "analogical" and "representational" response to the external world. The fabric of his sense/reason fusion is pure illusion, and as such calls for and is sustained only by a province of pure "play." Schiller will write later that man is only fully "man" when he plays, that one can *only* play with beauty, and that it is only *beauty* with which one can play. In the last analysis, Kant and Schiller both confront the sublime. The major difference is that, faced with its mortal flux, Kant wavers, calls up the supersensible, and then wisely dismisses the sublime altogether. Schiller plays. He dances in the graveyard, covering it over with a glorious realm of *Schein* or aesthetic illusion that can sustain beauty, order, living form, a human freedom characterized by a sense/reason harmony, all within the fiction-making activity of art and the imagination.

The Dissimulated *Ich*

> I have hazarded a few ideas on the origin and progress of Art . . . Wieland . . . would not look upon it as a poem, but as philosophical poetry, and compared it to Young's 'Night Thoughts.' . . . He said that the picturesque language, and the buoyant flight from one simile to another so dazzled him . . . He calls it poetry in the English style.[15]
>
> -- Schiller

Aesthetic *Schein* or semblance functioned only so long as Schiller continued to "play," only so long as he remembered that the self-generating *heauton* that grounded his system was illusion. But by the February 23 Letter, Schiller has "forgotten" that it is illusion, and his theory of illusory freedom becomes *de*lusion. Significantly, what Schiller forgets is that there *is* no ground beneath his theory, only the indeterminate nonground of the sublime. Discerning Schiller's lapse, Kerry divides the *Kallias Letters* into two distinct parts: the "logical," in which Schiller tries to remain within the rigor of Kant's transcendental methodology, and the "empirical," more indicative of Schiller's own "poetic" and "irrational" desires. In the latter sector, "analogies become facts, aesthetic configurations become 'things' . . . [a]nd this wholly contrasting, aesthetically valid and systematically untenable vision is adapted and assimilated to the abstract terminology of the strictly logical framework. Conceptual myths are generated in the vacuum between philosophical and poetic language" (Kerry 36).

Tellingly, this forgetting, in which subjective vision and objective reality blur, coincides with Schiller's *own* sudden interest in the *Ding an Sich* (the thing in itself) -- the same interest that had accompanied Kant's sudden shift to the ontological ground of the supersensible. This project of legitimating such aesthetic fantasies outside their "native and proper sphere" involves Schiller in illogicalities, in which

> [t]he 'thing' [*Person, Wesen, Ding*], which he wishes to raise above a subjective intuition, and yet, clearly, cannot equate with the materiality of the object, takes on a curious metaphysical existence, suspiciously like the prohibited 'Thing in itself' -- *'das innere Prinzip der Existenz an einem Dinge -- die innere Notwendigkeit der Form'*" (Kerry 60).

There are echoes here of what Guyer had discerned as Kant's sudden shift into the supersensible, and of the correlate connection, unexplained, between his aesthetic theory and the metaphysical distinction separating appearance and the "thing in itself" (Guyer 338).

Schiller's problem lies in his forgetting, in his projection of aesthetic ideas onto external reality, and in treating them as if they were systematic: "He derives formulae which appear to claim the same kind of authority as "*'Schönheit ist Freiheit in der Erscheinung,'*" Kerry writes, which is intelligible without assuming "'real' existences in nature." However, he displaces these regulative, subjective ideas, projecting them into external nature (Kerry 68). The problem lies in the fact that aesthetic laws are valid only in imagination. But attempting in the Letter of February 23 to find correlates for beauty in actual phenomena, he makes "the maximum claim of objectivity for the formal grounds of beauty" (Kerry 69). He writes:

> I trust that I have put you in a position of following me without difficulty when I speak of nature, of self -- determination, of autonomy and heautonomy, of freedom

and of artistic accuracy. You will also agree with me that this nature and this heautonomy of which I write to you are objective states of things; for they remain part of them even if the postulated subject should be entirely dismissed.[16]

This statement forces Schiller into a contradiction of his major premises. If he has never given a real meaning to the subjective term *'Heautonomie'* outside the aesthetic vision, how, Kerry asks, can "'heautonomy' now be located in the objective world, completely prior to and independent of the intuitions of the observer?" (Kerry 70).

To locate heautonomy, the reflective or merely self-producing *heauton*, in the objective world, to make it constitutive, is precisely what Kant had correctly realized that the merely regulative *a priori* principle of taste *cannot* do. It is precisely because of the fantastic character of such a claim that Kant limited the heautonomy of his principle to the purely subjective arena. By projecting heautonomy onto external phenomena, Schiller undermines the otherwise aesthetically valid ground of his theory of art's freedom, and sends his theory into the fantastic. Kerry writes:

> The special virtue of Schiller's reflections has been throughout that he has been establishing a mode of visualizing the world of objects which suspends the known enslavement of things to a general causality, and offers them 'free citizenship' in the aesthetic state. This has been made possible only by the demonstration of the interplay of faculties in the subject, allowing and reinforcing the welcome illusion . . . Now Schiller is attempting . . . to locate real freedom in nature, and that without any formal retraction of the systematic views he shares with Kant (Kerry 70).

A comparison of Lacoue-Labarthe's concept of forgetting and Kerry's characterization is instructive here. Lacoue-Labarthe outlines an artistic dissimulation "by which man supplements his feebleness, his fragility, his brevity of existence, by which in other words he compensates for his finitude." This dissimulation "defines itself as *a force of illusion,* but such that it can deceive itself, up to the point of taking itself for the force of truth." The notion is crucial for Schiller. The self-delusion Lacoue-Labarthe describes is primitive, aesthetic in character, and an inevitable response to the menace of the sublime -- to its subversion of unity in general. Any poet such as Schiller, by his artistic sensibility bent on finding unity and not division, instinctively counters such a menace through deliberate conceptual blurrings: "It is . . . the unconscious," Lacoue-Labarthe writes, "the artistic instinct, but rather considered here as an original *forgetting* that inevitably implies an *aesthetic response to terror* (the weakness of the intellect, the *absolute indifference of nature*, its infinite repetitive mortal flux), the inadmissible of art, this negative crumpling and absence of certification which is already *a nihilism wherein the 'lie' passes itself off for 'truth', the metaphor for the concept*, myth for science, etc., and wherein *the process of unsure initiates*" ("Detour," 51-2, italics mine). It is, in other words, not by chance that Kerry explains Schiller's philosophical forgetting in the same terms. Schiller's "lapse," he writes, "appear[s] rather as a manifestation of that strong desire for the transparency and penetrability of the natural universe," a "primitive and compulsive vision which, despite Schiller's best efforts, cannot be properly reconciled with the overall rationality of the discourse" (Kerry 71, 73). Kerry and Lacoue-Labarthe react similarly to Schiller's extraordinary lapse, because its implications are patent: the "lie" or dissimulation is intrinsic to the aesthetic impulse, particularly as the artist responds to the sublime.

The Divided Self

> Philosophy and art have not penetrated one another, and we are more than ever conscious of the want of an organ to act as a medium between the two.[17]
> -- Schiller

Schiller's figure of the *Reiner Wille* epitomizes his early attempts to realize a mediating aesthetics that could reestablish man's unified identity as the being who wills. His attempt to objectify what was only subjective harmony, going so far as to embody such harmony in the figure of a prelapsarian alter ego, is the first sign that Schiller's attempt at mediation has faltered. The second sign is more subtle, and more damaging in terms of his theory of aesthetic mediation. The figure of pure will was an aside in Schiller's thinking. In general, his theory of aesthetic mediation remained a controlled and systematic endeavor that gave way only incrementally under the duress of principles underlying the sublime. During the early *Kallias* speculations, Schiller took Kant's claim of a "harmony of the faculties" so literally that he thought more in terms of fusion than of mediation. With regard to moral matters, the aesthetic impulse or play drive (*Speiltrieb*) could effect a total *harmony* between sense and reason, not just a connection or mediation. But as the ten years of his aesthetic essays progressed, Schiller came to suspect that such a harmony was impossible. In the early essays he had buried his suspicion in far-fetched reassertions of the *Kallias* theory.[18] But increasingly troubled by the inevitable sense/reason divide behind Kant's sublime, he abandoned his *Kallias* claim that beauty could *harmonize* sense and reason for the compromise claim that it could at least *mediate* between them.

Not surprisingly, the major obstacle to Schiller's theory of aesthetic reconciliation (*Freiheit in der Erscheinung*) was Kant. Schiller had developed his theory of aesthetic freedom in response to Kant's austere concept of a moral autonomy which left no place for man's appetitive inclinations. From the *Critique of Judgment*, however, Schiller had inherited a problematic based on the essentially moral nature of Kantian aesthetics, a problematic which required Schiller to account for moral instances which preclude any consideration of the sensuous impulse. Such instances, as Schiller well knew, were antithetical to his theory of a sense/reason harmony, and hence his attempts to deal with them give rise to two distinct accounts which run throughout his philosophical essays: 1) the *Kallias* theory of beauty's reconciliation of our sensual/rational demands, and the semblance of freedom it offers, and 2) admissions of instances, related to the subversive effects of the sublime, which invalidate such reconciliation and expose its freedom as mere counterfeit.

Such unfavorable moral instances are intrinsically connected to Kantian sublimity. For Kant, the very act of sensuous denial is itself moral, since it uncovers our spiritual "Self" and allows the "Pure Will" to shine forth.[19] An identical sensuous and imaginative abnegation defines Kantian sublimity. In a judgment of the sublime, the sheer mass or power of the object devastates the senses, crushes the imagination, which falls back, utterly inadequate to the task of conceptualization. Extreme oppression, both of our physical and imaginative faculties, is integral to an aesthetic judgment which, for Kant, served exclusively to put us in mind of that noumenal aspect of our existence, the Reason, and its correlate within us, the Moral Law. In Kantian sublimity, the less our senses are involved and the more our imagination is stultified, the better.

Logically extending the enforced sense/reason dichotomy of his moral philosophy to the aesthetic realm, Kantian sublimity produces grave implications for Schiller's theory of beauty. Since the primary function of this negative aesthetic is in fact to expose and hence subvert the counterfeit nature of aesthetic harmony, the "secondary discourse of the sublime," as Weiskel observes, "is built on the failure of the beautiful and its reconciling functions" (Weiskel 45). In essence, Weiskel tells us, while "the beautiful intimates reconciliation, the sublime splits consciousness into alienated halves" (Weiskel 48). Riven, then, by Kant's unfavorable moral instances and their aesthetic expression in the sublime, Schiller's entire philosophical *oeuvre* assumes a bifurcated quality, with each essay vacillating between the *Kallias* concept of a sense/reason harmony, and the sensual/rational division required by the Kantian problematic. Predictably, the see-saw pattern of the essays begins to reveal a progressive subversion of Schiller's original theory, with each nod to Kant bringing an additional qualification, and each modification representing a more damaging retreat.

Ambiguity characterizes even the earliest essays. In "On the Pleasure We Derive from Tragic Objects" (1792), for instance, the *Kallias* sentiments resonate in Schiller's claim that ". . . the pleasure we find in what is beautiful . . . strengthens our moral sentiments."[20] The Kantian problematic dominates the essay, however, since the sublime nature of tragedy requires that it "embrace all that sacrifices a physical propriety to a moral one" (Dole, II, 93). Similarly, though the essay "Detached Reflections on Various Questions of Aesthetics" (1792-93) begins with *Kallias* intimations of the "agreeable," the "good" and the "beautiful," it quickly moves into the Kantian acknowledgement that the sublime "must be in opposition to our sensuousness" (Dole, I, 277-8). The bifurcation of these two works should indicate the ambiguity which pervades Schiller's early thinking, a schismatic process that assumes roughly two forms in the minor aesthetic essays. In the first, though Schiller fluctuates between the *Kallias* theory of beauty's reconciling powers and the divisive sublimity of the Kantian problematic, he ultimately reinstates the *Kallias* model via logical or terminological confusion, or both. "Grace and Dignity" (May, 1793) falls into this category, as do "On the Pathetic" (Summer, 1793),

"The Moral Utility of Aesthetic Manners" (1793) and "On the Necessary Limits of Beautiful Form" (1793). In the second, Schiller makes no attempt to preserve the *Kallias* theory and, predictably, the sublime predominates. "On the Pleasure We Derive from Tragic Objects" (1792), "On the Vulgar and Low in Art" (1792-93), "Detached Reflections on Aesthetic Questions" (1792-93), and "Of the Sublime" (Spring, 1793) exemplify this second type.[21]

Of the essays of 1793, a year during which by his own admission, Schiller felt Kant's influence most intensely,[22] "Grace and Dignity"[23] (begun scarcely three months after his final *Kallias* letter to Körner) offers the most striking instance of the profound effects of the Kantian problematic on Schiller's thinking. Here is Schiller's first clear and systematic segregation of his two incompatible accounts, whose disparity he had previously blurred. Here, more importantly, is Schiller's introduction of the "bridge" theory of beauty, a striking compromise of the *Kallias* theory that arises in direct connection with the subversive character of the Kantian sublime. Divided into two distinct halves entitled "Grace" ("*Anmut*"), and "Dignity" ("*Würde*"), the essay's format exhibits a telling bifurcation. "Grace," the external expression of the beauty of moral freedom which results from the serene and harmonious coexistence in man of "reason and sense, inclination and duty," accords perfectly with the *Kallias* theory. The moral freedom existing in "grace," which comes through the aesthetic reconciliation of man's warring impulses, is simply a reiteration of *Freiheit in der Erscheinung*.

But "Grace," the *Kallias* version of the essay, is only half the story, for Schiller must acquiesce to the instances, implied by the Kantian problematic, which are unfavorable to such harmony. "There may be conflicts," he admits, "between the law of nature . . and the law of reason" (Dole, I, 213). In such conflicts, one's "Dignity" must come to the fore, that outward expression of the "sublimity" of the will, which raises us above our sensuous inclinations. It is here, significantly, that Schiller introduces the sense/reason dichotomy required by Kant, since in "dignity," the senses and the reason are not only "no longer in harmony," but "it is precisely in their *opposition* that consists the expression of the moral force" (Dole, I, 218).

Just as the Kantian problematic evokes in "Grace and Dignity" Schiller's first sustained distinction between two unreconcilable notions, the sublime properties attendant upon that problematic give rise to a stunning modification of the *Kallias* theory. Observe Schiller's introduction of the second part of his essay:

> Dignity
>
> As grace is the expression of a noble soul, so is dignity the expression of a sublime feeling. It has been prescribed to man, it is true, to establish between his two natures a unison, to form always a harmonious whole . . . But this beauty of character . . . is but an ideal to which . . . he can never fully attain (Dole, I, 211).

With the introduction of the "sublime," come the beginnings of Schiller's most damaging qualification of the *Kallias* theory, the suggestion of a bridge notion[24] of the beautiful rather than a reconciliation, in which if beauty cannot actually "harmonize" our sensual and rational demands, it may perhaps offer some mediation between them. This severe diminution of beauty's efficacy will emerge as a full-blown acquiescence to Kant in *Aesthetic Education*, an inferior bridge model of the beautiful which is pitted against Schiller's own assertions of aesthetic harmony. And, indeed, by the time Schiller comes to write *Naive and Sentimental Poetry*, a mere mediational function, no longer even of beauty but of morality, will be all that remains of "reconciliation" in Schiller's system -- an endless bridge leading to an unattainable goal.

This barest of hints in "Grace and Dignity" that one might supplant a reconciling beauty with a mere mediatory function hardens, in *Aesthetic Education*, into a clear theoretical rift. In this most famous of Schiller's aesthetic essays, the two accounts are distilled into the clearly delineated and incompatible concepts of beauty as actual harmonizer of man's warring impulses,[25] and beauty as mere bridge,[26] intermediary stage between them.[27] Predictably, the harmony model, with its concomitant claims for *Schein*, play, the imagination, and appetitive man, sustains the original concept of heautonomy and the reconciling powers of the beautiful. The bridge model, Schiller's qualification in light of the Kantian problematic, consistently undermines each of the secondary characteristics of a reconciling beauty, and exhibits the predominant divisiveness of the sublime.

The harmony model is clearly one of accomplished unity. The aesthetic impulse and its object, beauty, actually reconcile sensuous and moral demands. "The play drive," Schiller tells us, "sets man free both physically and morally" (*AE*, 14, #5, 97) brings feelings and passions into harmony with ideas of reason, and reconciles laws of reason with sensuous interests" (*AE*, 14, #6, 99). The aesthetic makes man "a whole,[28] complete in himself, because it demands the cooperation of his two natures" (*AE*, 27, #10, 215). "Beauty weds [*verknüpft*] the two opposed conditions of feeling and thinking" in a "pure aesthetic unity," "unites" them so that "both conditions disappear entirely in a third one and no trace of separation remains" (*AE*, 18, #2, 123; 18, #4, 124-5). This can occur because ". . .in the realization of beauty or of aesthetic unity there is an actual union, an interchange between matter and form, passivity and activity" which proves the "compatibility of our two natures" (*AE*, 25, #6, 189). We need no longer wonder, Schiller explains, "how man succeeds in raising himself from the limited to the absolute, and opposing himself in his thought and will to sensuality, as this has already been produced in the fact of beauty" (*AE*, 25, #7, 189).

By contrast, the bridge model is one of division. Sensuous interest and moral demand are not reconciled but remain distinct, with beauty simply mediating between them. "Passing from mere life directly to pure form

. . . . is contrary to human nature," Schiller observes (*AE*, 25, #4, 185). "The transition from the passivity of sensuousness to the activity of thought and will can be effected," he asserts, "only by the intermediate stage of aesthetic freedom."[29] No longer a harmonizer of the sense and reason, beauty now becomes simply "a means of leading man from matter to form, from feeling to laws," of merely "paving the way" from feeling to thought, "leading the way" from sense to reason (*AE*, 19, #6, 131; 17, #4, 121; 19, #6, 131). If, however, "beauty provides man with a transition from sensation to thought," this "does not mean that beauty could ever bridge the gulf separating feeling from thinking. This gulf is infinite" (*AE*, 19, #6, 131). Far from the sensuous/rational unity of the *Kallias* harmony model, Schiller openly admits the profoundly divisive implications of the bridge model: "We can distinguish three different moments or stages of development through which the individual and the species must pass . . . if they are to complete the cycle of their destiny" (*AE*, 24, #1, 171). This destiny is not unity but fragmentation. As Schiller observes, man's ". . . step from the aesthetic to the logical and moral state (i.e., from beauty to truth and duty) . . . involves taking from himself, not giving to himself [*sich bloss zu nehmen und nicht zu geben*], fragmenting his nature, not enlarging it [*bloss seine Natur zu vereinzeln, nicht zu erweitern braucht*]" (*AE*, 23, #5, 163).

Sublimity and Self-Annihilation

> I am studying Kant's 'Powers of Judgment' . . . I feel, that . . . I have lost that boldness and living fire I formerly possessed. I now see what I create and form. I watch the progress of the fruits of inspiration, and my imagination is less free, since it is aware that it is being watched.[30]
>
> -- Schiller

It is not by chance that with the clear delineation of beauty's inferior bridge role in *Aesthetic Education*, the Kantian problematic and its coeval properties of sublimity slowly come to dominate Schiller's thinking. If as late as *Aesthetic Education* Schiller still resisted the influence of Kant's theory on the *Kallias* harmony model of beauty, the essays which follow clearly reveal that in the face of the sublime, the illusory center of heautonomy could not hold. There, the bridge compromise, with its built-in divisiveness, had become Schiller's only recourse. Moreover, the tenuous, even half-hearted hold that he had on the notion of a mere "mediation" is evident in "Vom Erhabenen" ("Of the Sublime," written Summer, 1793) in which Schiller dismisses the bridge function of beauty altogether and replaces it with a bridge of religion. "Of the Sublime,"[31] Schiller's first essay focussing solely on sublimity, reveals an *un*ambiguous capitulation to the Kantian problematic. However, the theoretical problems that beset Schiller in the essay and the solution he devises raise doubts not only about the viability of the remaining bridge model of beauty, but about Schiller's entire system.

Schiller first develops his theory along Kantian lines, distinguishing the "theoretical sublime" (*Theoretischerhabenen*) from the "practical sublime"

(*Praktischerhabenen*). Schiller's *Erhabenes der Erkenntniss* and *Erhabenes der Gesinnung* ("Of the Sublime" 172) essentially repeat Kant's "mathematical" and "dynamic" sublime, and hence except for the threat to his theory already implied by the Kantian sublime, the early section of the essay poses no new problem for Schiller. His later distinction, however, arrived at through a logical extension of Kantian sublimity -- the "pathetic" vs. the "contemplative" sublime -- poses a theoretical crisis implied by the notion of death, the ultimate province of the sublime, that no amount of aesthetic hedging can surmount. The "pathetic sublime," an idea Schiller had treated earlier, presents no obstacle, since it arises in face of an object that immediately threatens our existence. The "contemplative sublime" by contrast, arises in face of a condition that threatens us only in the attitude we take toward it. Such conditions are fate, the possibility of painful illness, and the certainty of death. The implications of the sublime's effect on Schiller's system here require our awareness of a final quality of sublimity, undoubtedly the most devastating: "Among the things the sublime enables us to discount is our life," Weiskel observes, and Schiller ultimately "developed Kant's view [of sublimity] into a justification of suicide under certain conditions" (Weiskel 95).[32] In "Of the Sublime," it is as if Schiller already senses the futility of his biophilic aesthetics, since he reaches for a non-aesthetic solution which itself illustrates the irreversible damage wrought by the Kantian problematic and its properties of the negative sublime.

Following Burke and Kant, Schiller had said that in order to experience the sublime we must feel fear, but not to the same extent as when our physical safety is endangered. However, Schiller now considers cases of the "contemplative sublime," "calamities and perils before which man can never be secure."[33] Since a certainty of our physical safety is necessary to the sublime, how do we ground that safety in cases of the contemplative sublime: "But on what do we ground our security," Schiller queries, "in the face of fate, . . . painful illness, grievous loss or death?"[34] Clearly aware that the "contemplative sublime" lacks the security necessary to the sublime experience -- how can we feel secure in face of inevitable death? -- Schiller now posits a *theological* foundation for that assurance, which crucially undermines not only the possibility of the *Kallias* theory, but that of the bridge model as well.

In the "contemplative sublime," he explains, we must ground our assurance on the sense of the "moral security" ("*moralische Sicherheit*") of our own immortality which is given by religion ("Of the Sublime" 180). "We view the terrifying without terror," he writes, "because we feel abstracted by thoughts of the imperishability of our being."[35] The informing bridge metaphor of religion appears in Schiller's explanation that "religion is that which seeks to establish a reconciliation [*Aussöhnung*], an agreement [*Übereinkunft*] between the claim of reason and the interest of the sensuous."[36] Schiller's addition of "*Übereinkunft*" to the almost synonymous "*Aussöhnung*" is not mere redundancy. Though *Übereinkunft* also means "agreement" or "reconciliation," the root "*überein*," which means to "cross, to cover up and extend beyond," reveals the bridge metaphor that guides his view of religion here. With the contemplative sublime, therefore, in order to sufficiently assuage our fear so that we may attain to the moral freedom given in the experience of death's sublimity, religion, with its promise of immortality, must first come in as a bridge between our sensuous and our spiritual existence ("Of the Sublime" 182). This solution poses grave problems for Schiller's aesthetic theory. In the "contemplative sublime" it is not an aesthetic response but a theological one, not art or beauty but religion which has assumed the bridge or mediating role.

In the face of the sublime's ultimate province, death, Schiller does not yet turn to moral suicide as he will in his final philosophical essay, "On the Sublime" (1793, 1801). Nevertheless, his treatment of it in "Of the Sublime" has theoretical repercussions far beyond those suggested by Weiskel. For when Schiller must take into account those instances which are absolutely unfavorable to the sense/reason harmony of beauty, he not only renounces any idea of reconciliation, but by substituting the concept of religion as the new sense/reason mediator, he also relinquishes the final vestiges of his theory, i.e., the inferior bridge role of beauty. Given the subversive qualities of the sublime, it is indeed no accident that in "Of the Sublime," beauty virtually disappears. The "contemplative sublime," with its crushing overtones of mortality, forces Schiller to replace beauty altogether with a bridge model of a completely unrelated concept. All that remains in this essay of his *Kallias* theory of aesthetics, is a non-aesthetic trace, a spectral "bridge" of religion.[37] As Schiller had observed in a poem, "Death is not aesthetic, my friends."[38]

Given Schiller's increasingly troubled approaches to the sublime, it is not surprising that his first extensive exploration of sublimity would unsettle the viability of even the bridge theory of beauty. But with *Naive and Sentimental Poetry* (1795-6)[39], not only had the bridge theory waned further, but the vaunted promises of a new autonomous self for man has paled as well. In this late essay, the bridge becomes a shadowy "path," leading essentially to nothingness, to what, in the more optimistic *Aesthetic Education*, Schiller called the "barren and naked land of abstraction" (*AE*, 10, #7, 71). The "path" is not one of art, moreover, of morality. At one level, the work is a comparison of the "naive" artist who, like Goethe,[40] still sustained the ideal sense/reason harmony which Schiller saw epitomized in Greek antiquity, and the "modern" or "sentimental" poet, like Schiller himself, who had long since lost such "natural" unity. At another level, the one that concerns us here, the piece is a nostalgic yearning, a hopeless quest for a vague and unattainable identity. The identity epitomized by the Arcadian ideal: the true, the beautiful, the good, the free was lost to phenomenal man; it was now a nebulous ideal, an "Elysium" toward which modern man limped upon an endless "path," no longer a "bridge," leading as far as Schiller could explain, nowhere (*N&SP* 153).

The journey prescribed in *Naive and Sentimental Poetry* signals the profound effects of the sublime on Schiller's original reconciliatory aesthetics. Like the sublime, the journey has no end, since Schiller's new ideal of "unity," sometimes called "the divine" (*N&SP* 85), is phenomenally and aesthetically unattainable: "This path," Schiller observes, "along which man . . . must pass" is an endless one, stretching into nothingness, leading to a goal before which "he must fall infinitely short," toward which he "approaches in endless progress," and which promises "an infinitude to which he never attains" (*N&SP*, 113, 85). The "unity," moreover, is no longer the sense/reason harmony of beauty but a "moral unity," which more clearly than ever before is not unity at all but the sense/reason divisiveness of Kant's moral philosophy. With the sentimental, Schiller now explains, "sensuous harmony in [man] is withdrawn, and he can only express himself as a moral unity, i.e., as striving after unity" (*N&SP* 11). The state of endless striving "after" such unity is not a "unity" but a division, characterized, like the sublime, not by fulfillment, but incompleteness, not by aesthetic freedom, but "moral regret" (*N&SP* 89).

The Sentimental's art becomes a signpost of his divided identity. Whereas "nature" had "set [man] at one with himself," Schiller writes, sentimental "art divides and cleaves him in two" (*N&SP* 112). Sublimity resonates in sentimental art's new tendency to divide and alienate: "The sentimental poet is . . . always involved with two conflicting representations, with actuality as a limit and with his ideas as infinitude" (*N&SP* 116). Like the artist's futile attempt to contain the formless and overwhelming, the sentimental must "reconcile the representation of imagination with an idea of reason and hence always fluctuate between two different conditions" (*N&SP* 116n). The vagueness of the "path along which the sentimental poet must pass" strikingly reflects what Schiller had called the "murky contours" of the sublime (*AE*, 25, #3, 185). But whereas the *Kallias* artist actually achieved a representation of the ideal -- the aesthetic process itself combined both the sensuous and rational drives -- the representations of the sentimental poet, and "modern" man, must always remain problematic. To Schiller, "It is the representation of the ideal that makes for the poet" (*N&SP*, 112). But that ideal, indeed, all the "material" of the sentimental poet, is unrepresentable. Sentimental art is the "art of the infinite," of "whatever is insusceptible of representation and ineffable, in a word, . . . [of] whatever . . . is called *spirit*." (*N&SP* 114-15).

Pervading *Naive and Sentimental Poetry*, Kant's sublime precludes any mediating impulse that might unify man's divided faculties and restore his proper identity. As in *Aesthetic Education*, where premonitions of sentimental yearning first appear, the "infinite opens up before our reeling imagination," leaving us with only "infinite longing," "Care and Fear" (*AE*, 24, #5, 175). The *Kallias* play drive which promised the restoration of man's "humanity" has been displaced with a "highly serious," even "humiliating" process of "resignation," in which "we look *upward* from the *limitation* of our condition," reminded by the fact that "we *change*, they [the naive] remain a unity" (*N&SP* 122, 87, 85). This is a far cry from the "third joyous kingdom of play and of semblance, in which man is relieved of the shackles of circumstance and released from all that might be called constraint, alike in the physical and in the moral sphere." This is a vastly different identity than the autonomous *Ich,* or self (*AE*, 27, #8, 215).

Schiller has clearly abandoned the idea of an ideal self. He has dismissed any hope of a bridge or even a "path" between sense and reason. He exhorts us rather to accept the division between noumenal and phenomenal, to face the evil of reality, since only in acquaintance with it may we obtain freedom (*N&SP* 100-01). "Then no more," he writes, "of the complaints of the difficulties of life . . . with free resignation you must subject yourself to all the ills of civilization" (*N&SP* 101-02). In what becomes an official doctrine of "resignation," he commands us, not unlike Kant, to "stand face to face with the evil fatality" ("On the Sublime" 209). "Be not afraid of the confusion around you, only of the confusion within you . . . abandoned by the ladder that supported you, no other choice now lies open to you, but with free consciousness and will to grasp the [moral] law, or fall without hope of rescue into a bottomless pit" (*N&SP* 101). Tellingly, this caveat is repeated in the final lines of the essay.

In the last analysis, Schiller concludes, the law is all we can cling to, cling or risk an "infinite fall into a bottomless abyss [which] can only terminate in complete destruction" (*N&SP* 190). This stark reversal, in which Schiller turns from a celebration of aesthetic freedom or "play" to a grim admonition to follow the law shows that the bridge, the path, or any movement toward realizing morality in physical existence, is gone. In the optimistic *Kallias Letters*, a bridge had not been necessary, since Schiller had hoped for a fusion of sense and reason through aesthetic play. Constructed upon an even more questionable foundation of indeterminacy than Kant's, Schiller's bridge of illusion began to reveal its increasingly tenuous character. The "sublime dignity" of this bridge not only manifests a highly damaging compromise, signalling that Schiller has indeed become aware of an abyss between sense and reason, it reveals that the sublime has begun to subvert the possibility of a unified self altogether. In "Of the Sublime," Kantian sublimity has fully infiltrated Schiller's system, usurping beauty's function entirely, and replacing it with the solace of religion.

Schiller's final attempt in *Naive and Sentimental Poetry* to reunify man's fragmented identity is short-lived. Indeed, the self disappears altogether by the essay's conclusion with the resigned admission of the unbridgeable character of human nature's two warring faculties. The gulf, moreover, is clearly the province of the Kantian sublime, and to Schiller, in his final philosophical essay "On the Sublime" (1793, 1801), the only logical conclusion in face of it is "moral suicide." He was dealing with a thinker whom he called "the Draco of his time," a tyrant whose moral philosophy proposes "the idea of duty . . . with a harshness enough to ruffle the Graces and one which could easily tempt a feeble mind to seek for moral perfection in the somber paths of an ascetic and monastic life." Clearly, he wrote archly in a letter addressing Kant's moral philosophy, "one could be assured of doing one's duty only if one did it with aversion"

(Dole, I, 205-206).[41] Thus, while he accedes to Kant's restrictions, a sanguine Schiller can in no way submit to Kant's austere philosophy. The concept of *moral* rather than *aesthetic* resignation left to him in his final philosophical essay, clearly a resignation brought about by principles underlying Kant's sublime, is tantamount to death.

NOTES

1. *Wie werde ich nun von dieser Sinnlichen Abhangigkeit zu der moralische Freiheit einen Übergang finden?* Letter to Prince von Augustenberg, November 11, 1793, in *Schiller's Briefe*, ed. Erik Jonas, (Stuttgart, Leipzig, Berlin, Vienna: Deutsche Verlags-Anstalt, n.d.), III, 385. Hereafter, *Briefe*.

2. Paul Guyer, *Kant and the Claims of Taste*, 35.

3. Lacoue-Labarthe, "Le Detour," in *Le Sujet de Philosophie* (Paris, 1979), 31-74, p. 52. Hereafter, "Detour." See Lacoue-Labarthe, "The Detour," trans. Gary Cole in Lacoue-Labarthe, *The Subject of Philosophy* (Minnesota, 1993).

4. Schiller, "The Stage as a Moral Institution" (*Works*, II, 53).

5. Long before responding to the sense/reason dichotomy prescribed in Kantian ethics, Schiller had begun to examine the idea of a reciprocal sense/reason relation. In "*Philosophie der physiologie*" (1779) he sought "the point within the reciprocal action of body upon mind, and mind upon body" that would "'save' the freedom of the will." But he was still working with the problem of associationist theory, and had not clearly defined his basic tenets. See Elizabeth Wilkinson, Introduction, in Schiller, *On the Aesthetic Education of Man* (Oxford 1967), xxxii. Hereafter, *AE*. The following year found Schiller on the same theme with "On the Connection between the Animal and Spiritual Nature in Man" (1780), an essay designed to "bring into a clearer light the remarkable contributions made by the body to the working of the soul." See Schiller, *Aesthetical and Philosophical Essays*, ed. Nathan Haskell Dole, 2 vols. (Boston

1902), II, 133. Again, however, though Schiller had shown that the body participates in the spirit, that "animal impulses awaken and develop the impulses of the soul" ("Connection between the Animal and Spiritual" 142), he had not established a systematic connection between man's sensuous vocation and his moral autonomy. Hereafter, references to translations of Schiller's minor aesthetic essays are taken from the Dole edition, unless otherwise noted, and will appear as Dole.

[6.] The *Kallias Letters* refers to correspondence between Schiller and his friend Gottfried Körner from January through March, 1793. In the Letters, Schiller proposes to write a dialogue entitled "*Kallias oder über die Schönheit*," and outlines a number of the points to be included. The dialogue was never written, but Schiller's remarks, preserved in the *Kallias Letters* to Körner, contain the germinal ideas of what was to become his basic aesthetic theory. The most important letters, as Ellis has observed, are Dec. 21; Jan. 11 and 25; Feb. 8, 18, 19, 23, and 28. Several further letters in which Schiller mentions the *Kallias* project prove helpful in explaining why Schiller did not continue it. These are Mar. 15 and 22; April 7; May 5 and 27; June 20. Only the Letters of Feb. 8, 18, and 23 are relevant to the present discussion. For a thorough examination of Schiller's "Kallias" theory, see J. M. Ellis, *Schiller's Kalliasbriefe and the Study of His Aesthetic Theory* (The Hague, 1969), and S. S. Kerry, *Schiller's Writings on Aesthetics* (Manchester, England: 1961). Hereafter, Ellis, and Kerry.

[7.] *Analogie einer Erscheinung mit der Form des Reine Willens oder der Freiheit ist Schönheit (in weitester Bedeutung). Schönheit also ist nicht anders, als Freiheit in der Erscheinung.* Schiller, Letter to Körner, Feb. 8, 1793, in *Briefwechsel Zwischen Schiller und Körner* (München, 1973), 163. References to the texts of the *Kallias Letters* will be taken from this edition and cited as *Kallias*.

[8.] Elsewhere in the Feb. 8 Letter to Körner, Schiller emphasizes the analogous and illusory nature of Beauty's heautonomy: "*So ist diese Analogie eines Gegenstandes mit der Form der pr(aktischen) Vernunft nicht Freiheit in der Tat, sondern bloss Freiheit in der Erscheinung, Autonomie in der Erscheinung.* Kallias*, p. 162.

[9.] *Kallias*, Feb. 18, p. 167. The same emphasis appears in a number of remarks. As Schiller explains: "Diese grosse Idee der Selbstbestimmung strahlt uns aus gewissen Erscheinungen der Natur zuruck, und diese nennen wir Schönheit." And elsewhere:

> Zeigt sich nun ein Objekt in der Sinnenwelt bloss durch sich selbst bestimmt, stellt es sich den Sinnenso dar, dass man an ihm keinen Einfluss des Stoffes oder eines Zweckes bemerkt; so wird es als ein Analogen der reinen Willenbestimmung (ja nicht als Produkt einer Willenbestimmung) beurteilt. Weil nun ein Wille, der sich nach blosser Form bestimmen kann, frei heisst, so ist diejenige Form in der Sinnenwelt, die bloss durch sich selbst bestimmt erscheint, eine Darstellung der Freiheit; den dargestellt heisst eine Idee, die mit einer Anschauung so verbunden wird, das beide eine Erkenntnisregel miteinander teilen.

[10] Kant admits to "the forming force" (*die bildende Kraft*) of reason or transcendental imagination. See Philippe Lacoue-Labarthe, "Typography," in *Typography: Mimesis, Philosophy, Politics* (Cambridge, MA: 1989), 70; *(Mimesis des Articulation* (Paris, 1975).

[11] Coleridge, Jan. 6, 1823. In *Table Talk* (Princeton, NJ: 1990), I, 26.

[12] Wallace Stevens, "Notes Toward a Supreme Fiction." VII *The Palm at the End of the Mind*. Ed. Holly Stevens. (New York, 1972), 230.

[13] Schiller also rests "*Die Schöne Seele*" and "*Moralische Schönheit*" (the Beautiful Soul and Moral Beauty), the basic components of his entire system on the *Reiner Wille*.

[14] "Typography," in *Typography* (Cambridge, 1989), 127.

[15] Schiller, Letter to Körner, Feb 25, 1789, *Correspondence of Schiller with Körner*, ed. Simpson (London, 1849), 342.

16. *Ich hoffe Dich nunmehr in den Stand gesetzt zu haben, mir ungehindert zu folgen, wenn ich von Natur, von Selbstbestimmung, von Autonomie und Heautonomie, von Freiheit und von Kunstmässigkeit spreche. Du wirst auch mit mir darüber einig sein, dass diese Natur und diese Heautonomie objektive Beschaffenheiten der Gegenstände sind, denen ich sie zuschreibe; denn sie bleiben ihnen, auch wenn das vorstellende Subjekt ganz hinweggedacht wird. Kallias,* Feb. 23, 1793, p. 182.

17. Letter to Goethe, Jan. 20, 1802, in *Correspondence between Schiller and Goethe, from 1794 to 1805*, trans. Dora Schmitz (London, 1877), I.

18. There are hints of beauty's incompleteness both in the bridge function of beauty in *Aesthetic Education*, and in the discrepancy between grace and dignity in "Grace and Dignity." But Schiller conceals beauty's incompleteness in the bridge model with a ringing assertion of the powers of *Schein*, or aesthetic semblance, in his two concluding Letters. He also obscures the grace/dignity distinction by blurring of the properties of the noble soul and the great soul (both termed "*Schöne Seele*"), and can therefore conclude that since dignity (displayed by the great soul) includes grace (which characterizes the noble soul) and vice versa, the concept of a *Kallias* harmony stands.

19. Kant writes: "the sublimity and inner worth of the command [of the Moral Law] is more manifest in a duty, the fewer are the subjective causes for obeying it and the more against." Immanuel Kant, *Groundwork of the Metaphysics of Morals*, trans. H. J. Paton (New York, 1964), 425, 60.

20. Schiller, "Of the Cause of the Pleasure We Derive from Tragic Objects," in *Aesthetical and Philosophical Essays*, Dole, II, 88.

21. When precisely in 1793 any of the minor essays were completed is a matter of speculation. All, according to the editors of the *Nationalausgabe Werke*, seem to have been in progress in 1793. And some appear to have preceded others. "On the Necessary Limitations in the Use of Beauty of Form," for instance, seems to follow the inception of "Grace and Dignity," given Schiller's remark in a letter to Körner of October 4, 1793: "*Ich habe jetzt wieder eine kleine Schrift etwa wie Anmut und Würde angefangen.*"

22. On December 3, 1793, Schiller wrote to Prince von Augustenberg: "*Ich bekenne gleich vorläufig, dass ich im Hauptpunkt der Sittenlehre volkommen kantisch denke.*" Significantly, Schiller's admission of Kant's dominance in his thought is later crossed out. See Schiller, *Werke, Nationalausgabe*, Hrsgb., Benno von Wiese (Weimar, 1962), XXI, 324. References to Schiller's essays in the *Nationalausgabe* edition will be cited as *Werke*, with the appropriate volume number.

23. Schiller, "Grace and Dignity," Dole, II, 168-211.

24. Schiller had frequently employed the metaphor of a "bridge" to describe beauty's function. As early as 1793, he had written to Prince von Augustenberg: "Wie werde ich nun von dieser sinnlichen Abhangigkeit zu der moralische Freiheit einen Übergang finden?" ("How will I now find a bridge from this sensuous dependence to moral freedom?"), in *Schiller's Briefe*, ed. Jonas, III. p. 385.
See also Schiller's "The Stage as a Moral Institution," in which he remarks: "Man, neither altogether satisfied with the senses, nor forever capable of thought, wanted a middle state, a bridge between the two states, bringing them into harmony" (Dole, II, 53).

25. Letters 9, 14-15, 22, 26-27.

26. Letters 16-21, 23-24.

27. Scholars have long been aware of Schiller's two disparate accounts of beauty's function in *Aesthetic Education*. Wilkinson and Willoughby allude to a number of them in the very thorough and informative Introduction to their translation of *Aesthetic Education*. However, though acknowledging the discrepancy, they interpret critical emphasis of it as philosophical nit-picking. This is a rather wrong-headed approach to Schiller, I believe. The discrepancy between the two accounts is clearly there. The point is not to obscure its presence, as do Wilkinson and Willoughby, with accounts of Schiller's art of "paradox" (*AE*, xlix), views of *Aesthetic Education* as a "labyrinth" (lvii), a dismembered Grecian torso (lviii), a poetic dialectical "dance" (cxxii-cxxxii), etc. (which may perfectly well be true on one level), but to take Schiller's work on the philosophical level (in which Schiller clearly intended it) and then to ask why such contradictions occur. What do they imply, not only for the possibility of

Schiller's original theory, but in terms of the larger consequences, i.e., the implications for any reconciliatory theory of art, of which so many existed in the immediately following period of romanticism?

28. The harmony model appears early in the essay (Letters 9, 14, 15), while Schiller sustains a rather straightforward but poetically informed rhetoric. It gives way to the bridge model for most of the remainder (Letters 16-21, 23-24) where, tellingly, Schiller attempts Kant's transcendental method. Schiller is able to revive the harmony model at the conclusion only by underscoring its illusory character, i.e., the fact that the freedom of beauty's harmony or *Freiheit in der Erscheinung* is grounded merely in semblance or *Schein*. Reflecting the idealistic thrust of Schiller's intensely humanistic *Kallias* theory, the early harmony Letters are carried by the rhetorical pitting of metaphors of organic wholeness against those of mechanical fragmentation. To heal man, says Schiller, we must unite, not "dissect" him: "man is not a clock; one cannot stop one part of the mechanism (i.e., sensuous) in order to repair another (i.e., rational)." Clearly revealing the encroachment of Kant's influence, these metaphors disappear from the essay after Letter 9 (a Letter intrinsically Schillerian), giving way to abstruse attempts at transcendental logic and an emergent imagery of war.

If Carlyle's crusty estimation of *Aesthetic Education* must be put down as irascible, his attacks on Schiller's logic-chopping contain some truth. To Carlyle, if "the end and aim of Kantian philosophy seems not to make abstruse things simple, but to make simple things abstruse," Schiller's aim in *Aesthetic Education* seems little better, given its ". . . dreadful array of first principles, the forest huge of terminology and definitions, where the panting intellect of weaker men wanders as in pathless thickets and at length sinks powerless to the earth, oppressed with fatigue and suffocated with scholastic miasma." See Calvin Thomas, The Life and Works of Schiller (New York, 1904), 283. After Letter 11, *Aesthetic Education* indeed reveals a thicket of fractured Kantian logic, a number of errors of which provide clear evidence of Schiller's faltering struggle to evade the Kantian problematic.

Though chiefly characterized by a rigorous attempt at transcendental method after Letter 11, Schiller's subsequent writing in the essay is not without rhetorical imagery. Interestingly, however, the organic/mechanical metaphors of the early harmony Letters give way in the bridge Letters to imagery of warfare. The aesthetic, for instance, must "guard against the encroachment upon the frontiers of either drive [sensuous or rational] by the other." And elsewhere, Schiller exhorts us to "let man play the war against matter on the territory of matter, so he does not have to fight this dread foe on the sacred soil of freedom" (23, #8, 169). Assuredly, it is a battle of man's warring natures with which Schiller attempts to deal in *Aesthetic Education*, a *Streit der Fakultäten*, as Kant would have it. But it also is a battle of Schiller's own principles against Kantian ones.

29. *AE*, 23, #1, 163.

30. Schiller, Letter to Körner, May 23, 1792, in *Correspondence of Schiller with Körner*, 3 vols. (London, 1849).

31. "*Vom Erhabenen,*" *Werke*, XX, 170-195. Hereafter, "Of the Sublime."

32. In a compelling study, Joel Black argues that the logical conclusion of the sublime can be murder as well as suicide. See Black, *The Aesthetics of Murder* (Baltimore, 1992), 15.

33. "*Nun gibt es aber Unglücksfalle und Gefahren, vor denen sich der Mensch niemals sicher wissen kann,*" "Of the Sublime," 179.

34. "*Aber worauf wollte man seine Sicherheit vor dem Schicksal . . . vor schmerzhaften Krankheiten, vor empfindlichen Verlusten, vor dem Tode grunden?*" "Of the Sublime" 180.

35. "*Wir sehen das Furchtbare ohne Furcht an, weil wir . . . Gedanken an die Unzerstörbarkeit unsers Wesens entzogen fühlen.*" "Of the Sublime" 181.

36. "*Die Religion ist es, der zwischen den Forderung der Vernunft und dem Anliegen der Sinnlichkeit eine Aussöhnung eine Übereinkunft zu stiften sucht.*" "Of the Sublime" 181. "Religion is that which seeks to establish an agreement or a bridge between the advancement of reason and the demands of sensuality."

37. Wilkinson's and Willoughby's focus on *Aesthetic Education* obscures the theoretical implications of such essays as "Of the Sublime": ". . . never having assigned primacy to aesthetic values," they write, "he [Schiller] never -- like a Schelling or a Pater -- found himself in the position of having to recant in favor of religion or morality" (*AE*, clxxxi). Schiller clearly recanted in favor of both.
   The idea that to introduce immortality and religion is to hobble the *Kallias*

theory of beauty is further underscored in Goethe's evaluation of Schiller's aesthetics. During an extended period of correspondence on Schiller's exploration of the aesthetic impulse, Goethe wrote to his friend: "The aesthetic state of mind calls for none of those arguments of comfort which have to be drawn from speculation . . . it is only when the sensuous and the moral elements in man come into conflict, that help has to be sought from pure reason. A healthy and beautiful nature . . . requires no moral code, no Law for its nature . . . *you might as well have added that it requires no godhead, no idea of immortality wherewith to support and maintain itself.*" See Letter to Schiller, July 9, 1796, in *Correspondence between Goethe and Schiller*, trans. Dora Schmitz (London, 1877), I, 199, italics mine.

38. Schiller, "Genius with the Inverted Torch."

39. Schiller, *Naive and Sentimental Poetry*, in *Friedrich von Schiller: Naive and Sentimental Poetry and "On the Sublime*," trans. Elias (New York, 1966), 83-190. Hereafter, *N&SP*.

40. Much could be said, at this level, about the justificatory character of the piece, particularly with regard to what Bloom would call Schiller's "strong precursor poet," Goethe. Such concerns, however, are beyond the scope of this study.

41. Schiller's chaffing at Kant's ideas is worth noting. Kant's denigration of the senses was, to Schiller, not only excessive and unnecessary, but wrong-headed. The idea of a "pleasure" that could possibly be taken in doing anything "with aversion," in this case one's duty, was dubious at best. The contradictory nature of Kant's stringent sense of moral duty as expressed in the sublime's "negative pleasure" is clarified by Derrida: "we are concerned with pleasure, pure pleasure, the being-pleasure of pleasure. The third *Critique* was written for pleasure's sake, and so must it be read. A pleasure which is somewhat arid -- without concept and without enjoyment (jouissance) -- and somewhat strict, but it teaches us once more that there is no pleasure without restriction . . . What is it to exist, for Kant?" (*Parergon*, in *October* IX, 9, 15).

4

COLERIDGE AND THE DISJUNCTIVE PERSONALITY

> Schiller has the material sublime.[1]
>
> -- Coleridge

> I go further than Hartley, and believe the corporeality of thought.[2]
>
> -- Coleridge

Though unsuccessful, Kant's and Schiller's mediating strategies are designed to reunite humanity's divided identity, to reconcile its warring physical and spiritual aspects through a third, mediating principle of aesthetic harmony. It is true that in his general philosophy, Kant wants the senses and the reason divided in matters of moral judgment, a division reflected in the sublime as an aesthetic expression of such judgment. But in the third *Critique*, he insists on an ultimate unity between man's appetitive impulses and his moral obligation. The difference between his own and Schiller's ideas of such unity is simply how it should come about -- whether through the celebration of the senses as in Schiller, or through their denigration, as in Kant.

Self and the Sole True Something

> The sole true *Something*, this in Limbo Den,
> It frightens Ghosts as Ghosts here frighten men.
>
> -- Coleridge

> The language of the Senses, first, the only possible vehicle of early instruction . . . : secondly, as the proper language for that which is superscientific, namely, Morality (for only to the Things without us as Objects of our senses does our practical duty extend).[3]
>
> -- Coleridge

The concept of self in Kant's and Schiller's systems depended on the concept of a mediating or bridging principle. In Kant's theory, the fundamental element of human identity, transcendental unity of apperception, was founded on such mediation. In Schiller's, the zenith of man's identity, or his "humanity," resided in a third reconciling property created by the aesthetic impulse, or play drive. Coleridge's theory of identity follows the identical bridging function, operating on the principle of "trichotomy." His system was "trichotomous not only in its main divisions," Alice D. Snyder writes, but in its subdivisions as well." "'In *all* things,'" he argued, "'we *all* of us arrange in the same way -- A, and the opposite of A (Say, B) and that in which A and B co-exist.'"[4] This arrangement required a method: "All things, in us, and about us," he wrote, "are a Chaos, without Method: so long as the mind is entirely passive, so long as there is an habitual submission of the Understanding to mere events and images, as such, without any attempt to classify and arrange them, so long the Chaos must continue" (in Snyder 29, 3). The tripartite scheme Coleridge had devised was a method by which to mend the conflicting processes within the mind: "Method results from a balance," he wrote, "between the passive impression received from outward things, and the internal activity of the mind in reflecting and generalizing." Mirroring the same mediating system as Kant's and Schiller's, Coleridge's trichotomous method would create that balance.

He drew the scheme not only from Kant and Schiller, however, but from a number of German writers.[5] Identifying a synthesizing process that could reconcile the divided elements of man's identity, Coleridge carved out of Kant's, Fichte's, and Schelling's philosophy a harmony of the *Ich* and the *nicht-Ich* ('I' and not-'I') in a third and higher identity. According to "the venerable sage of Koenigsberg," he wrote:

> . . . transcendental philosophy demands . . . that two forces should be conceived which counteract each other . . . The problem will then be to discover the result or product of two such forces . . . and as rest or neutralization cannot be the result; no other conception is possible but that the product must be a tertium aliquid . . . [which] can be no other than an interpenetration of the counteracting powers, partaking of both (*BL*, I, 299-300).

This restatement of Kant is Coleridge's celebrated definition of the imagination, filtered through the theories of Fichte and Schelling. "Two forces or concepts in dynamic tension both find themselves in the imagination," James Engell and Walter Jackson Bate write,

> which reconciles and unifies them: the self or mind (I AM) with nature or the cosmos, the subjective with the objective. In Fichte, the imagination reconciles the *Ich* and the *nicht-Ich*, which hovers as a single power between them." The imagination resolves all contradictions: mind/nature; real ideal; subject object etc. It is the 'ultimate synthesis' in the dialectic of mind and nature (*BL*, I, 299, n1).

Coleridge was aware of Schiller's problems in *Naive and Sentimental Poetry*,[6] and of his increasing trouble in balancing his own harmonizing theory with Kant's philosophy. Yet clearly, his awareness did not deter him from attempting his own *Übergang* or bridge that might link subject and object. Indeed, the idea of an aesthetic link which might harmonize the sensuous and rational, self and other, human and divine, became the guiding principle of his work. Sanguine assertions of organic totality inform his writing, often, as contemporaries and later critics would observe, to the detriment of his poetry.[7] With each attempt, however -- through the symbol, which participates in both subject and object; through the imagination, which as repetition in the finite mind of the infinite I AM, links human and divine; and most importantly, for our purposes, through the poet's identity, which links subjective and objective arenas of existence -- Coleridge failed as resoundingly as Kant and Schiller.

The Bridge of Imagination

> For a very long time . . . I could not reconcile personality with infinity; and my head was with Spinoza, though my whole heart remained with Paul and John.[8]
>
> -- Coleridge

Though known for his thoughts on the reconciling imagination, Coleridge did not originate the idea of the imagination as a mediating process. He was following a similar train of thought among German thinkers. The concept of a fusing or harmonizing imagination had occupied not only Kant and Schiller, but, among others, Bruno, Hamann, Schelling and Herder.[9] It is not by chance, however, that Coleridge's particular spin on the imagination's reconciling powers had its origins in the theological idea of Christ as mediator between man and God: "*Christ als Mittelpunkt*" ("Christ as middle point"), as Herder expressed it (Engell 221, 223). Following his German predecessors, Coleridge opened the *Biographia's* Chapter Thirteen, the celebrated chapter dealing with his theory of the imagination, with a telling Greek epigraph from a hymn of Synesius: "I reverence the hidden system of noble things which is God. Descend to some *middle ground* which I can reach."[10]

Coleridge's outline in the *Statesman's Manual* of the imagination's middle ground or bridging function shows that he intended it to reconcile the same elements of human identity that Schiller sought to unify in his own attempt to reconstruct the divided self: the province of man's physical appetites (the phenomenal) and of man's rational and moral obligations (the noumenal). The imagination, Coleridge wrote, is

> . . . that reconciling and mediatory power, which incorporating the Reason in Images of the Sense, and organizing (as it were) the flux of the Senses by the permanence and self-circling energies of the Reason, gives birth to a system of symbols, harmonious in themselves, and consubstantial with the truths of which they are the conductors.[11]

Coleridge's writings are replete with statements proclaiming the imagination's capacity to bridge the sensuous and the spiritual. It is "the imagination . . . [which] combining many circumstances tends to produce that ultimate end of all human thought and feeling, unity" (in Engell 354), a "power" which "reveals itself in the balance or reconciliation of opposite or discordant qualities: of sameness with difference; of the general with the concrete; the idea with the image; the individual with the representative" (*BL*, II, 16-17).

The imagination alone can seize the "Idea" of Coleridge's Dynamic Philosophy, an idea which "contemplates the Alpha and Omega (one-all; Finite-Infinite: Subject-Object; Mind-Matter; Substance-Form; Time-Space; Motion-Rest; Futuration-Presence; & c&c) -- and it is indifferent which of the pairs you take, for they are Symbols of the same Truth produced by different Positions."[12] The imagination, "in philosophical language . . . an intermediate faculty" (*BL*, I, 124-25) "acts chiefly by creating out of many things . . . a oneness, even as nature," a oneness in which "the two alternatives [the above and cognate oppositions] are joined suddenly and audaciously by the 'connecting energy' [of its] power of 'genial method'" (in Engell, 354-5). Art, the product, or process, of imagination, itself produces the same self/other bridge: it "is the Mediatress, the reconciliator of Man and Nature," the "middle nature between a Thought and a Thing, or as before, the union and reconciliation of that which is Nature and that which is exclusively Human" (*CN*, III, T, 4397, 4397, f48). Clearly, a bridging or mediating activity constituted the imagination's central function, in Coleridge.

Following the completion of the *Biographia*, however, he withdrew his assertions of its power to reconcile the noumenal and phenomenal elements of man's nature. Prefiguring Hugo's later assertion that "Christianity puts an abyss between the soul and the body, an abyss between man and God,"[13] Coleridge found that he could not continue to support the idea of the reconciling imagination *and* a "pure" or Christian concept of God. Coleridge, for whom man is virtually "unintelligible without Christianity's story of the Fall," had, despite his quest for unity, to concur with the abyss marked later by Hugo (*TT*, May 1, 1830, p. 65). Rather than summon God to help him establish an imaginative bridge between the subject's spiritual and sensuous aspects as he had with the hymn of Synesius, it was wiser to dispense with the imagination's bridging role altogether, to leave the mediation, if indeed mediation were possible, to God.

Coleridge had already found the imagination increasingly suspect, especially in matters of religion. It was too ready to encroach on the strictly theological, too ready to "create any unity or representation and call it God," as it had in the "pantheism" of Schelling and Wordsworth. To Coleridge, only Wordsworth's character saved him from his tendency to pantheism in such poems as "Tintern Abbey" and the Immortality Ode (*BL*, II, 139). This particular "defect of Wordsworth's poetry," he wrote, was luckily overcome by Wordsworth's "strong sense," without which "his mysticism would become sickly -- mere fog and dimness!" (*BL*, II, 142).[14] In the last analysis, the imagination and its bridging capacity had become not only "unnecessary, [but] treacherous."

With his theory of aesthetic unity between noumenal and phenomenal increasingly tentative, Coleridge virtually dropped the word "imagination" from his writing after 1818, precisely because its mediating role did not, and rightfully could not, obtain in the province of religion. Engell notes accurately: "By revealing and creating harmony between the material and spiritual realms, imagination progressed up to the absolute being, but could not synthesize or see a synthesis in God. 'The dialectic Intellect by the exertion of its own powers exclusively can lead us to a general affirmation of the Supreme Reality of an absolute Being. But here it stops'" (Engell 363).

As in Schiller, Coleridge's abandonment of a reconciling imagination parallels the process of Kant's sublime. Even before the *Biographia*'s completion, Coleridge noted a telling instance of the imagination's limits, writing that "in basic attempts to answer this question [of unity or the 'Whole'] the imagination goes on adding and adding and as if to hide from itself its perpetual failure, & to evade the perpetual recurrence of the same question . . . it takes the *salto mortale* and vaults at once into the transcendental Ideal, of Infinity" (*CN*, III, T, 4047, f138). Echoing Schiller's tactical revelation in "Of the Sublime" ("*Vom Erhabenen*") that his own principle of aesthetic harmony had failed, Coleridge abandons his own aesthetic bridge for a religious leap. As his apt Italian metaphor "*salto mortale*" (somersault) connotes, the leap is both chaotic and deathly, much as Schiller's notion of the sublime as suicide. In the face of the sublime, all imaginative "adding," all aesthetic effort proves useless. Commanded by Reason to embody the transcendental non-place of the "Whole" or "Infinity," "the imagination is called forth, . . still offering what is still repelled, again creating what is again rejected."[15] Aware of the imagination's inability to span the sense/reason gulf, Coleridge prophesies an ultimate solution in a leap into religion. But it is a "deathly leap."

The Self as Mediator

> Thesis VI: 'The principle . . . manifests itself in the SUM OR I AM; which I hereafter indiscriminately express by the words spirit, self and self-consciousness.[16]
>
> -- Coleridge

Just as inevitably, and more significantly for the sublime's relation to the romantic self, sublimity topples Coleridge's concept of the poet as mediator. It is true that the imagination's mediating power rests on the poet's identity, with the "artist becom[ing] something like a keenly ground lens, an 'I' focused by the imagination" (Engell 359). But the poet's self is also paradigmatic of ideal human identity. The self of the poet "brings the whole soul of man into activity, [and] with the subordination of each faculty to each other. . . , diffuses a tone and spirit of unity that blends and. . .fuses, each to each to each" (*BL*, II, 15-16). The poet's "conscious self" becomes "an intermediary for words and things,"[17] "the link that combines the two" (*CN*, III, T, 4397, f51).

Coleridge's most systematic attempt to establish the concept of the ideal self as mediator appears in the ten Schelling Theses of the *Biographia*. The attempt is also his most damagingly obscure. Following Schelling, Coleridge grounds a reconciliation between subject and object on Schelling's version of Kant's transcendental apperception: what Schelling implies is the poet's "absolute self-consciousness." But Coleridge's attempt to adopt Schelling for his own ends is fraught with problems. Relying on Schelling's system for his notion of the self as a mysterious "tertium aliquid" or "dark adyt" in which "extremes meet," Coleridge's concept of man's identity as a third mediating principle remains, by his own admission, "visionary." Even if the mediating self's "higher knowledge" *could* unify the "world-self opposition," such unity would still remain "abstractly opposed to the understanding" (*CN*, III, 3400, 3405, 4166).[18]

Much as it had with Schiller, Schelling's pantheistic and mystical tendencies had begun to unravel Coleridge's argument. Following a similar attempt to use Schelling, Schiller had written to Goethe:

> "I attacked Schelling about an assertion he makes in his Transcendental Philosophy, that 'in Nature one starts from the Unconscious in order to raise it to the Conscious; whereas, in Art, one proceeds from the Conscious to the Unconscious.' Here, it is true, he speaks only of the contrast between the product of Nature and that of Art; in so far he is quite right. I fear, however, that idealists, such as he is, take too little notice of experience . . . " (Letter to Goethe, Jena, March 27, 1801, #809).[19]

Echoing Schiller's mistrust of Schelling's spongy ideas, Coleridge attempts to augment his Schellingian bridge of absolute self-consciousness with the more rigorous principles of Kant -- he seeks, as had Schiller, to use Kant to ground the bridge more firmly. The results, however, prove equally damaging to Coleridge's system.

Completing Schelling with Kant

> Quere? Is Descartes' Postulate, 'Quicquid clare percipio, verum est, et reale' reconcilable with the Critical philosophy of Kant? -- If not, either Kant or Schelling must fall.[20]
>
> -- Coleridge

Paul Hamilton has correctly discerned the negative effects of Coleridge's combination of Schelling and Kant. Although it was Schelling, not Kant, who believed in the absolute identity of the principles of mind and nature, "both sides of the [Schelling-Kant] antimony can exist happily on their own," he writes. Contradictions arise, however, when Coleridge "tries to bring the two halves together."[21] Kathleen Wheeler, on the other hand, finds Coleridge's use of Kant to "complete" Schelling remarkably successful. Her argument helps illuminate the problems Coleridge faced, for by adhering too closely to Coleridge's idea of "totality," she confronts the same problems.

Wheeler notes two instances in which Coleridge ostensibly completes Schelling with Kant. In the first, Coleridge skips from the binary opposition of Schelling's centripetal/centrifugal metaphor to a "trinary" system in which *Kant* becomes the third, or synthesizing factor. Coleridge, Wheeler argues, uses Schelling's metaphor only "as a base from which to appeal to Kant's negative qualities," bringing Kant into the discussion in order to introduce "the missing element in Schelling, the tertium aliquid, the third factor or synthesis." Though his switch to Kant carries the tertium aliquid "even further" than Kant might allow, Wheeler writes, Coleridge successfully employs Kant "as a *corrective* to and *completion* of Schelling" (Wheeler 45). Yet, it is Coleridge himself who marks the opposition between Kant and Schelling, basing it on Kant's irreconcilability with Descartes: "Quere? Is Descartes' Postulate, 'Quicquid clare percipio, verum est, et reale' [Whatever I perceive clearly and distinctly is true and real] reconcilable with the Critical philosophy of Kant? -- If not, either Kant or Schelling must fall" (*CN*, III, T, 4259).

Wheeler takes as a second instance Coleridge's note to refine his idea of opposing forces and their tertium aliquid synthesis:

> It will hereafter be my business to construct by a series of intuitions the progressive schemes, that must follow from such a power with such forces, till I arrive at the fullness of *human* intelligence. For my present purpose I *assume* such a power as my principle, in order to deduce from it a faculty. . . (*BL*, I, 286, my italics)

To Wheeler, this passage closing the *Biographia*'s chapter twelve demonstrates that Kant is

> appealed to once again immediately following a Schelling borrowing, to complete and correct Schelling, and once again Coleridge expands the use of 'intuition' (which is at the root of his difference with Kant on the nature of ideas as merely regulative or constitutive) and carries metaphysics into divinity (Wheeler 45).

The two-fold problem of Wheeler's reading illuminates Coleridge's faltering argument. First, the ten Schelling Theses could scarcely be called a "borrowing" or brief aside, comprising as they do the bulk of the most philosophically rigorous chapter of the *Biographia*. The fact that they constitute the main body of Coleridge's argument underscores his heavy, and unwise, reliance on Schelling's idealism. Second, it is precisely these

Kantian "negative qualities" or oppositions which Coleridge, like Schiller, must both incorporate, i.e., "bridge" and thus control (*BL*, I, 297).

What Wheeler sees as Coleridge's "dizzying" manner of carrying Kant's scheme "even further than Kant," of "expanding" Kant's concept of intuition to the point of "carrying metaphysics into divinity," is not a sign of the poet's control, of an audacious but successful solution to the dilemma, but of a tentativeness in Coleridge's argument, stemming from the conflicting demands to ground his system more firmly than Schelling had done, and yet to avoid Kant's restriction of the concept of "unity" to the merely subjective arena. Wheeler misses the damaging qualifications in the second passage that she quotes from Coleridge. There are two signs. First, at the beginning of the Ten Theses, Coleridge had "assumed" nothing. He had asserted all claims flatly, and directly. At this later point in the chapter, however, his claims are qualified and more tentative, indicating his growing knowledge of the weakness of his claim. Second, early in the chapter "Sacred self-consciousness" was "*Being*," and not merely "knowing." It possessed ontological rather than epistemological status (*BL*, I, 252, 264). Its "Knowledge" was absolute -- "all knowledge" (*BL*, I, 252, 255). In his later discussion, it has become simply "human" knowledge, the same limitation that Kant imposes on what man can know.

Losing the Self

> [W]e must . . . affirm an absolute something that is in and of itself at once cause and effect (*causa sui*) subject and object, or rather the absolute identity of both . . . [N]atural philosophy places the sole reality of things in an ABSOLUTE, which is at once causa sui et effectus [father of himself, son of himself] -- in an absolute identity of subject and object, which it calls nature, and which in its highest power is nothing else than self-conscious will or intelligence.[22]
>
> -- Coleridge

Coleridge's leap to a Kantian framework does not complete his theory of a unifying self-consciousness but subverts it. His hedging in Wheeler's second quote is the culmination of a series of prior Kantian unsettlings throughout the later Theses. Following Schelling in Thesis Eight, Coleridge had said that the absolute self given in self-consciousness was both finite *and* infinite (*BL*, I, 280). Similarly, in Thesis Nine, Coleridge had asserted that the principle of Being and Knowing (or self) was a direct principle of transcendental philosophy, in contrast to the "assumed" principle of Thesis Ten quoted above (*BL*, I, 281). However, toward the conclusion of Thesis Nine, Coleridge suggests that he does not wish to be construed as referring to "God" with the term "absolute Being" (something that had not bothered him before), and so, drawing clearly on Kant, he brings in a highly damaging qualification of his earlier concept of a unifying self: "We are not investigating an absolute principium essendi [principle of being]; for then I admit, many valid objections might be started against our theory; but an absolute principium cogniscendi [principle of knowing]" (*BL*, I, 282).

With this Kantian reduction, Coleridge's all-important notion of "being" is dropped, leaving him with only "knowing," or knowledge. Following Thesis Ten, however, even this absolute knowing given by self-consciousness is then itself qualified: "The transcendental philosopher," Coleridge begins, "does not enquire, what ultimate ground of our knowledge there may lie out of our knowing, but what is the last in our knowing itself, beyond which *we* cannot pass . . . It is asserted only, that the act of self-consciousness is for *us* the source and principle of all *our* possible knowledge" (*BL*, I, 282-4). Employing this Kantian qualification, Coleridge turns from "all knowledge," the absolute knowledge given by Schellingian self-consciousness, to merely "human" knowledge, "our" knowledge, which, under Kant's aegis, is as tenuous as ever.

It is not by chance that after both major qualifications, which reflect Kant's damaging retreat to the supersensible in the third *Critique* and Schiller's turn to religion in "Of the Sublime," Coleridge turns directly to concepts of religion. Following the first passage quoted by Wheeler, in which Coleridge dismisses Being as the issue of self-consciousness, Coleridge writes: "We begin with I KNOW MYSELF, in order to end with the absolute I AM. We proceed from the SELF, in order to lose all self in GOD" (*BL*, I, 283). Following Wheeler's second Coleridge quote, demonstrating what she calls the system's "Kantian completion and correction," Coleridge submits to an even more fervid theological capitulation, quoting again in Greek (usually a sign of trouble in Coleridge) from another hymn of Synesius:

> Be full of goodness unto me, Blessed One, be full of goodness unto me, Father, if beyond what is ordered, beyond what is destined, I touch upon what is thine (*BL*, I, 282).

Much as Schiller had learned in his struggles with Kant, Coleridge accedes to the discipline and restraint required by systematic theory. Called back to those limits by his attempt to incorporate Kant into his Schellingian system, and brought up short by the principles in Kant's sublime that subvert harmony, Coleridge does indeed carry his system "into divinity." But it is not a controlled balance of Schellingian and Kantian principles, not a "completion" of Schelling by Kant, but a schismatic struggle that sends him into religion. By the time of *Table Talk* (1822), the effect of Coleridge's turn is all too evident: "In finite Forms," he writes in the later work, "there is no real and absolute Identity. God alone is Identity. In the former, the prosthesis is a bastard prosthesis, a quasi-Identity only" (*TT*, 161).

Equally detrimental to his theory of a unified self is the fact that "having delivered this flight into high German transcendentalism" as Read aptly puts it,[23] Coleridge transforms the following *Biographia* chapter, in which he promises to unveil the imagination's tertium aliquid -- the link between man's warring impulses -- into the celebrated evasion of the bogus letter from a friend. The promised theory of the imagination becomes a single paragraph in which he hastily distinguishes the "primary" and "secondary" imagination from mere "fancy." The subsequent remarks with which he immediately concludes the chapter contain a similar evasion:

> Whatever more than this, I shall think fit to declare concerning the powers and privileges of the imagination in the present work, will be found in the critical essay on the uses of the Supernatural in poetry and the principles that regulate its introduction: which the reader will find prefixed to the poem of *The Ancient Mariner*.

The essay on the supernatural was, of course, never written. But

Coleridge's associative connection of Schelling's absolute selfhood, the imagination's power, and the supernatural, foreshadows his sense of the extravagance required to reconstruct the self in situations of the sublime.

Ignore Thyself

> Lord, help my unbelief![24]
>
> -- Coleridge

> The dialectic Intellect by the exertion of its own powers exclusively can lead us to a general affirmation of the Supreme Reality of an absolute Being. But here it stops.[25]
>
> -- Coleridge

As with Schiller, Kant's philosophy did indeed "take hold of [Coleridge] with a giant's hand," as Coleridge had remarked, but not in the manner he had wished (*BL*, I, 155). Initially resisting the "letter" of Kant, clinging much as Schiller, to what he saw as the "spirit," Coleridge writes of the "venerable old man,"

> In spite therefore of his own declarations, I could never believe, it was possible for him to have meant no more by his Noumenon, or THING IN ITSELF, than his mere words express; or that in his own conception he confined the whole plastic power to the forms of the intellect, leaving for the external cause, for the materiale of our sensations, a

matter without form, which is doubtless inconceivable. I entertain doubts likewise, whether in his own mind, he even laid all the stress, which he appears to do on the moral postulates.

Refusing to believe the remoteness of Being in Kant's system, the stringent limits on the all-important "plastic" power, the "unexplainable" stress on the moral postulates, Coleridge's rationalizations are designed to deny Kant's clear rejection of any mind-nature fusion. Why, for example, had Kant limited his concept of apperception (self-consciousness) to the subjective arena, and why he had denied it any participation in the will? Surely by "apperception," Coleridge reasoned, Kant must have *meant* something like Schelling's dynamic system, for had not Kant mentioned in his *Metaphysische Anfangsgrunde der Naturwissenschaft* that "all reality of objects of external sense...is to be conceived as a moving force?" (*BL*, I, 129, n3).

Kant "must" have concluded that any notion of the unity of apperception as an act of self, an act grounded in the will as Coleridge and Schelling both held in opposition to Kant -- was more prudently "*left behind in a pure analysis, not of human nature in toto, but of the speculative intellect alone.*" Surely Kant *would* have embraced the notion, had his *Critique* included more than the arena of "reflection and natural consciousness" (*BL*, I, 154). Or perhaps, Coleridge speculated more wildly, in leaving a mind-nature fusion out, in limiting any dynamic concept to the subjective realm, Kant was merely speaking "symbolically," his advancing age and the political pressures of the time preventing him from clearly stating a harmonizing view which would have accorded with Schelling's and his own (*BL*, I, 156-7). In spite of his explanations, however, Coleridge's ideal "spirit" of Kant dissolves in the *Biographia*'s chapter twelve. What remains, the harsher Kantian "letter" and the sublime that expresses it, eats away at Coleridge's faltering concept of a subject/object mediation.

To Paul Hamilton, the *Biographia* straddles the gulf between

Schellingian and Kantian positions, and the abyss that separates them constitutes the arena of the sublime. But Hamilton fails to note that the capitulation to Kantian principles, by undermining the principle of aesthetic mediation, opens the abyss in the first place. One of the earliest illuminations of this disruption is the diminishment of Coleridge's argument for a mediating self. Coleridge had argued that only through the poet's apperceptive identity do extremes meet, a meeting wrought by the "heaven-descended KNOW THYSELF" of aesthetic response and imagination. However, such self-reflexive creativity cannot stand when, like Schiller, Coleridge must admit to intuition's merely regulative and subjective character.

The admission bodes ill for Coleridge's concept of the self, when we recall that he considers intuition an essential tool of self-consciousness. Wheeler's second quotation of Coleridge, in which Coleridge admits to the self's merely human knowledge and thus to the fact that his theory of intuition is grounded on assumption, reveals *not* that he has strengthened his Schellingian theory of absolute self-consciousness with a Kantian corrective, but that in the "tertium aliquid," the "third something" rising out of the opposing forces, Coleridge has in fact produced nothing but religion. This retreat to the divine emerges in a telling transformation of Coleridge's use of the dictum, "KNOW THYSELF." The adage appears first as the idea of losing oneself and finding it in God. It then becomes "Know thyself and so shalt thou know thy God." Finally, in the 1832 poem "Self Knowledge," the prescription to know thyself -- Coleridge's only systematic presentation of an aesthetic principle that can mediate between subject and object -- has been dropped completely. At this point, Coleridge writes: "Ignore thyself and strive to know thy God!" (*Poetical Works* 487).

When, in chapter twelve of the *Biographia*, Coleridge concludes that the subject/object link provided by self-consciousness "needs no further proof," that it is "morticed and annexed," we should note that the mortar or connection is internal. The bridge has not crossed to the objective realm

(*BL*, I, 284). Though Coleridge has constructed a link of apperception or of the self, his compromises in light of Kant's restrictions have turned it back on the subject, giving it a circular trajectory, like a snake with its tail in its mouth.[26] This symbol[27] of eternity, moreover, is not a happy one.[28] Any sense of the bridge progressing further along the metaphysical path of divinity is out of the question, since as Coleridge himself had remarked, the only "Gravity in the machine" is the weightless province of "religion" (*CL*, IV, 759).

Regardless of whether the Ten Theses were written as part of the projected *Logosophia*, the zenith, as Coleridge hoped, of his life's work,[29] it is still unlikely that Coleridge, in the words of Shawcross, "arranged" that "no matter in what order he wrote the *Biographia*, . . . the philosophy of the first volume concludes with divinity just as the second volume builds to a crescendo in chapter 24 with the proclamation of Christ and God the Father."[30] It is more reasonable that in view of the Kantian limitations on his aesthetics of unity, Coleridge had no choice. In fact, Coleridge judged a unity of religion to be only a kind of spectre -- much like the spectral non-bridge of religion to which Schiller turned in "Of the Sublime." "Poor unlucky metaphysics!" Coleridge writes at the conclusion of the *Biographia*, "[you] are nothing but . . . divinity." As even Shawcross has observed, one cannot "anchor a philosophy in the bottomless sea of faith."[31]

Scholars have long noted the direct lineage of Kant's negative sublime and modern existentialism.[32] Coleridge, laboring under the immediate influence of this negative aesthetics, could not avoid prefiguring certain existential tendencies, notably the sense of a gulf between self and other, man and God. Too many of Coleridge's remarks suggest his ironic attitude toward an accomplished subject/object unity, and his scorn of those who "officious for equivalents," blindly pursue such a "conjunction disjunctive" (*CN*, III, 4239; *BL*, II, 19). "For Coleridge, as later for Kierkegaard," Herbert Read writes, "there was inherent in the human situation an ineluctable Either/Or, and to deny it, as did the pantheistic Schelling only 'expresses the striving of the philosopher himself to hide these consequences from his own mind.'"[33]

However reluctantly, Coleridge ultimately answered his own question of whether Kant or Schelling would fall. Riven by the implications of Kant's sublime, Coleridge's Schellingian bridge of self-consciousness, of imagination and of symbolic language -- all fundamental aspects of his concept of the self -- dissolved into the fog of religion. Though Coleridge remained a devout Christian to the end, his response to the capitulation was a mute one. Henry Nelson Coleridge, compiling the first edition of *Table Talk* one year after Coleridge's death, added the following anecdote from 1830:

> 'I have no difficulty,' said [Coleridge], 'in forgiveness. Neither do I find or reckon the most solemn faith in God as a real object, the most arduous act of the reason and will. O no, my dear, it is to pray, to pray as God would have us; this is what at all times makes me turn cold to the soul. Believe me, to pray with all your heart and strength, with the reason and the will, to believe vividly that God will listen. . . --- this is the last, the greatest achievement of the Christian's warfare upon earth. Teach us to pray, O Lord!' And then he burst into a flood of tears, and begged me to pray for him. O what a sight was there! -- H.N.C. (*TT* 91)

NOTES

1. Coleridge, *Table Talk and Omniana*, ed. T. Ashe (London, 1905), 15. Hereafter, *TT*.

2. Cited in Arthur Clayborough, *The Grotesque in Art and Literature* (Oxford, 1965), 162. Hereafter, Clayborough.

3. Coburn comments: "The young Col[eridge] (1796) thought the senses were to be overcome in the individual and the race, and educational process in which "Fancy is the Power / That first unsensualises the dark mind" ("Destiny of Nations") . . . He came to see the senses as having an essential constructive part in the understanding . . . Hence presumably the use of magic in early instruction" (*CN*, IV, 4642, T, N).

4. See Alice D. Snyder, ed., *S. T. Coleridge's Treatise on Method as Published on the Encyclopaedia Metropolitana* (London, 1934), 3. Hereafter, Snyder.

5. Coleridge's knowledge of German literature and philosophy is, of course, legend. Among other works he translated by Schiller, are "The Homeric Hexameter," "The Ovidian Hexameter," "The Visit of the Gods," and the play *Wallenstein*. Walter Scott considered *Wallenstein* "more grand in the translation of Coleridge than in the original of Schiller." See Scott, "Paul's Letters to His Kinsfolk," *Miscellaneous Prose Works* (London, 1834-46), V, 307. Hearing that Coleridge was translating another German work, Scott remarked: "I hope it is so

. . . Coleridge made Schiller's *Wallenstein* far finer than he found it, and so he will do by this!" (See J. G. Lockhart, *Memoirs of the Life of Sir Walter Scott* (Boston, 1927). A partial list of the German works Coleridge devoured during his prodigious reading bouts includes Lessing ("That most formidable of heretics," Ewen, 60); Herder's *Kalligone* (see Coleridge *Marginalia*); Kant, Fichte, Tieck, August Schlegel, Friedrich Schlegel (see his *Athenaeum Marginalia* I, 131); Hans Sachs; Schelling; Steffens; Solger (*CL*, IV, 737-39; 744-46; 666-7, 794); Novalis's *Heinrich von Ofterdingen* (*CL*, IV, 870); the Tieck-Wackenroder *Phantasien*, borrowed June 1817 (*CL*, IV, 743, 911); Gessner; Bürger; Wieland; Goethe: Coleridge knew his *Farbenlehre* (*CL* IV, 911), was said to be translating *Faust* (Ewen, 51), and considered him a lesser writer than Schiller (Ewen, 33). For a fuller list of Coleridge's extensive familiarity with German writing, see Coleridge, *Marginalia* I, p. 131; A. C. Dunstan, "The German Influence on Coleridge," *Modern Language Review* XVII, 272- and XVIII, 183- (1922-23); Frederic Ewen, *The Prestige of Schiller in England, 1788-1859* (New York, 1932); G. N. G. Orsini *Coleridge and German Idealism* (Carbondale, 1969); J. L. Haney, *The German Influence on Samuel Taylor Coleridge* (Philadelphia, 1902); and Ralph Coffman, ed., *Coleridge's Library: A Bibliography of Books Owned and Read by Samuel Taylor Coleridge* (Boston, 1987).

6. Coleridge knew Schiller's "Grace and Dignity," *Aesthetic Education*, and *Naive and Sentimental Poetry* and had translated Schiller's *Wallenstein*. See Elizabeth Wilkinson, "Introduction" in *Schiller, Aesthetic Education*, cliv; and Coleridge, *CN*, ed. cit. 1,451 ff, Appendix A: "Coleridge's Knowledge of German as Seen in the Early Notebooks"; G. N. G. Orsini, *Coleridge and German Idealism* (Carbondale, 1969); John Louis Haney, *The German Influence on Samuel Taylor Coleridge* (New York, 1966).

7. To Walter Pater, whose powerful debt to Coleridge included the burden of Coleridge's failure: "Everywhere [Coleridge] is restlessly scheming to apprehend the absolute; to affirm it effectively, to get it acknowledged. Coleridge failed in that attempt, happily for him, for it was a struggle against the increasing life of the mind itself . . . How did his choice of a controversial interest, his determination to affirm the absolute, weaken or modify his poetic gift?" See Pater, "Coleridge's Writings" (1866), quoted in Bloom, *Figures*, 2-3.

8. By 1807, Spinoza had taken his place besides Descartes in the ranks of the atheists. See Coleridge's Letter to Cottle, *Biographia Epistolaris* (London, 1911), II, 18.

9. See James Engell, *The Creative Imagination: Enlightenment to Romanticism* (Cambridge, Mass: 1981). Hereafter, Engell.

10. Translated by Engell, 363. I do not use the Princeton *Biographia* translation, which tends to obscure the mediating function Coleridge emphasizes. Their translation: "I venerate the hidden ordering of intellectual things, but there is some *medial element* that may not be distributed." See *BL*, I, 296. My italics.

11. Coleridge, *The Statesman's Manual*, ed. R. J. White (Princeton, NJ, 1972), 29. Hereafter, *SM*.

12. Coleridge, *Aids to Reflection*, in Engell, 334.

13. Victor Hugo, *Preface to Cromwell*, in *Théâtre Complet* (Paris, 1963-4), I, 425; see also Suzanne Guerlac, *The Impersonal Sublime* (Stanford: 1990), 13-68.

14. Coleridge's intense reaction against Wordsworth's "mysticism" suggests the type of antipathy that characterizes those with the same flaw. For a thorough study of Coleridge's own flirtation with pantheism and his subsequent rejection of it, see Thomas McFarland, *Coleridge and the Pantheist Tradition* (Oxford, 1969). Hereafter, McFarland, *Pantheist*.

15. Coleridge, *Shakespearean Criticism* (Cambridge, MA, 1930), II, 138.

16. *BL*, 1, 272-3; 280.

17. Shawcross, Preface, *Biographia Literaria* (London, 1907), lxxvii.

18. Coleridge writes that the link is seen by a "higher knowledge" which alone provides a "unification of the world-self opposition." See Kathleen Wheeler,

Sources, Processes and Methods in Coleridge's Biographia (Cambridge, 1980), p. 75. Hereafter, Wheeler.

[19.] See Wheeler, 45.

[20.] *CN*, III, T, 4259.

[21.] See Paul Hamilton, *Coleridge's Poetics* (Stanford, 1983); 61, 187. Hereafter, Hamilton

[22.] *BL*, I, 285.

[23.] Read, *The True Voice of Feeling* (New York, 1953), p. 175.

[24.] *CN*, III, T, 3353, f5lv.

[25.] *BL*, I, 363n.

[26.] Paul de Man notes another facet of this self-returning bridge, observing in Coleridge a "pseudo-dialectics of subject and object" which is in fact merely an intersubjective relation of subject with subject. Here, "the relationship with nature has been superseded by an intersubjective, interpersonal relationship that, in the last analysis, is a relationship of the subject toward itself. Thus the priority has passed from the outside world entirely within the subject, and we end up with something that resembles a radical idealism" ("Temporality" 196). Focussing less on Coleridge's error than on the tendency of critics to be taken in by the romantic myth of a reconciliation of opposites, much as Wheeler de Man observes:

> Wasserman's claim for Coleridge as the reconciler of what he calls 'the phenomenal world of understanding with the noumenal world of reason' is based on a quotation in which Coleridge simply *substitutes another self for the category of the object*, and thus removes the problem from nature altogether, reducing it to a purely intersubjective pattern.

> 'To make the object one with us, we must become one with the object -- ergo an object. Ergo the object must be itself a subject -- partially a favorite dog, principally a friend, wholly God, the Friend.' Wordsworth was never guilty of thus reducing a theocentric to an interpersonal relationship ("Temporality" 198, my italics).

We end up in Coleridge with more than "radical idealism," however, for this fall into self leads precisely to the "conscious madness" (*"folie lucide"*) remarked by de Man in Baudelaireian hyperbole. The dead-end of self, however, is even more marked in Thesis VI of Chapter Twelve of the *Biographia*, and in the *Notebooks*, III, where Coleridge characterizes the "tertium aliquid" -- simply the imagination, the poet's self, the symbol: all are cognate in terms of mediating capacity -- as "neither wholly objectivized, nor wholly restored to its identity -- but . . . a perpetual Duplicity, Object and therefore Subject -- Subject and therefore Object" (*CN*, III, 4265, f24). However, it should be noted that Coleridge does not sustain this "mystification" of the reconciliation of opposites, and in fact, produces a body of work characterized by his awareness of its fictionality.

[27.] At one point to Coleridge, words had been things, thereby establishing the subject/object link. But his later remarks reveal his increasing uncertainty with respect to the unifying power of language. One might compare the remark that "Words are not mere symbols of things and thoughts, but themselves things" (*CN*, III, T, f96), with the observation that "Words are but the shadows of notions" (*BL*, I, 243). Equally suggestive is his remark that "The powers of conscious intellect increase by the accession of . . . a new word . . . I have been struggling . . . to find some exact word for each meaning -- but no!" (*CN*, III, T, 3268, f60v). For the relation of representation to the interaction between subject and object, and the complex subversion of representation caused by the subject/object breakdown in Kant's sublime, see Suzanne Guerlac, "Theories of the Sublime," *The Impersonal Sublime* (Stanford, 1990), 10.

[28.] Coleridge had claimed precisely this circularity as the ideal end of poetry. On March 7, 1815, he writes to Joseph Cottle: The common end of all narrative, nay, of all, Poems is to convert a series into a Whole: to make those events, which in real or imagined History move on in a Strait, assume to our Understandings a circular motion -- the snake with it's [sic] Tail in it's Mouth." (*CL*, IV, 545). It is perhaps this circular model for both narrative and poetry that leads Coleridge to guide what should have been a necessarily linear theory of mediation into the damaging circularity of self-reflection.

29. *CL*, IV. See Letters 974, 976, 978, pp. 585, 589, 591.

30. *BL*, Shawcross, Preface, lxiii-lxxiv.

31. *BL*, II, 240, n; Shawcross, Preface, lxxiv.

32. See Donald Reiman, *Intervals of Inspiration* (Greenwood, FL: 1988); Thomas Weiskel, *The Romantic Sublime* (Baltimore, 1978); Wimsatt & Brooks, *Literary Criticism: A Short History* (New York, 1957); Herbert Read, *The True Voice of Feeling* (New York, 1953).

33. Coleridge, *The Friend*, in Read, *The True Voice of Feeling* (New York, 1953), 182.

5

THE EXTRAVAGANT SELF

Alas, what great calamities have misty words produced, that say so much that they say nothing -- clouds, rather, from which hurricanes burst.[1]

-- Coleridge

But evil are the swellings, both in body and diction, which are inflated and unreal, and threaten us with the reverse of our aim.[2]

-- Longinus

The verticality that Frye discerns in romanticism takes the form of hyperbole, not only as trope of extravagance but as existential stance. Longinus gave considerable attention to hyperbole's relation to the sublime's vertical character, to its natural alignment with sublimity's heights and depths. The sublime eschewed the linear, he wrote. It was found in the pinnacles of speech, in "noble diction," "elevated language," "lofty expression," and "amplification" (Longinus 80-86). It inhabited languages' nadirs, its expressions of "deep and grave thoughts," and the absence of language, as in the silence of Ajax in the underworld, which, Longinus wrote, "is great and more sublime than words" (Longinus 81). Later views of the sublime reiterated this connection of sublimity to the vertical and hyperbolic.[3] Eighteenth-century theorists called it an expression of heights. It was "raised, elevated or exalted" to a "high place" -- the stuff of the hyperbolic (*OED* Sublime 3122). It dealt with "ideas, truths, subjects, etc. belonging to the highest regions of thought, reality or human activity" (*OED* Sublime 4, 3123). Its "style," Chambers wrote in 1728, "requires big and magnificent words," in essence, the unabashedly extravagant (*OED* Sublime 6, 3123).

Big and magnificent words could frequently elude the artist's control, however, a fact also noted by the sublime's early theorists. From the beginnings of its eighteenth-century vogue, the sublime was hailed as a lofty aesthetic of "flight" (*OED*, Sublime 1c, 3123). But such paeans downplayed the other, less laudable characteristic of sublimity. If its early theorists praised the sublime for its flights, they also knew that such soaring had an inverse characteristic as well. Barely a decade after Boileau's translation of Longinus, Burnet complained in 1684: "We were beginning to fly into a sublime pitch of a strong but false rhetoric" (*OED* Sublime 3123). In 1724, Collins criticized the sublime's neglect of the literal and its tendency towards exaggerated and even false meaning, writing that theologians had "despised the literal sense of the Old Testament and employed their inventions to find out sublime senses thereof" (*OED* Sublime 4, 3123).

The sense of hyperbole's potential weakness went back to Longinus. Although praising the sublime's loftiness, he frequently lamented the potential duplicity of its hyperbolic character. He applauded sublime writing for its capacity to glorify when applied properly to sublime situations. But he warned that hyperbole was to be used with the greatest caution, since its murkiness had a tendency to deceive, and its excess tended to produce the bathetic rather than the grand. Improperly managed, he cautioned, hyperbole had a tendency to "swing round and produce its contrary effect" (Longinus 98).

The Posture of Excess

> If a poet has the unhappy chance to choose for his picture certain natures that are merely superhuman and cannot possibly be represented, he can only avoid exaggeration by ceasing to be a poet.[4]
>
> -- Schiller

Longinus' caveats against sublime bombast pervaded eighteenth-century and romantic views of the sublime. Yet, while most critics reiterated charges of "strained language" and "distorted meaning," some offered important insights into what appeared to be a growing problem as the eighteenth century drew to a close. John Dennis's suggestive analysis of the overblown writing he found among his contemporaries is among the most prescient. To Dennis, Nicolson writes,

> The Moderns . . . had the talent and genius necessary for the highest poetry. Their trouble was that they had departed from the true wellspring of great poetry, religion. . . . As he said in his criticism of Longinus, contemporary poets were attempting the results of the sublime without experiencing the causes. Their lips were moved to a language of 'Fury, Rapture, Transport, Ravishment.' But their souls had not been affected. The passions that moved them -- if, indeed, passion moved them at all -- were 'ordinary' Passions. Religious ideas, the true sources of the Sublime, were 'extraordinary Ideas,' arousing 'extra-

ordinary Passions,' expanding the faculties of man to their highest pitch, exalting the soul until the poet both thought and felt beyond the limitations of man.[5]

Dennis' explanation of his contemporaries's bombastic sublimity as deriving from the absence of theological groundwork is significant. This absence, and the strained language that attended it, became the hallmark of the romantic sublime.

Despite complaints such as Dennis's, bombast in eighteenth-century sublime writing was generally accepted, and often even indulgently celebrated. It was thought to be a natural accompaniment to the inspiration that produced the sublime. Burnet's generous estimation of a colleague's overblown language is typical of such a stance: "However, hyperboles here might easily be forgiven. The Alps appear to be Nature's extravagancies, and who should blush to be guilty of Extravagancies, in words that make mention of hers?"[6]

However, while eighteenth-century writers blushed and asked to be forgiven for hyperbole, the romantics had no choice. They could not avoid the hyperbolic, either in their reception to the world around them, or in their sense of the romantic subject who responded to that world. Romantic extravagance differed from its counterpart in eighteenth-century writing. It was not mimetic, not an attempt to imitate an overwhelming scene or situation. To use Meyer Abrams's figure, its guiding metaphor was not the mirror but the lamp, and a black light at that, a wild and often uncontrolled expression of the despair that such encounters provoked in the romantic subject, and the sense of the gap they opened between the spectator of sublimity and universal meaning. Hyperbole offered the only trope suitable to such a dilemma. It was the only figure even vaguely appropriate to a situation in which, as Coleridge noted, "the poet's unusual state of excitement justifies and demands a correspondent difference of language."[7] The golden years of youth in Wordsworth's *Prelude* required no hyperbole. Their belated representation, however, was another story, one of "hollow exaltation dealing forth / Hyperboles of praise *comparative*."[8] The correspondent difference in language frequently became bombast, as many of Coleridge's own unfortunate attempts at sublimity illustrate.

Dennis's astute sense that his colleagues' increasingly overblown rhetoric stemmed from the waning of an authorizing godhead points directly to the similar absence underlying the romantic sublime. The absence came to define not only the romantic literary style but the existential stance. It also explains the frequent bombast of romantic attempts at sublime writing. Schiller, pushing Dennis's type of analysis still further, dealt at length with the fact that the tendency to produce the extravagant and even the bombastic was not only unavoidable, but integral to the romantic or sentimental character. "If a poet," Schiller wrote of his own sentimental era,

> has the unhappy chance to choose for his picture certain natures that are merely *superhuman* and *cannot possibly* be represented, he can only avoid exaggeration by ceasing to be a poet, and not trusting the theme to his imagination. Otherwise one of the two things would happen: either imagination, applying its limits to the object, would make a limited and merely *human* object of an absolute object -- which happened with the gods of Greece -- or the object would take away limits from fancy, that is, render it null and void, and this is precisely exaggeration (*N&SP* 166).

What Schiller discerned in the Sentimental's inevitable exaggeration was a hyperbolic stance, a predetermination to hyperbole that emerges in the sentimental or romantic era.

Writing three years before the dawn of English romanticism in the *Lyrical Ballads*, Schiller basically delineated the English romantic character:

> The sentimental genius . . . is exposed to the danger . . . of going . . . beyond possibility or otherwise falling into extravagant enthusiasm. This error of *overtension* is . . . founded in a specific idiosyncrasy of its procedure (*N&SP* 164).

"Overstrain," "overtension," or in essence hyperbole, Schiller had discovered, was endemic to the sentimental or romantic response to the sublime. It was an aesthetics, and an occasional poetic turgidity, that not only mirrored but underscored the lack of theological "cause" that Dennis had discerned. Like Schiller's reflection of Dennis's critique, Coleridge was also to single out the potential danger of sublimity to the romantic or "modern" sensibility of his era. Such writers, Coleridge wrote, "receive neither the Letter nor the Spirit, turning the one into Oriental hyperbole, in order to explain away the other."[9]

A Desperate Philosophy

> From my very childhood I have been accustomed to *abstract* and as it were unrealize whatever of more than common interest my eyes dwelt on; and then by a sort of transfusion and transmission of my consciousness to identify myself with the Object.[10]
>
> -- Coleridge

It is true that the frequent product of such excess in English romanticism is bathos. Thomas McFarland cites numerous instances in Coleridge's poetic aspirations to the sublime, in particular, which he describes as "turgid," "frenzied," "hysterical," and "shrill," as indeed they are.[11] Yet, it would seem important to consider the implications behind such language. The romantics, and especially Coleridge, were acutely aware of their propensity to overblown writing, and of the fact that it persisted despite their efforts to contain it. More important, whether they were aware of the problem or not, the phenomenon stemmed not entirely from lack of skill or self-indulgence but, as Schiller had already demonstrated, from the philosophical project of romanticism itself. It was a project aptly expressed by the aporia of the sublime.

Coleridge provides an excellent case in point. He was painfully conscious of what McFarland calls his "deleterious aspirations toward the sublime," and of the futility of the pains he had taken to correct it. Yet, he had "done all he could to rectify the tendency," to no avail. Noting the same poem that McFarland complains of, "Religious Musings" (1794-6), Coleridge admitted "to its full extent" the justice of the reviewers' attacks on the "EXCESS OF ORNAMENT in addition to STRAINED AND ELABORATE DICTION." In response to his censors' "friendly admonitions," he explained that he "pruned the double epithets with no sparing hand, and used [his] best efforts to tame the swell and glitter both of thought and diction" (*BL*, I, 7-8). There was nothing, however, as Coleridge's frustrated explanations show, that could have alleviated the poem's excess. Its hyperbole was inherent in its topic.

Coleridge's own explanation of his inability to tame the poem, which McFarland suggests but leaves undeveloped, shows the full implications of this inability for romantic identity. Frenetic hyperbole, Coleridge writes, inevitably occurs in attempts to combine poetry and philosophy: "Satisfied that the thoughts, such as they were, could not have been expressed otherwise, or at least more perspicuously," he writes, "I forgot to enquire, whether the thoughts themselves did not demand a degree of attention unsuitable to the nature and objects of poetry" (*BL*, I, 7-8). The remark is germane to the dilemma of the self. As Coleridge was beginning to discover, analytic causality, the process by which we construct a coherent concept of personal identity, could not be superimposed on the sublime's unrepresentability. The subjective structures of linear meaning on which conventional selfhood is based were rendered null by the meaninglessness encountered in an experience of sublimity. This discovery, one of which

Coleridge is only fitfully aware here, constitutes the hyperbolic moment, the hyperbolic stance that guides the autofigurational project of romanticism's negative sublime. Coleridge constantly lamented the precarious balance on which his extravagant language rested, and on which the subject's nature depended: "'Alas, what great calamities have misty words produced," he wrote, "that say so much that they say nothing -- clouds, rather, from which hurricanes burst'" (*BL*, II, 31, n2).

He was not alone among the romantic writers. Shelley's embarrassing "fall upon the thorns of life" in "Ode to the West Wind," his soarings in "Epipsychidion" (which J. Hillis Miller finesses as "orgasmic") are random instances. The tranquil Wordsworth, as Bloom notes quite accurately, could sink even further than Coleridge. Coleridge's "awfulness is at least sublime," Bloom writes; "it is not the drab, flat awfulness of Wordsworth at *his* common worst," those passages in *The Excursion* and even in *The Prelude* "(heresy to admit this!) . . . that we hastily skip by, with our zeal and relief in getting at the great moments."[12] Even in his overt deference to Wordsworth, Coleridge also notes the customary flat-footedness of Wordsworth's hyperbole, in which the reader's "feelings are alternately startled by climax and hyperclimax," leaving the rather bumptious impression of having prepared oneself for leaping down three stairs and only leaping down one (*BL*, II, 123, 123n).

In the last analysis, if Coleridge "whoops," as Bloom writes of "Religious Musings" and other Coleridge poems,[13] it is "because he vaults." Reflecting the verticality of romantic autofiguration, he vaults because "he is a high-jumper of the Sublime" (*Figures* 7). If Coleridge's soarings become the earthbound rush of the "ostrich," to which he so frequently compare himself (*BL*, I, xlvii, 46, 46n), the displeasure of the resulting clumsiness should scarcely provide a focal point of concern. What is significant is the fact that such hyperbolic vaulting begins to uncover the self-constructive character of romanticism, a project related not only to the trope of hyperbole (although the trope provides a useful marker), but to the hyperbolic stance underpinning it.

Subliming the Self

> I have thoughts of thee,
> Of thee, thy learning, gorgeous eloquence,
> . . . .
> The self-created sustenance of a mind
> Debarred from Nature's living images,
> Compelled to be a life unto itself.[14]
>
> -- Wordsworth, to Coleridge

The hyperbolic moment of romanticism's negative sublimity is one of imbalance, as if the conventional status of things, and along with it the conventional posture of the poet, begins to waver. A change begins to occur, which, as Ruskin was later to make clear in his celebrated discussion of a new, more "grotesque" or less traditionally "beautiful" aesthetics, was not altogether negative:

> However great a man might be, there are always some subjects which *ought* to throw him off balance; some by which his poor human capacity of thought should be conquered, and brought into the inaccurate and vague state of perception, so that the language of the highest inspiration becomes broken, obscure and wild in metaphor.[15]

Whether or not such imbalance "ought" to occur, it nonetheless does in the romantic sublime, and in the face of it both Schiller and Coleridge reveal the beginnings of a peculiar transformation.

What the hyperbolic moment of romantic sublimity puts in question is the poet's capacity to represent what he sees or experiences, his ability to translate the moment's chaos into some acceptable order of human meaning. Eugenio Donato shows the relation of this inability to a further manifestation of hyperbole: transformation or metamorphosis. Citing Grimm's definitions of *übersetzen* (translation), Donato writes:

> *Übersetzen* has as diffuse and extensive a semantic field as the word *translatio* has in Latin or 'translation' has in English. Again, according to Grimm, among its meanings we find 'to transport from one place to another,' 'to transform,' 'to metamorphose,' 'to use a stronger or exaggerated expression: hyperbole,' 'to jump over or above something.' And incidentally, here Grimm significantly gives the example *'den Abgrund übersetzen,'* hence to jump over an abyss or a groundless space.[16]

The meanings of *übersetzen* link romantic hyperbole to metamorphosis and to the *salto mortale* which, as Coleridge shows, is intrinsic to the sublime. The hyperbolic moment can involve both, being sufficiently precarious to warrant the metamorphic and the uncanny. At such moments, Schiller warns accurately, "the sentimental genius abandons actuality in order to rise upward to ideas." Ideally, such "ideas" are intended to restore the equilibrium threatened by the confrontation with a sublime object or force. "But," Schiller writes, "the sentimental [or romantic] genius will not always remain sufficiently *dis*passionate to maintain himself uninterruptedly and uniformly within the conditions that are entailed in the concept of *human nature* and to *which reason, even in its freest effects, must here always remain bound*" (*N&SP* 164-5, my italics).

The response to the sublime sweeps the poet beyond reason, beyond rationality. More important, it sweeps him beyond the conditions of the human. "If," as we recall Schiller remarking, "a poet has the unhappy chance to choose for his picture certain natures that are merely *superhuman* and *cannot possibly* be represented, he can only avoid exaggeration by ceasing to be a poet" (*N&SP* 166). Ceasing to be a poet, what then does he become? Wordsworth's intuitive description of Coleridge provides an apt response: "The self-created sustenance of a mind / Debarred from Nature's living images / Compelled to be a life unto itself (*Prelude*, VI, 264-314).

Writing of the romantic sensibility, Schiller and Coleridge describe a subject that, debarred from the natural, has become a life unto itself. It is alien, or other. Its foreignness stems from a process that is intrinsic, Schiller writes, to the sentimental or romantic era. It is "founded in a specific idiosyncrasy of [sentimental or romantic] procedure (*N&SP* 164). Overwhelmed and unbalanced by an element (for want of a better term) that is absolutely not its own, the sentimental or romantic subject is excluded from the natural because it has become other, or "contranatural," as Coleridge describes it. The impetus that propels this transformation, the moment of the romantic or negative sublime, produces a hyperbolic assault in which the subject is overpowered by what it *recognizes* cannot be given anthropomorphic significance. Such assaults give rise in the poet to a process of becoming "other," of assuming another nature, or an alternative identity.

There is, in the sublime's hyperbolic moment, a displacement of the overwhelmed or annihilated self -- the self defined by conventional reason -- by something nonhuman or other than self. The change occurs as a way of overcoming the uncertainty of such a moment, a moment "wherein," as Lacoue-Labarthe writes, "the process of the *unsure* initiates." As a metamorphosis of the poet, the process of this substitution reflects the hyperbole peculiar to *übersetzen* or translation. Its transformation is uncanny, as Donato writes -- a "leap over an abyss or groundless space." What is more, it is deliberate. It entails a *willful* "forgetting" and "dissimulation," in which the romantic subject becomes other than self, other than the conventionally ordering poet -- becomes *imposteur absolu*.

A Death's Head Identity

> Coleridge is evidently mad and unintelligible, but I venture to say you will never repent giving him sixteen pages a month.[17]
> -- John Lockhart

Mad and unintelligible, the contranatural self that results from the sublime's reduction of the romantic subject is clarified by examining a derivative of the sublime, "sublimation." Sublimation here does not mean the process of substitution or transformation that Freud describes, the process by which an unacceptable or threatening wish or drive is sublimated into a more acceptable one -- although such substitution occurs in the sublime with regard to other problems. "Sublimation" here specifically refers to its effects on the integrity of the self, to the effect of being "sublimed" or "sublimated." To sublimate in this sense is to "reduce to essence," "refine away into something unreal or non-existent, "reduce to unreality" (*OED*, "sublimate," 3122-3123). Such sublimation has nothing to do with an "exaltation" of the self. More accurately, Michel Deguy writes,

> in the majority of cases [of the sublime], it is a question of death. The mortal condition and the moment of perishing are always at stake when the *sublime* appears.[18]

Like Schiller, Coleridge was well aware of the devastation -- not the exaltation -- that attended the sublime's "sublimation" of the subject. And it is not by chance that he repeatedly drew on the idea of "subliming" in the sense of chemical reduction to describe the self's annihilation in such moments.

Coleridge's use of the metaphor of chemical subliming to describe associationist philosophy's calamitous effect on the self illuminates the parallel effect that he saw in the sublime. He used the same metaphor for both assaults. It shows further that for Coleridge, the meaninglessness of both was tantamount to death. Given materialist philosophy's dismissal of categories of meaning as mere constructs, Coleridge wrote, "Hartleain associationism look[ed] death into everything."[19] According to Hartley's "dualistic hypothesis" -- that "lawless law" of materialist associationism that, incidentally, echoes Lyotard's description of sublimity's "rule of non-regulation" -- "the soul becomes a mere ens logicum . . . / a caput mortuum" (*BL*, I, 116). According to Engell and Bate,

> Caput mortuum is the residuum remaining after the distillation or sublimation of any substance, or, figuratively, any worthless residue. The transferred use was current in C's day" (*BL*, I, 117, 117n).

Yet, while Engell's and Bate's explanations are accurate, Coleridge had a further meaning of caput mortuum in mind as well, a definition more in keeping with Deguy's characterization of sublimity. That meaning, the sublime's inherent association with the subject's mortality, emerges in Coleridge's attack on French materialist philosophy: "even in its height of self-complacency as chemical art," Coleridge wrote, "greatly am I deceived if it has not from the very beginning mistaken the products of destruction, cadavera rerum [dead bodies of things] for the elements of composition."

Reflecting his view of the "deadening" nature of Hartley's philosophy, Coleridge drew on sublimity's intrinsic associations with death to characterize French materialist philosophy. Such philosophy, he wrote, was the "caput mortuum of human nature evaporated." Again, his diction is germane. Engell and Bate press the chemical and alchemical meanings of caput mortuum in this usage as well, writing that the Latin term means

> [l]iterally 'death's head' -- the alchemical term for the residuum left after distillation (but C has confused the distillate with the residuum). The metaphor is, however, clear: French thinkers, like alchemists, in a false quest of truth, have burned off the human, leaving only the animal, nature in their alembics (*SM* 76-77, 77n).

In the interest of Coleridge's accuracy with alchemical terminology, Engell and Bate gloss over caput mortuum's literal meaning of "death's head," the universal symbol of human mortality. Taken in its meaning as this symbol, Coleridge's use of caput mortuum shows the implications behind his two connected uses of "sublimation." Just as the meaninglessness of materialist philosophy sublimates the subject into an inhuman caput mortuum or death's head -- a sign of man's mere mutability -- the sublime as aesthetic paradigm of unmeaning sublimates or transforms the subject into inhuman "other" -- into what lies beyond the recuperative myths of immortality.

Romanticism and a Sublimation Strange

> Hyperbole is the movement by which thought ravishes itself.[20]
>
> -- Michel Deguy

The central role that Coleridge gave the subliming of the subject in romantic aesthetics is illustrated in the *Biographia Literaria*. Here,

Coleridge attributes the capacity to sublimate the subject to the imagination itself. This form of imagination is obviously a murkier aspect of romantic creativity, a side revealing Coleridge's awareness that the death's head sublimation of the self haunted not only materialist philosophy but the romantic project in general.

Like the imagination's eruption in Wordsworth's Simplon Pass, the onset of the imagination's subliming force in the *Biographia* requires a knowledge of the events leading up to it. Much as with Wordsworth, the impetus for the incident is Coleridge's own chariness of the imagination's more daunting qualities, the darker creative powers that he had already confronted in the Mariner and Christabel, and which are associated with madness and a chaotic complexity that defies all attempts to theorize or contain it within formal understanding. Given such characteristics, the imagination in Coleridge's view becomes the perfect source of a sublime, and a subliming, encounter.

As so much of Coleridge's thought, the process of the encounter is circuitous, but ultimately patent. In this latter part of volume one of the *Biographia*, Coleridge has promised to present a "theory of imagination" or, in essence, to bring the imagination under the control of a rational, philosophically ordered system. Such a project, however, requires that he wrestle theoretically with the imagination's anti-theoretical properties, described above. In what is a clear and strategic effort to avoid such a confrontation, Coleridge postpones the project of outlining his theory by referring to a bogus letter from a friend, who advises him not to attempt such a "critically demanding" exposition in so popular a work. Coleridge heeds the "letter," and drops all mention of the imagination, filling most of the following chapter (thirteen) with the "letter's" contents. Toward the conclusion of this chapter, however, realizing that he can no longer avoid at least a remark about the imagination -- he has, after all, promised a rigorous account of its properties and powers -- Coleridge pens the terse paragraph which becomes his celebrated distinction between the fancy and the imagination, and concludes both chapter thirteen and the *Biographia*'s first volume.

At first glance, the evasion seems to have succeeded. With the opening of the second volume, Coleridge appears to have escaped the topic of his theory of imagination, and hence the threat of sublimity, altogether. Buoyed by his strategy's apparent success, Coleridge promises, in the early paragraphs of chapter fourteen, to provide a series of relatively benign topics -- an account of the "Occasion of the *Lyrical Ballads*" and some "Philosophic definitions of a poem and poetry with scholia" (*BL*, II, 5). The different care he gives the two topics is important. Dealing with little more than a string of anecdotes, Coleridge treats the occasion of the *Lyrical Ballads* at length. Each detail of the famous volume's inception is described lingeringly. But his "philosophic definitions of the poem and poetry," which are potentially more theoretically demanding and which could quite easily lead back to his theory of the imagination, turn out to be a few random remarks. In a similar fashion and for the same reason, his promised formal "scholia," with an equal potential to produce the spectre of the imagination, are never produced. The uneven treatment that Coleridge gives the two topics, the one anecdotal and the other theoretical, indicates the further evasion of any connection with a theory of the imagination.

Unwisely, however, and perhaps again buoyed by the control he seems to have recaptured, Coleridge decides to conclude the chapter with a panegyric on "the Poet" who, in Coleridge's own system and as he apparently forgets, is most often conflated with the imagination itself. It is thus not by chance that the panegyric becomes Coleridge's Simplon Pass, leading him inadvertently back to the overwhelming concept that he had apparently escaped. The poet, he writes,

> . . . diffuses a tone and spirit of unity that blends, and (as it were) *fuses*, each into each, by that synthetic and magic power, to which we have exclusively appropriated the name of imagination.

The Extravagant Self

With the term "imagination" finally confronting him, Coleridge's evasive tactics are instantly suspended. His rational or critical powers paralyzed, he is "halted," much as was Wordsworth on the mountain path.

With a hyperbolic force that erupts despite Coleridge, despite his measured attempts at formal definitions and scholia, a rhapsodic sentence commences. Beyond all logic, all measure, all "reason," the sentence swells to over one hundred and twenty-five words, as Coleridge struggles to "theorize," or to gain control, of what is clearly the sublime core of romantic aesthetics:

> This power, first put in action by the will and understanding, and retained under their irremissive, though gentle and unnoticed, controul (*laxis effertur habenis*) reveals itself in the balance or reconciliation of opposite or discordant qualities: of sameness, with difference; of the general, with the concrete; the idea, with the image; the individual, with the representative; the sense of novelty and freshness, with old and familiar objects; a more than usual state of emotion, with more than usual order; judgement ever awake and steady self possession, with enthusiasm and feeling profound or vehement; and while it blends and harmonizes the natural and the artificial, still subordinates art to nature; the manner to the matter; and our admiration of the poet to our sympathy with the poetry (II, 16-17).

At the conclusion of this astonishing sentence, Coleridge, beyond words and indeed, "sublimed," turns immediately to a quotation of a poem about the soul by Sir John Davies. Meant to augment his failed philosophic containment of the imagination, the quote in fact illustrates in images deliberately summoned by Coleridge himself, the metamorphosis he has undergone as a result of the powers of the "POETIC IMAGINATION:"

> 'Doubtless', as Sir John Davies observes of the soul (and *his words may with slight alteration be applied, and even more appropriately to the poetic Imagination.*)
>
> Doubtless this could not be but that *she turns*

> *Bodies to spirit by sublimation strange,*
> *As fire converts to fire the things it burns,*
> As we our food into our nature change.
>
> *From their gross matter she abstracts their form,*
> And draws a kind of quintessence from things;
> Which to her proper nature *she transforms*
> To bear them light on her celestial wings.
>
> Thus does she, when *from individual states*
> *She doth abstract the universal kinds;*
> Which then re-clothed in divers names and fates
> Steal access through out senses to our minds.
>
> P. 18 Finally, GOOD SENSE is the BODY of poetic genius, FANCY its DRAPERY, MOTION its LIFE, and IMAGINATION the SOUL that is every where, and in each; and forms all into one graceful and intelligent whole (17-18, italics mine).

Given his clear loss of control at this point in the chapter, the meaning of the quotation is clear. Coleridge has called up the subliming images of Davies's poem in recognition of the moment's hyperbolic and transforming character, and in admission of the fact that he has, however temporarily, himself been transformed.

The images Coleridge draws from Davies's poem illustrate what Donato characterizes as hyperbole's metamorphic power. Coleridge, his "gross matter" or body abstracted, has been sublimed by the "maddening" nature of the imagination. The change becomes clear when compared to Coleridge's reference to an identical self-transformation in "Kubla Khan":

> *Could I revive within me*
> *Her symphony and song,*
> To such a deep delight 'twould win me
> That with music loud and long,
> I would build that dome in air,
> That sunny dome! those caves of ice!
> And all who heard should see them there,

> *And all should cry, Beware! Beware!*
> *His flashing eyes, his floating hair!*
> *Weave a circle round him thrice,*
> *And close your eyes with holy dread,*
> *For he on honey-dew hath fed,*
> *And drunk the milk of Paradise* (my italics).[21]

As with "Kubla Khan," Coleridge in the *Biographia* passage has, despite his "rational" intentions, indeed "revived" within himself the imagination's symphony and song. And it *has* "won," or changed him. Through its irrational power, he *has* built with "music loud and long" -- and Bloom's sense of "whooping" changes tone here -- the identical (if less poetically compelling) fantasy that he invoked in "Kubla Khan." No longer the flightless, theorizing "ostrich" as he described himself in contrast to "nightingale" Wordsworth, Coleridge, with this mighty sentence on the poet, becomes the flashing-eyed poet of the romantic imagination. "Magic," "contranatural," even "fearful," the "synthetic" Coleridge has allowed his "individual state" to be subsumed by Davies's "universal" ambiance. As Deguy notes with the sublime, it is a type of death. The "residuum" "Coleridge" that remains after this sublimation is the *other* "self" -- the self of the sublime.

Most significant, Coleridge's autoscopic transformation is, to a large extent, willed.[22] Frye shows unquestionably that Coleridge recognizes and deliberately invokes the daemonic alter-ego of himself that he creates in "Kubla Khan." The poet's awareness of such a change and his intention to bring about the situation that creates it is clarified by what Frye calls romanticism's "recognition poems." Such poems, Frye writes,

> reverse the usual associations of dream and waking, so that it is experience that seems to be the nightmare and the vision that seems to be the reality . . .
> A very important group of recognition poems are the poems of self recognition, where the poet himself is involved in the awakening from experience into a visionary reality. Examples include Collins's *Ode on the Poetical Character*, Coleridge's

Kubla Khan, and Yeats's *Tower* and *Sailing to Byzantium*.[23]

Much as Collins and the later Yeats, Coleridge recognizes and "hails" the "superhuman" identity he has assumed, both in the *Biographia* and in the "Kubla Khan" dream passage. We may compare Yeats's transformation:

> *Consume my heart away*; sick with desire
> And fastened to a dying animal,
> It knows not what it is; and *gather me*
> *Into the artifice of eternity.*
>
> Once out of nature *I shall never take*
> *My bodily form from any natural thing* . . .
> But such a form as Grecian goldsmiths make . . .
> Or set upon a golden bough to sing. . .[24]
>
>   -- "Sailing to Byzantium"

> Before me floats *an image*, man or shade,
> Shade more than man, more image than a shade;. . .
> *I hail the superhuman*;
> I call it *death-in-life and life-in-death.*
>
> *Miracle, bird* or golden handiwork,
> More miracle than bird or handiwork,
> Planted *on the starlit golden bough* . . .[25]
>
>   -- "Byzantium,"

with Coleridge's:

> The Night-mare LIFE-IN-DEATH was she
> Who thicks man's blood with cold . . .
> 'The game is done! I've won! I've won!'
> Quoth she, and whistles thrice. . .
> *(Listen, O stranger! to me.)* . . .

> 'I fear thee, ancient Mariner!
> I fear thy skinny hand!
> And thou art long and lank, and brown,
> As is the ribbed sea sand . . .
> I fear thee and *thy glittering eye* . . .'[26]
>
> -- *Rime of the Ancient Mariner*

> *An old Man with a steady Look sublime. . .*
> He stops his earthly Task to watch the Skies --
> But he is blind -- *a statue hath such Eyes* -- . . .
> He gazes still, his eyeless Face all eye. . .
> *Wall'd round* and made a spirit-jail secure
> By the mere *Horror of blank Nought at all* --[27]
>
> -- *Limbo*

Like Yeats, Coleridge -- who referred to himself as "the gray-haired passenger" or essentially, the Mariner -- hailed his aesthetic alter-ego as "Life in Death, and Death in Life."

We should recall that the metamorphosis of the poet that such sublime encounters bring about, as Schiller continually reminds us, is integral to sentimental or romantic aesthetics. Coleridge is careful to make clear that it is *not* the "soul" that causes such a transformation, the sense that Davies's words had originally implied. It is rather the "*POETIC IMAGINATION*," as Coleridge admittedly twists Davies's words to mean, that "turns / Bodies to spirit by sublimation strange, / As fire converts to fire the things it burns (*BL*, II, 16-17). It is, in other words, the sublime ground of romantic aesthetics itself that transforms -- the same *Abgrund* that toppled Kant's analogical philosophy of man's unified self in the *Critique of Judgment*. The "idiosyncrasy" of such an aesthetics, Schiller implies, is the decimation of the subject's traditionally unified identity.

On the authority of his own words and those of Davies, whom Coleridge deliberately chooses to cite at this crucial instance, the death of the poet's conventional self is portrayed as a clear subliming. It is a direct, and in Coleridge's somewhat ambivalent estimation, a *desirable* consequence of the sublime. Like the uncanny alter-ego of Yeats's "Sailing to Byzantium" -- the ancient sage who, like Coleridge's ubiquitous double[28] in the Mariner, appears repeatedly throughout Yeats's writing -- Coleridge has been "consumed away." Like Yeats's sage, the contranatural self that is left to Coleridge does not -- *will* not -- partake of "any natural thing."

Although Coleridge attributes his sublimation strange to the poetic imagination, he does not, in this particular instance, sustain his overt acknowledgment of the imagination's metamorphic power. Recovering from the disorientation of the moment, he reverts to the "sensible" language characteristic of conventional meaning. Echoing the deliberately limited vision of the speaker in Blake's "The Divine Image," Coleridge reinstalls the image of perfect, and safe, *human* existence -- the "human form divine" of Blake's myopic speaker:[29] "Finally," Coleridge concludes the chapter, "GOOD SENSE is the BODY of poetic genius, FANCY its DRAPERY, MOTION its LIFE, and IMAGINATION the SOUL that is everywhere, and in each; and forms all into one graceful and intelligent whole (*BL*, II, 18).

The ruse is telling, however. Coleridge has appropriated Davies' metaphor of the soul in order to humanize the imagination's otherwise uncanny power, and to limit its province to the noumenal aspects of existence, the limitation that, ironically, he had protested in Kant. As so many of Coleridge's efforts, however, the attempt proves contradictory. With the extended image of human being, he attempts to impose "good sense" on what essentially lacks sense, the human form on what is non-human, and totality on that which is, in fact, limitless.

The hyperbolic character of this instance, the sublimation or metamorphosis of the "sensible" poet who is struck by the profound inadequacy of "sense" in a confrontation with the sublime, seems unquestionable. And not accidentally, the same sense of becoming "other," of moving beyond the "possible," beyond the real in such a moment, pervades Schiller's characterization of sentimental or romantic sensibility. It is worth recalling Schiller's words here:

> The sentimental genius abandons actuality in order to rise upward to ideas . . . but . . . [he] will not always remain sufficiently dispassionate to maintain himself uninterruptedly and uniformly within the conditions that are entailed in the concept of human nature" (*N&SP* 164-65).

The tendency of the sentimental or romantic to go beyond the possible, the human, is generic, "founded in a specific idiosyncrasy of its procedure" (*N&SP* 164). By its nature, sentimental genius is always "exposed to the danger of going beyond possibility." "All poets," Schiller writes,

> who draw their material too one-sidedly from the world of thought . . . are . . . in danger . . . of falling into this bypath . . . If driven so far . . . it [the sentimental work] contravenes the conditions of all possible experience and consequently, in order to make it actual, human nature would have to be totally abandoned, then such a thought is no longer poetic but overstrained [hyperbolic] -- provided, that it has declared itself as representable and poetic . . . (*N&SP* 165).

Reflecting Schiller's characterization of an emerging sentimental sensibility, the effect of the sublime's hyperbolic moment clearly propels the romantic poet beyond the human. It also indicates, in no uncertain terms, a poetics that did *not* declare itself as representable and poetic, at least in the traditional sense.

According to Longinus: "Whenever the form of a speech is poetical and fabulous and breaks into every kind of impossibility, such digressions have a strange and alien air" ("On the Sublime" 87). To Longinus and even to Schiller, both of whom mistrusted the hyperbolic, hyperbole's "strange and alien air" was still a "digression," a "bypath" as Schiller called it, even though he defined sentimental genius in terms of this bypath. Yet, with the onset of a full-blown romanticism, particularly as it appears in Coleridge, the tendency became less a detour than a major avenue of expression. Like the existential stance that such expression prefigures, it is a poetics of "an indirect (ironic) communication," as Louis Mackey writes of the later Kierkegaard, "a system of signifiers that obviates reference."[30] As Coleridge saw, and had begun to render through a newly aestheticized sense of identity, romanticism's hyperbolic sublimity also discloses a system that obviates the conventional self.

NOTES

[1] *BL*, II, 31, n2.

[2] "On the Sublime," in *Critical Theory Since Plato*, ed. Adams (New York, 1991), 76-99; 78. References are taken from the Adams anthology unless otherwise noted.

[3] See "sublime," *The Compact Edition of the Oxford English Dictionary* (Oxford, 1971), II, 3122-3123. Hereafter, *OED*.

[4] *N&SP*, 166.

[5] Nicolson, 284-5.

[6] Burnet, *Sacred Theory of the Earth*, in Nicolson, 278-9.

[7] See Hamilton, 152.

[8] Wordsworth, *The Prelude: 1799, 1805, 1850* (New York, 1979), 1805, VI, 663-4, my italics.

[9] *Aids to Reflection and the Confessions of an Inquiring Spirit*, ed. H. N. Coleridge (Rpt. 1825; London, 1884), 101. Hereafter, *AR, Confessions*.

[10] *CN*, III, 4181, #7, N.

[11] McFarland, *Romanticism and the Forms of Ruin*, 238-45.

[12] *Figures of Capable Imagination* (New York, 1976), 7. Hereafter, *Figures*.

[13] Bloom counts "well over one hundred exclamation points in just over four hundred lines" of "Religious Musings".

[14] *Prelude*, VI, 264-314.

[15] Ruskin, in Nicolson, 287.

[16] Eugenio Donato, "Idioms of the Text," *Glyph*, 2, 1977, 1-13, p. 6.

[17] Lockhart to Blackwood, cited in Marion Lochhead, "Coleridge and John Gibson Lockhart," *New Approaches to Coleridge* (London, 1981), 69. Original source, M. Oliphant, *Annals of a Publishing House: William Blackwood and His Sons* (1897), i, 218.

[18] Michel Deguy, "The Discourse of Exaltation," in *Of the Sublime: Presence in Question* (New York: State University of New York Press, 1993), 9. Hereafter, Deguy.

[19] *CL*, IV, 575; *The Friend*, ed. Barbara Rooke (London & Princeton, NJ: 1969), I, 106; II, 71-2. Hereafter, *Friend*.

[20] Deguy, "The Discourse of Exaltation," 9.

21. Coleridge, "Kubla Khan," *The Complete Poetical Works of Samuel Taylor Coleridge* (Oxford, 1966), I, ll. 43-54, p. 298.

22. See Robert Rogers's discussion of "autoscopy" or the "visual hallucination of the physical self" in *A Psychoanalytic Study of the Double in Literature* (Detroit, 1990), 14, *passim*; Maud Bodkin, *Archetypal Patterns in Poetry: Psychological Studies of Imagination* (London, 1951); E.T.A. Hoffmann, "The Sandman," in *Tales of E. T. A Hoffmann* (Chicago, 1972); Otto Rank, *The Double* (Chapel Hill, 1979); Bryan Tyson, "'The Frightful Co-Existence of the To Be and the Not to Be,'" in *Philosophical Approaches to Literature* (Lewisburg, 1984).

23. Northrop Frye, "The Drunken Boat": The Revolutionary Element in Romanticism" (Englewood Cliffs, 1970), 302.

24. William Butler Yeats, "Sailing to Byzantium," ll. 21-30, in *The Collected Poems of W. B. Yeats* (New York, 1969), 218.

25. William Butler Yeats, "Byzantium," ll. 9-10, 15-16, in *The Collected Poems of W. B. Yeats* (New York, 1969), 280.

26. Coleridge, *Rime of the Ancient Mariner*, II, ll. 193-198, 224-28; italics signify earlier ms. version. See *The Complete Poetical Works of Samuel Taylor Coleridge* (Oxford, 1966) I, p. 194, 194n.

27. Coleridge, "Limbo," ll. 20-22, 26, 32-33, *The Complete Poetical Works of Samuel Taylor Coleridge* (Oxford, 1966) I, 430.

28. See Bodkin, *Archetypal Patterns in Poetry*; Rank, *The Double*; Robert Rogers, *A Psychoanalytic Study of the Double in Literature*.

29. Compare Blake:
>For Mercy has a Human heart
>Pity a human face,

And Love, the human form divine
And Peace, the human dress.

The Poetry and Prose of William Blake. (New York, 1970), 12. See Bloom, *Blake's Apocalypse* (New York, 1963).

[30.] See Roger Poole, review of *Kierkegaard's Truth: The Disclosure of the Self*, ed. Joseph H. Smith, *Times Literary Supplement* (March 5, 1982), 260.

BIBLIOGRAPHY

AUTHORS

BLAKE

The Complete Writings of William Blake. Ed. Geoffrey Keynes. London and New York: Oxford University Press, 1972.
The Poetry and Prose of William Blake. Ed. David E. Erdman. New York: Doubleday and Co., 1970.
Bloom, Harold. *Blake's Apocalypse: A Study in Poetic Argument*. New York: Anchor Books, 1963.

BURKE

A Philosophical Enquiry into the Origin of Our Ideas of the Sublime and Beautiful. Ed. J. T. Boulton. Notre Dame and London: University of Notre Dame Press, 1968.
A Philosophical Enquiry into the Origin of Our Ideas of the Sublime and Beautiful. *Works*. London: Bohn, 1964. I; 49-178.

COLERIDGE

Works

The Complete Poetical Works of Samuel Taylor Coleridge. Ed. Ernest Hartley Coleridge. 2 volumes. Oxford: Oxford University Press, 1966.

The Poetical Works of Samuel Taylor Coleridge. Ed. Ernest Hartley Coleridge. Oxford: Oxford University Press, 1978.

Aids to Reflection and the Confessions of an Inquiring Spirit. Ed. H. N. Coleridge. Rpt. 1825; London: George Bell & Sons, 1884.

Biographia Literaria. Eds. James Engell and Walter Jackson Bate. 2 vols. Princeton, NJ: Princeton University Press, 1983.

Biographia Literaria. Ed. John Shawcross. 2 vols. London: Oxford University Press, 1965.

The Friend. Ed. Barbara E. Rooke. 2 vols. Princeton, NJ: Princeton University Press, 1969.

Inquiring Spirit: A Coleridge Reader. Ed. Kathleen Coburn. Rpt. 1951; New York: Minerva Press, 1968.

Lay Sermons. Ed. R. J. White. Princeton, NJ: Princeton University Press, 1972.

Lectures 1809 - 1819 on Literature. Ed. R. A. Foakes. 2 vols. Princeton, NJ: Princeton University Press, 1987.

The Literary Remains of Samuel Taylor Coleridge. Ed. Henry Nelson Coleridge. 4 vols. Rpt. 1836; New York: AMS Press, 1967.

Marginalia. Ed. George Whalley. 5 vols. Princeton, NJ: Princeton University Press, 1980-.

The Notebooks of Samuel Taylor Coleridge. 4 Vols. Ed. Kathleen Coburn. New York: Routledge & Kegan Paul, 1957-.

Shakespearean Criticism. Ed. T. M. Raysor. 2 vols. Cambridge, MA: Harvard University Press, 1930.

The Statesman's Manual. Lay Sermons. Ed. R. J. White. Princeton, N.J.: Princeton University Press, 1972.

S. T. Coleridge's Treatise on Method as Published on the Encyclopaedia Metropolitana. Ed. Alice D. Snyder. London: Constable & Co., 1934.

Coleridge's Table Talk and Omniana. Ed. T. Ashe. London: George Bell and Sons, 1905.

Table Talk. Ed. Carl Woodring. 2 vols. Princeton, NJ: Princeton University Press, 1990.
Collected Letters of Samuel Taylor Coleridge. Ed. Earl Leslie Griggs. 6 vols. Oxford: Clarendon Press, 1956-.

Biographies, Memoirs, Correspondence

Alsop, Thomas. *Letters, Conversations and Recollections of S. T. Coleridge*. New York: Harper & Brothers, 1836.
Coffman, Ralph J., ed. *Coleridge's Library: A Bibliography of Books Owned and Read by Samuel Taylor Coleridge*. Boston, MA: G. K. Hall, 1987.
Cottle, Joseph. *Reminiscences of Samuel Taylor Coleridge and Robert Southey*. New York: Wiley and Putnam, 1847.
Gillman, James. *The Life of Samuel Taylor Coleridge*. 2 vols. London: William Pickering, 1838.
Haney, John Louis. *The German Influence on Samuel Taylor Coleridge*. New York: Haskell House, 1966.
Hanson, Lawrence. *The Life of S. T. Coleridge: The Early Years*. New York: Russel and Russel, 1962.
Hazlitt, William. "Mr. Coleridge." *Selected Essays of William Hazlitt: 1778 - 1830*. Ed. Geoffrey Keynes. London: Nonesuch Press, 1970.
Holmes, Richard. *Coleridge: Early Visions*. 2 vols. New York: Viking Press, 1990. I.
_____. *Shelley: The Pursuit*. New York: E. P. Dutton, 1975.
_____. *Coleridge*. Oxford: Oxford University Press, 1982.
Lockhart, J. G. *Memoirs of the Life of Sir Walter Scott*. 5 vols. Boston: J. H. Francis and Co. 1927.
Watson, Lucy Eleanor Gillman. *Coleridge at Highgate*. New York: Folcroft Library Editions, 1970.

Secondary Sources

Burwick, Frederick, ed. *Coleridge's Biographia Literaria: Text and Meaning*. Columbus: Ohio State University Press, 1989.

Bate, W. Jackson. *Coleridge*. Rpt. 1968; Cambridge, MA: Harvard University Press, 1987.

Beer, John, ed. *Coleridge's Variety: Bicentennary Studies*. Pittsburg: University of Pittsburg Press, 1975.

Deaschamps, Paul. *La Formation de la pensée de Coleridge (1772-1804)*. Paris: Didier, 1964.

de Man, Paul. "Review of Harold Bloom's *Anxiety of Influence*." *Blindness and Insight: Essays in the Rhetoric of Contemporary Criticism*. Minneapolis: University of Minnesota Press, 1983; 187-229.

_____. "The Rhetoric of Temporality." *Blindness and Insight*.

Dunstan, A. C. "The German Influence on Coleridge." *MLR* XVII, 272- and XVIII, 183- (192-23).

Engell, James. *The Creative Imagination: Enlightenment to Romanticism*. Cambridge, MA: Harvard University Press, 1981.

Frei, Hans W. *The Eclipse of Biblical Narrative: A Study in Eighteenth and Nineteenth Century Hermeneutics*. New Haven: Yale University Press, 1974.

Fruman, Norman. *Coleridge, The Damaged Archangel*. New York: George Braziller, 1971.

Gallant, Christine, ed. *Coleridge's Theory of Imagination Today*. New York: AMS Press, 1989.

Gatta, Jr., John. "Coleridge and Allegory." *Modern Language Quarterly*, 38 (1977): 62-77.

Hamilton, Paul. *Coleridge's Poetics*. Stanford: Stanford University Press, 1983.

Haney, John Louis. *The German Influence on Samuel Taylor Coleridge*. Philadelphia: Haskell House, 1966.

Kermode, Frank. *The Sense of an Ending: Studies in the Theory of Fiction*. Rpt. 1966; London: Oxford University Press, 1970.

Kernan, Alvin B. *The Plot of Satire*. Rpt. 1965; New Haven: Yale University Press, 1974.

Kroeber, Karl. *Romantic Narrative Art*. Madison, WI: University of Wisconsin Press, 1966.

Lacoue-Labarthe, Philippe and Jean Luc Nancy. *The Literary Absolute: The Theory of Literature in German Romanticism*. Trans. Philip Barnard and Cheryl Lester. New York: State University of New York Press, 1988.

_____. *The Subject of Philosophy*. Ed. Thomas Trezise. Ed. Consultant. Linda M. Brooks. Trans. Hugh Silverman, et. al. Minneapolis: University of Minnesota Press, 1993.

_____. *Le Sujet de Philosophie*. Paris: Flammarion, 1979.

_____. *Typography: Mimesis, Philosophy, Politics*. Ed. Christopher Fynsk. Ed. Consultant Linda M. Brooks. Trans. Barbara Harlow, et.al. Cambridge, MA: Harvard University Press, 1989.

_____. *Mimesis des Articulation*. Paris: Flammarion, 1975.

Lockridge, Laurence. *Coleridge the Moralist*. Ithaca: Cornell University Press, 1977.

Logan, Sister Eugenia. *A Concordance to the Poetry of S. T. Coleridge*. St. Mary of the Woods, Indiana: St. Mary of the Woods College, 1940.

McFarland, Thomas. *Romanticism and the Forms of Ruin: Wordsworth, Coleridge and Modalities of Fragmentation*. Princeton, NJ: Princeton University Press, 1981.

_____. *Coleridge and the Pantheist Tradition*. Oxford: Oxford University Press, 1969.

Miller, J. Hillis. *The Disappearance of God: Five Nineteenth-Century Writers*. Cambridge, MA: Harvard University Press, 1963.

Mellers, Wilfred. "The Influence of the Future." Review of David B. Greene, *Temporal Processes in Beethoven's Music*. New York: Gordon & Breach 1983. *TLS*, June 29, 1984, p. 723.

Modiano, Raimonda. *Coleridge and the Concept of Nature*. Tallahassee: Florida State University Press, 1985.

_____. "Coleridge and Milton: The Case Against Wordsworth in the *Biographia Literaria*." *Coleridge's Biographia Literaria: Text and Meaning*. Ed. Frederick Burwick. Columbus: Ohio State University Press, 1989; 150-71.

Newlyn, Lucy. "Parodic Allusion: Coleridge and the 'Nehemiah Higgenbottom' Sonnets, 1797." *Charles Lamb Bulletin*. New Series No. 56. (October, 1986): 255-59.

Reiman, Donald H. *Intervals of Inspiration: The Skeptical Tradition and the Psychology of Romanticism.* Greenwood, FL: Penkevill Publishing Co., 1988.

Said, Edward. *Beginnings: Intention and Method.* Baltimore: Johns Hopkins University Press, 1975.

Snyder, Alice D., ed. *S. T. Coleridge's Treatise on Method as Published on the Encyclopaedia Metropolitana.* London: Oxford University Press, 1934.

Sultana, Donald, ed. *New Approaches to Coleridge: Biographical and Critical Essays.* London: Vision Press, Limited, 1981.

Wheeler, Kathleen. *Sources, Processes and Methods in Coleridge's Biographia.* Cambridge: Cambridge University Press, 1980.

DE QUINCEY

De Quincey, Thomas. "A Brief Appraisal of Greek Literature." *De Quincey, Selected Essays on Rhetoric.* Ed. Frederick Burwick. Southern Illinois University Press, 1967; 289-342.

_____. "A Brief Appraisal of the Greek Literature in its Foremost Pretensions." *Works.* Ed. David Masson. London: Adam & Charles Black, 1897. X, 300-302.

_____. "System of the Heavens as Revealed by Lord Rosse's Telescope." *Works.* Ed. David Masson. London: Adam and Charles Black, 1890. VIII, 7-34.

HAZLITT

Hazlitt, William. *The Complete Works of William Hazlitt.* Ed. P. P. Howe. 21 vols. London: J. M. Dent and Sons, 1930-34.

Carnall, Geoffrey. "The Impertinent Barber of Baghdad: Coleridge as Comic Figure in Hazlitt's Essays." *New Approaches to Coleridge: Biographical and Critical Essays.* London: Vision Press, Limited, 1981; 38-48.

HEGEL

Hegel, G.W.F. *The Difference between Fichte's and Schelling's System of Philosophy*. Trans. H. S. Harris and W. Cerf. Albany: State University of New York Press, 1977.
_____. *Lectures on the Fine Arts*. 2 vols. Trans. T. M. Knox. Oxford: Oxford University Press, 1975.
_____. *Logic: Being Part One of the Encyclopaedia of the Philosophical Sciences*. Trans. William Wallace. Rpt. 1873; Oxford: Clarendon Press, 1978.

KANT

Works

Anthropology from a Pragmatic Point of View. Trans. Victor Lyle Dowdell. Carbondale: Southern Illinois University Press, 1978.
The Contest of the Faculties. Kant's Political Writings. Ed. Hans Reiss. Trans. H. B. Nisbet. London: Cambridge University Press, 1977; 176-90.
The Critique of Judgment. Trans. J. C. Meredith. Rpt. 1952; Oxford: Clarendon Press, 1957.
Kritik der Urteilskraft. Hrsg. Gerhard Lehmann. Stuttgart: Philipp Reclam, 1976.
The Critique of Pure Reason. Trans. Norman Kemp Smith. Rpt. 1929; New York: St. Martin's Press, 1965.
Dreams of a Spirit-Seer, Illustrated by Dreams of Metaphysics. Ed. Frank Sewall. Trans. Emanuel F. Goerwitz. London: Swan Sonnenschein & Co., 1900.
Groundwork of the Metaphysics of Morals. Trans. H. J. Paton. New York: Harper & Row, 1964.
The Old Saw: That May Be Right in Theory But It Won't Work in Practice. Trans. B. Ashton. Philadelphia: University of Pennsylvania Press, 1974.

Secondary Sources

Bretall, R. W. "Kant's Theory of the Sublime." *The Heritage of Kant*. Ed. George Tapley Whitney and David F. Bowers. Rpt. 1939; Princeton, NJ: Princeton University Press, 1962.

Cassirer, Heinrick Walter. *A Commentary on Kant's Critique of Judgment*. London: Methuen, 1938.

Crawford, Donald W. *Kant's Aesthetic Theory*. Madison, WI: University of Wisconsin Press, 1974.

Crowther, Paul. *The Kantian Sublime: From Morality to Art*. Oxford: Clarendon Press, 1989.

de Man, Paul. "Phenomenality and Materiality in Kant." *Hermeneutics: Questions and Prospects*. Amherst: University of Massachusetts Press, 1984.

Derrida, Jacques. *Raising the Tone of Philosophy: Late Essays by Immanuel Kant, Transformative Critique by Jacques Derrida*. Baltimore: Johns Hopkins University Press, 1994.

Guyer, Paul. *Kant and the Claims of Taste*. Cambridge, MA: Harvard University Press, 1979.

Jones, Hardy E. *Kant's Principle of Personality*. Madison: University of Wisconsin Press, 1971.

Kipperman, Mark. *German Idealism and English Romantic Poetry*. Philadelphia: University of Pennsylvania Press, 1986.

Makkreel, Rudolf A. *Imagination and Interpretation in Kant: The Hermeneutical Import of the Critique of Judgment*. Chicago: University of Chicago Press, 1990.

Orsini, G. N. G. *Coleridge and German Idealism: A Study in the History of Philosophy with Unpublished Materials from Coleridge's Manuscripts*. Carbondale: Southern Illinois University Press, 1969.

Wolff, Robert Paul. *Autonomy and Reason: A Commentary on Kant's Groundwork of the Metaphysics of Morals*. New York: Harper and Row, 1973.

_____. *Kant's Theory of Mental Activity: A Commentary on the Transcendental Analytic of the Critique of Pure Reason*. Cambridge, MA: Harvard University Press, 1963.

KEATS

The Poetical Works and Other Writings of John Keats. 8 vols. Ed. H. B. Forman, Rev. M. B Forman. New York: Charles Scribner's Sons, 1938-1939.
Selected Poems and Letters. Ed. Douglas Bush. Boston: Houghton Mifflin, 1959.

LAMB

Lamb, Charles. *The Letters of Charles and Mary Ann Lamb.* 3 vols. Ed. Edwin W. Marrs, Jr. Ithaca: Cornell University Press, 1975-78.
Lucas, E. V., ed. *Charles Lamb and the Lloyds.* London: Smith, Elder & Co., 1798.

PEACOCK

The Works of Thomas Love Peacock. Eds. H. L. B. Brett-Smith and C. E. Jones. 10 vols. New York: Gabriel Wells, 1924-1934.
Letters to Edward Hookham and Percy Bysshe Shelley. Boston: Bibliophile Society, 1910.

ROBINSON

Henry Crabb Robinson on Books and Their Writers. 3 vols. Ed. Edith J. Moreley. London: E. M. Dent and Sons, 1938.
Blake, Coleridge, Wordsworth, Lamb, Etc., Being Selections from the Remains of Henry Crabb Robinson. Ed. Edith J. Morley. Rpt. 1922; New York: AMS Press, 1967.
The Correspondence of Henry Crabb Robinson with the Wordsworth Circle, 1808-1866. Ed. Edith J. Moreley. 2 vols. Oxford: Clarendon Press, 1929.

Crabb Robinson in Germany, 1800-1805: Extracts from His Correspondence. Ed. Edith J. Moreley. 2 vols. London: Oxford University Press, 1929.
Diary, Reminiscences, and Correspondence of Henry Crabb Robinson. Ed. Thomas Sadler. 2 vols. New York: Hurd and Houghten, 1877.
The Diary of Henry Crabb Robinson: An Abridgement. Ed. Derek Hudson. London and New York: Oxford University Press, 1967.

SCOTT

Scott, Sir Walter. *Miscellaneous Prose Works.* 6 vols. Edinburgh: Cadell and Co., 1827.

SCHILLER

Works

"*Vom Erhabenen.*" *Werke.* Hrsgb. B. von Wiese. Weimar: Hermann Bohlaus, 1962; XX, 170-95.
Kallias oder über die Schönheit; Über Anmut und Würde. Hrsgb. K. L. Berghahn. Stuttgart: Philipp Reclam, 1971.
Über die äesthetische Erziehung des Menschen. Friedrich Schiller: Sämtliche Werke. 5 band. *Philosophische Schriften, Vermischte Schriften.* Hrsgb. Wiese. München: Winkler Verlag, 1975: V; 311-409.
On the Aesthetic Education of Man: In a Series of Letters. Trans. E. Wilkinson and L. A. Willoughby. Oxford: Clarendon Press, 1967.
"*Über das Erhabene.*" Wiese. München, 1975: V; 213-31.
"On the Sublime." *Friedrich von Schiller: Naive and Sentimental Poetry and "On the Sublime."* Trans. J. A. Elias. New York: Frederick Ungar, 1966; 193-212.
Über naive und sentimentalische Dichtung. Sämtliche Werke. Wiese. München, 1975. V; 433-518.
Naive and Sentimental Poetry. Friedrich von Schiller: Naive and Sentimental Poetry and "On the Sublime." Trans. J. A. Elias. New York: Frederick Ungar, 1966; 83-190.

Bibliography

Schillers Briefe. Hrsgb. E. Streitfeld u. V. Zmegac. Königstein: Athenäeum Verlag, 1983.
Briefwechsel zwischen Friedrich Schiller und Wilhelm von Humboldt. Berlin: Aufbau-Verlag, 1962; I, II.
Briefwechsel zwischen Schiller und Körner. Hrsgb. Klaus L. Berghahn. München: Winkler Verlag, 1973.
Correspondence between Schiller and Goethe, from 1794 to 1805. Trans. L. Dora Schmitz. London: George Bell and Sons, 1877; I.
Correspondence of Schiller with Körner. 3 vols. London: R. Bentley, 1849.
Life of Schiller; Poetical Works. The Complete Works of Friedrich von Schiller. Ed. Nathan Haskell Dole. Boston: Aldine Publishing Co., 1910; I.
Aesthetical Philosophical Essays. In *The Complete Works.* Ed. Dole; V.
Don Carlos. The Classic Theater: Five German Plays. Ed. E. Bentley. 2 vols. Garden City, NY: Doubleday, 1959; II.
Sketches and Anecdotes of Goethe, the Schlegels, Wieland and Other Contemporaries. Ed. Leonard Simpson, Esq. 3 vols. London: Richard Bentley New Burlington Street, 1849.
The Piccolomini and *The Death of Wallenstein.* Trans. Samuel Taylor Coleridge. *Schiller: The Complete Works.* Ed. Nathan Haskell Dole. Boston: Aldine Publishing Co., 1910: IV; 2-426.
Wallenstein: A Historical Drama in Three Parts. Trans. Charles E. Passage. New York: Ungar, 1958.
Wallenstein: ein dramatisches Gedicht. Munich: Deutsche Taschenbuch Verlag, 1966.

Secondary Sources

Brooks, Linda M. "Sublime Suicide: The End of Schiller's Aesthetics." *Friedrich von Schiller and the Drama of Human Existence.* Ed. Alexej Ugrinsky. New York: Greenwood Press, 1988; 91-103.
_____. "Sublimity and Theatricality: Romantic Pre-Postmodernism" *MLN* 105:5 (Winter, 1990): 939-64.
Cohen, Ted and Paul Guyer. *Essays in Kant's Aesthetics.* Chicago: University of Chicago Press, 1982.
Dunstan, A. C. "The German Influence on Coleridge." *MLR* XVII, 272- and XVIII, 183- (1922-23).

Ellis, J. M. *Schiller's Kalliasbriefe and the Study of His Aesthetic Theory.* The Hague: Mouton, 1969.
Ewen, Frederic. *The Prestige of Schiller in England, 1788-1859.* New York: Columbia University Press, 1932.
Haney, John Lewis. *The German Influence on Samuel Taylor Coleridge.* New York: Haskell House, 1966. Rpt. Philadelphia, 1902.
Henrich, Dieter. "Beauty and Freedom: Schiller's Struggle with Kant's Aesthetics." *Essays in Kant's Aesthetics.* Eds. Ted Cohen and Paul Guyer. Chicago: University of Chicago Press, 1982.
Kerry, S. S. *Schiller's Writings on Aesthetics.* Manchester, England: Manchester University Press, 1961.
Kulenkampff, Jens, ed. *Materialen zu Kant's 'Kritik der Urteilskraft.'* Frankfurt am Main: Suhrkamp, 1974.
Lovejoy, A. O. "Schiller and the Genesis of German Romanticism." *Essays in the History of Ideas.* New York: Putnam, 1960; 207-228.
Orsini, G. N. G. *Coleridge and German Idealism: A Study in the History of Philosophy with Unpublished Materials from Coleridge's Manuscripts.* Carbondale: Southern Illinois University Press, 1969.
Passage, Charles E. *Friedrich Schiller.* New York: Frederick Ungar, 1975.
Thomas, Calvin. *The Life and Works of Schiller.* New York: Henry Holt, 1904.

SHELLEY

The Complete Poetical Works of Percy Bysshe Shelley. 4 vols. Ed. Neville Rogers. Oxford: Clarendon Press, 1972.
Shelley: Poetical Works. Ed. Thomas Hutchinson. London: Oxford University Press, 1967.
The Letters of Percy Bysshe Shelley. 2 vols. Ed. Frederick L. Jones. Oxford: Clarendon Press, 1964.

STEVENS

The Palm at the End of the Mind. Ed. Holly Stevens. New York: Vintage Books, 1972.

WORDSWORTH

The Prelude: 1799, 1805, 1850. Ed. Jonathan Wordsworth, et.al. New York: W. W. Norton, 1979.

YEATS

The Collected Poems of W. B. Yeats. New York, Macmillan, 1969.

SUBJECTS

THE SELF

In Coleridge

Barfield, Owen. *What Coleridge Thought.* Middletown, CT: Wesleyan University Press, 1971.
Bygrave, Stephen. *Coleridge and the Self: Romantic Egotism.* New York: St. Martin's Press, 1986.
Christensen, Jerome. *Coleridge's Blessed Machine of Language.* Ithaca: Cornell University Press, 1981.
Ferris, David S. "Coleridge's Ventriloquy: The Abduction from the *Biographia, SiR,* 1 (Spring, 1985): 217-39.
Fichte, J. G. *Science of Knowledge with First and Second Introductions.* Ed. and Trans. P. Heath and J. Lachs. New York: Meredith, 1970.
Galperin, W. H. "'Desynonymizing' the Self in Wordsworth and Coleridge." *SiR,* vol. 26, no. 4 (Winter, 1987), 513-27.
Hayter, Alethea. *Opium and the Romantic Imagination.* Berkeley and Los Angeles: University of California Press, 1970.

Kessler, Edward. *Coleridge's Metaphors of Being.* Princeton, N.J.: Princeton University Press, 1979.

Lockridge, Laurence S. "Coleridge and the Perils of 'Self Realization.'" *Coleridge's Theory of Imagination Today.* New York: AMS Press, 1989; 257-75.

??????????. *Coleridge the Moralist.* Ithaca: Cornell University Press, 1977.

Prickett, Stephen. *Coleridge and Wordsworth: The Poetry of Growth.* Cambridge: Cambridge University Press, 1970.

Potter, Stephen. *Coleridge and S. T. C.* New York: Russel and Russel, 1965.

Riede, David G. *Oracles and Hierophants: Constructions of Romantic Authority.* Ithaca: Cornell, 1991.

Rzepka, Charles J. *The Self as Mind: Vision and Identity in Wordsworth, Coleridge and Keats.* Cambridge, MA: Harvard University Press, 1986.

Schelling, F. W. J. *System of Transcendental Idealism.* Trans P. Heath. Charlottesville: University Press of Virginia, 1978.

Schultz, Max F. *The Poetic Voices of Coleridge.* Detroit: Wayne State University Press, 1964.

Wallace, C. Miles. "Coleridge's *Biographia* and the Evidence for Christianity." *Interspace and the Inner Sphere: Essays on Romantic and Victorian Self.* Eds. Norman A. Anderson and Margene E. Weiss. Macomb, IL: Western Illinois University Press, 1978.

In Schiller

Brooks, Linda Marie. "Autobiographical Hyperbole: Schiller's *Naive and Sentimental Poetry.*" *Reading After Foucault: Institutions, Disciplines, and Technologies of the Self in Germany, 1750-1830.* Ed. Robert Leventhal. Detroit: Wayne State University Press, 1994; 193-211.

Dewhurst, Kenneth and Nigel Reeves. *Friedrich Schiller: Medicine, Psychology, and Literature, with the First English Edition of His Complete Medical and Psychological Writings.* Berkeley: University of California Press, 1978.

Heyn, Gisa. *Schiller als Psychologe.* Zurich: Juris Verlag, 1966.

Reidel, Wolfgang. *Die Anthropologie des jungen Schiller: zur Ideengeschichte der medizinischen Schriften und der 'Philosophischen Briefe'*. Wurzburg: Konighausen und Neumann, 1985.

Reider, Heinz. *Schiller: Religion und Menschenbild*. Wien: W. Braumiller, 1966.

Reiner, Hanz. *Duty and Inclination: Discussed and Refined in Special Regard to Kant and Schiller*. The Hague: Nijoff, 1983.

Taubeneck, Steven A. "From Schiller to Derrida: Geneology and Deconstruction of the Individual." *Friedrich von Schiller and the Drama of Human Existence*. Eds. Alexej Ugrinsky and Natalie Datlov. New York: Greenwood Press, 1988; 103-09.

In Kant

Grene, Marjorie. "On Some Distinctions between Men and Brutes." *Ethics* 57, no. 2 (January 1947): 121-27.

Haezrahi, Pepita. "The Concept of Man as an End-in-Himself." *Kant: A Collection of Critical Essays*. Ed. Robert Paul Wolff. Garden City, NY: Doubleday, 1967; 291-313

Hoernle, R. F. A. "Kant's Concept of the 'Intrinsic Worth ' of Every 'Rational Being.'" *The Personalist* 24, no. 2 (April 1943): 130-146.

Jones, Hardy E. *Kant's Principle of Personality*. Madison: University of Wisconsin Press, 1971.

Maclagen, W. G. "Respect for Persons as a Moral Principle -- I." *Philosophy* 35, no. 134 (July 1960): 193-217.

_____. "Respect for Persons as a Moral Principle -- II." *Philosophy* 35, no. 135 (October 1960): 289-305.

Morris, Bertram. "The Dignity of Man." *Ethics* 57, no. 1 (October 1946): 57-64.

Sturma, Dieter. *Kant Über Selbstbewusstsein: Zum Zuzammenhang von Erkenntniskritik und Theorie des Selbstbewusstseins*. New York: Olms and Hildesheim, 1985.

In Romanticism

Baxter, Edmund. *De Quincey's Art of Autobiography*. New York: Barnes and Noble, 1990.
Bloom, Harold. *Poetry and Repression: Revisionism from Blake to Stevens*. New Haven and London: Yale University Press, 1976.
Bodkin, Maud. *Archetypal Patterns in Poetry: Psychological Studies of Imagination*. Rpt. 1934; London: Oxford University Press, 1951.
Cooke, Michael. *The Romantic Will*. New Haven: Yale University Press, 1976.
Cooper, Andrew M. *Doubt and Identity in Romantic Poetry*. New Haven: Yale University Press, 1988.
de Man, Paul. "Time and History in Wordsworth." *Romanticism and Contemporary Criticism*. Baltimore: The Johns Hopkins University Press, 1993.
_____. "Autobiography as De-facement." *The Rhetoric of Romanticism*. New York: Columbia University Press, 1984; 67-83.
_____. "Impersonality in Blanchot." *Blindness and Insight*; 60-79.
_____. "Ludwig Binswanger and the Sublimation of the Self." *Blindness and Insight*; 36-50.
Garber, Frederick. *The Autonomy of the Self: From Richardson to Huysmans*. Princeton, NJ: Princeton University Press, 1982.
Horn, William Dennis. "William Blake and the Problematic of the Self." *William Blake and the Moderns*. Eds. R. J. Bertholf and Annette S. Levitt. Albany: State University of New York Press, 1982.
Izenberg, Gerald. *Impossible Individuality: Romanticism, Revolution and the Origins of Modern Selfhood*. Princeton, NJ: Princeton University Press, 1992.
Jay, Paul. *Being in the Text: Self-Representation from Wordsworth to Roland Barthes*. Ithaca: Cornell University Press, 1984.
Molnar, Géza von. *Romantic Vision, Ethical Context*. Minneapolis: University of Minnesota Press, 1987.
Reiman, Donald H. *Intervals of Inspiration: The Skeptical Tradition and the Psychology of Romanticism*. Greenwood, FL: Penkevill Publishing Co., 1988.

Tyson, Bryan. "'The Frightful Co-Existence of the To Be and the Not to Be': Antinomy and Irony in De Quincey's 'Sir William Hamilton.'" *Philosophical Approaches to Literature*. Ed. W. E. Cain. Lewisburg: Bucknell University Press, 1984.

And the Double

Bodkin, Maud. *Archetypal Patterns in Poetry: Psychological Studies of Imagination*. Rpt. 1934; London: Oxford University Press, 1951.
Hoffman, E. T. A. "The Sandman." *Tales of E. T. A. Hoffman*. Ed and Trans. Leonard J. Knight and Elizabeth C. Knight. Chicago: University of Chicago Press, 1972; 93-126.
Lacoue-Labarthe, Philippe. *'Retrait' of the Artist, in Two Persons*. Trans. Mira Kamdar. Frac Rhône-Alpes: Editions mem/Arte Facts, 1981.
Rank, Otto. *The Double*. Trans. and Ed. Harry Tucker Jr. Rpt. 1971; Chapel Hill: University of North Carolina Press, 1979.
Rogers, Robert. *A Psychoanalytic Study of the Double in Literature*. Detroit: Wayne State University Press, 1990.

General

Adams, Henry. *The Education of Henry Adams*. Eds. Ernest Samuels & Jayne N. Samuels. Boston: Houghton Mifflin Co., 1973.
Anderson, Norman A. and Weiss Margene E., eds. *Interspace and the Inner Sphere: Essays on Romantic and Victorian Self*. Macomb, IL: Western Illinois University, 1978.
Barker, Stephen. *Autoaesthetics: Strategies of the Self After Nietzsche*. New Jersey and London: Humanities Press, 1992.
Brilliant, Richard. *Portraiture*. Cambridge, MA: Harvard University Press, 1991.
Brooks, Linda Marie, ed. *Alternative Identities: The Self in Literature, History, Theory*. New York: Garland Press, 1995.
Cadava, Eduardo, et. al. eds. *Who Comes After the Subject?* New York: Routledge, 1991.
Copjec, Joan, ed. *Supposing the Subject*. London: Verso, 1994.

Cox, Stephen D. *The Stranger Within Thee: Concepts of the Self in Late 18th-Century Literature*. Pittsburg: University of Pittsburg Press, 1980.

Fleishman, Avrom. *Figures of Autobiography: The Language of Self-Writing in Victorian and Modern England*. Berkeley: University of California Press, 1983.

Dean, Carolyn. *The Self and Its Pleasures: Bataille, Lacan, and the History of the Decentered Subject*. Ithaca: Cornell University Press, 1992.

Elbaz, Robert. *The Changing Nature of the Self: A Critical Study of the Autobiographic Discourse*. Iowa City: University of Iowa Press, 1987.

Franck, Isaac. "Self-Realization as Ethical Norm: A Critique." *The Philosophical Forum*, 9 (1977): 1-25.

Finkelstein, Joanne. *The Fashioned Self*. Philadelphia: Temple University Press, 1991.

Corngold, Stanley. *The Fate of the Self: German Writers and French Theory*. New York: Columbia University Press, 1986.

Irwin, John T. "Self Evidence and Self Reference: Nietzsche and Tragedy, Whitman and Opera." *New Literary History*, 11 (1979).

Lévi-Strauss, Claude. *The Savage Mind*. Rpt. 1962; Chicago: University of Chicago Press, 1973.

Levine, George, ed. *Constructions of the Self*. New Brunswick, NJ: Rutgers University Press, 1992.

Lang, Berel. *Writing and the Moral Self*. New York: Routledge, 1991.

Lynd, Helen Merrell. *On Shame and the Search for Identity*. New York: Harcourt Brace and Co., 1958.

Noonan, Harold. *Personal Identity*. London: Routledge, 1991.

Olney, James. *Metaphors of Self: The Meaning of Autobiography*. Princeton, NJ: Princeton University Press, 1972.

_____, ed. *Autobiography: Essays Theoretical and Critical*. Princeton, NJ: Princeton University Press, 1980.

Parfit, Derek. *Reasons and Persons*. Oxford: Clarendon Press, 1984.

Ricouer, Paul. *Oneself as Another*. Trans. Kathleen Blamey. Chicago: University of Chicago Press, 1992.

Singer, Alan. *The Subject as Action: Transformation and Totality in Narrative Aesthetics*. Ann Arbor: University of Michigan Press, 1993.

Smith, Joseph H., ed. *Kierkegaard's Truth: The Disclosure of the Self*. New Haven: Yale University Press, 1981.

Smith, Paul. *Discerning the Subject*. Minneapolis: University of Minnesota Press 1988.
Solomon, Robert C. *Continental Philosophy Since 1750: The Rise and Fall of the Self*. Oxford: Oxford University Press, 1988.
Spacks, Patricia Meyer. *Imagining a Self: Autobiography and Novel in Eighteenth-Century England*. Cambridge: Harvard University Press, 1976.
Taylor, Charles. *Sources of the Self: The Making of the Modern Identity*. Cambridge, MA: Harvard University Press, 1989.
Vaihinger, Hans. *The Philosophy of 'As If'*. Rpt. 1924; London: Routledge & Kegan Paul Ltd., 1965.

THE SUBLIME

In Coleridge

Bloom, Harold. "Coleridge: The Anxiety of Influence." *New Perspectives on Coleridge and Wordsworth: Selected Papers from the English Institute*. Ed. Geoffrey Hartman. New York: Columbia University Press, 1972; 247-69.
Dunstan, A. C. "The German Influence on Coleridge." *Modern Language Review* XVII, 272- and XVIII, 183- (1922-23).
Haeger, J. H. "Anti-Materialism, Autobiography and the Abyss of Unmeaning in the *Biographia*." *Coleridge's Biographia Literaria: Text and Meaning*. Ed. Frederick Burwick. Columbus: Ohio State University Press, 1989; 75-88.
Knapp, Steven. *Personification and the Sublime: Milton to Coleridge*. Cambridge, MA: Harvard University Press, 1985.
Lovejoy, A. O. "Coleridge and Kant's Two Worlds." *Essays in the History of Ideas*. New York: Putnam, 1960; 254-277.
Modiano, Raimonda. "Humanism and the Comic Sublime." *SiR* 2 (Summer, 1987); 231-245.
_____. "Coleridge and the Sublime: A Response to Thomas Weiskel's *The Romantic Sublime*. *The Wordsworth Circle* 9, no. 1 (Winter, 1978); 110-120.
_____. "Coleridge's Conception of the Sublime." *Coleridge and the Concept of Nature*. Tallahassee: Florida State University Press, 1985; 101-138.

Shaffer, Elinore S. "Coleridge's Revolution in the Standard of Taste." *Journal of Aesthetics and Art Criticism* 28 (1969); 213-221.
Starobinski, Jean. *Portrait de l'Artiste en Saltimbanque.* Geneva: Skira, 1970.
Thorpe, Clarence DeWitt. "Coleridge on the Sublime." *Wordsworth and Coleridge.* Ed. Earl Leslie Griggs. Princeton, NJ: Princeton University Press, 1939; 192-220.
Yarlott, Geoffrey. *Coleridge and the Abyssinian Maid.* London: Methuen, 1967.

In Schiller

Schiller, Friedrich von. "On the Sublime" (*"Über das Erhabene"*) and *"Vom Erhabenen"* Werke. Hrsgb. B. von Wiese. Weimar: Hermann Bohlaus, 1962; XX, 170-95.
Brooks, Linda M. "Sublime Suicide: The End of Schiller's Aesthetics." *Friedrich von Schiller and the Drama of Human Existence.* New York, 1988.
_____. "Sublimity and Theatricality: Romantic Pre-Postmodernism." *MLN.*
Cohen, Ted and Paul Guyer. *Essays in Kant's Aesthetics.* Chicago: University of Chicago Press, 1982.
Henrich, Dieter. "Beauty and Freedom: Schiller's Struggle with Kant's Aesthetics." In Ted Cohen and Paul Guyer. *Essays in Kant's Aesthetics.*
Kerry, S. S. *Schiller's Writings on Aesthetics.* Manchester, England: Manchester University Press, 1961.

In Kant

Abrams, Meyer. "Kant and the Theology of Art." *Notre Dame English Journal*, XIII (1981): 75-106.
Crowther, Paul. *The Kantian Sublime: From Morality to Art.* Oxford: Clarendon Press, 1989.
de Man, Paul. "Phenomenality and Materiality in Kant," in *Hermeneutics: Questions and Prospects.* Amherst: University of Massachusetts Press, 1984.

Kant, Immanuel. *Observations on the Feeling of the Beautiful and the Sublime*. Trans. John T. Goldthwait. Berkeley: University of California Press, 1960.

Makkreel, Rudolf. "Imagination and Temporality in Kant's Theory of the Sublime," *The Journal of Aesthetics and Art Criticism*. XLIII/3 (Spring, 1984): 305-315.

_____. *Imagination and Interpretation in Kant: The Hermeneutical Import of the Critique of Judgment*. Chicago, 1990.

Nahm, Milton C. "'Sublimity' and the 'Moral Law' in Kant's Philosophy." *Kant-Studien* 48 (1956-57); 502-24.

General

Adorno, Theodor W. *Aesthetic Theory*. Trans. C. Lenhardt. Eds. Gretl Adorno and Rolf Tiedemann. London: Routledge and Kegan Paul, 1986.

Altieri, Charles. "Reach Without a Grasp." Review. Paul Fry. *The Reach of Criticism: Method and Perception in Literary Theory*. Diacritics (Winter, 1984); 58-66.

Arac, Jonathan. "The Media of Sublimity: Johnson and Lamb on *King Lear*." *SiR* (Summer, 1987); 209-221.

Brooks, Peter. *The Melodramatic Imagination: Balzac, Henry James, Melodrama, and the Mode of Excess*. New York: Columbia University Press, 1985.

Carritt, E. F. *The Theory of Beauty*. Rpt. 1914; London: Methuen, 1962.

Croce, Benedetto. *Aesthetic*. Trans. Douglas Ainslie. New York: Macmillan, 1929.

Dale, Peter Allen. "*Sartor Resartus* and the Inverse Sublime." In *Allegory, Myth, and Symbol*. Ed. Morton W. Bloomfield. Cambridge, MA: Harvard University Press, 1981; 293-312.

De Brun, Frans. "Hooking the Leviathan: The Eclipse of the Heroic and the Emergence of the Sublime in Eighteenth-Century Literature." *Eighteenth Century: Theory and Interpretation* 2 (Spring, 1987); 195-215.

Derrida, Jacques. "Freud and the Scene of Writing." *Writing and Difference*. Trans. Alan Bass. Chicago: University of Chicago Press, 1978; 196-278.

———. "Cogito and the History of Madness." *Writing and Difference*, 31-64.
Donato, Eugenio. "Idioms of the Text." *Glyph* II, 1977; 1-13.
Ferguson, Frances. *Solitude and the Sublime: Romanticism and the Aesthetics of Individuation*. New York: Routledge, 1992.
———. "A Commentary on Suzanne Guerlac's 'Longinus and the Subject of the Sublime.'" *NLH* 16 (1985); 291-97.
———. "Legislating the Sublime." *Studies in EighteenthCentury British Art and Aesthetics*. Ed. Ralph Cohen. Berkeley: University of California Press, 1985.
———. "The Sublime of Edmund Burke, or the Bathos of Experience." *Glyph 8* (1981); 62-78.
———. "The Nuclear Sublime." *Diacritics* 14, no. 2 (Summer, 1984).
Foucault, Michel. *Madness and Civilization: A History of Insanity in the Age of Reason*. Trans. Richard Howard. New York: Random House, 1965.
Guerlac, Suzanne. "Longinus and the Subject of the Sublime." *NLH* 16 (1985); 275-89.
Harpham, Geoffrey Galt. "Asceticism and the Sublime." *The Ascetic Imperative in Culture and Criticism*. Chicago: University of Chicago Press, 1987.
Hertz, Neil. *The End of the Line: Essays on Psychoanalysis and the Sublime*. New York: Columbia University Press, 1985.
———. "A Reading of Longinus," *Critical Inquiry* 9 (March, 1983); 579-97.
———. "The Notion of Blockage in the Literature of the Sublime." *Psychoanalysis: The Question of the Text*. Ed. Geoffrey Hartman. Baltimore: Johns Hopkins University Press, 1978.
Hipple, Walter John Jr. *The Beautiful, the Sublime and the Picturesque in Eighteenth-Century British Aesthetic Theory*. Carbondale, IL: Southern Illinois University Press, 1957.
Jameson, Frederic. "Baudelaire as Modernist and Postmodernist: The Dissolution of the Referent and the Artificial Sublime." *Lyric Poetry: Beyond New Criticism*. Eds. C. Hosek & P. Parker. Ithaca: Cornell University Press, 1985.
Kristeva, Julia. *Powers of Horror: An Essay on Abjection*. Trans. Leon S. Roudiez. New York: Columbia University Press, 1982.

Lamb, Jonathan. "The Gothic Sublime and Sterne's Fiction." *ELH* 48 (1981); 110-143.
Levine, Steven Z. "Seascapes of the Sublime: Vernet, Monet, and the Oceanic Feeling." *New Literary History*, 2 (Winter, 1985); 377-401.
Librett, Jeffrey S., ed. trans. *Of the Sublime: Presence in Question.* New York: State University of New York Press, 1993.
Lindenberger, Herbert. *Opera: The Extravagant Art.* Ithaca: Cornell University Press, 1984.
Longinus. "On the Sublime." Trans. W. R. Roberts. *Critical Theory Since Plato.* Ed. Hazard Adams. Rpt. 1971; New York: Harcourt, Brace Jovanovich, 1991; 76-99.
Lyotard, Jean-François. "Answering the Question: What is Postmodernism?" Trans. Régis Durand. *The Postmodern Condition: A Report on Knowledge.* Trans. Geoff Bennington and Brian Massumi. Minneapolis: University of Minnesota Press, 1984.
_____. "Das Erhabene und die Avantgarde." *Merkur* (1984); 151-64.
Mason, Jeffrey D. *Melodrama and the Myth of America.* Bloomington: Indiana University Press, 1993.
Meager, R. "The Sublime and the Obscene." *British Journal of Aesthetics* 4, no. 3 (1964); 214-27.
Monk, Samuel Holt. *The Sublime: A Study of Critical Theories in XVIII-Century England.* Rpt. 1935; Ann Arbor: University of Michigan Press, 1960.
Morris, David B. *The Religious Sublime: Christian Poetry and Critical Tradition in 18th-Century England.* Lexington: University Press of Kentucky, 1972.
Murdoch, Iris. "The Sublime and the Good." *Chicago Review* XIII, iii (1959); 42-55.
Nicolson, Marjorie Hope. *Mountain Gloom and Mountain Glory: The Development of the Aesthetics of the Infinite.* Rpt. 1959; New York: Norton, 1963.
O'Hara, Daniel T. "The Poverty of Theory: On Society and the Sublime." *Contemporary Literature* (Fall, 1985); 335-50.
Paulson, R. "Versions of a Human Sublime." *NLH* 16 (1985).
Pease, Donald. "Sublime Politics." *boundary 2* 12.3-13.1 (1984); 259-279.

Rousseau, George S. "Quotation Marks: Burke's Enquiry and the Aesthetics of Pain," *Journal for the History of the Behavioral Sciences* (April, 1985); 117-35.
Said, Edward W. *Orientalism.* New York: Vintage Press, 1978.
Shapiro, Gary. "From the Sublime to the Political: Some Historical Notes." *NLH* 16 (1985); 213-35.
Siebers, Tobin. *The Romantic Fantastic.* Ithaca: Cornell University Press, 1984.
Simpson, David. "Updating the Sublime." *SiR* 2 (Summer, 1987); 245-259.
Sparshott, F. E. *The Structure of Aesthetics.* Toronto: University of Toronto Press, 1963.
Sussman, Henry. *Psyche and Text: The Sublime and the Grandiose in Literature.* New York: State University of New York Press, 1993.
Sutton, M. "Inverse Sublimity in Victorian Humor" *Victorian Studies*, 10 (2); 1966.
Silverman, Hugh and Gary Aylsworth, eds. *The Textual Sublime: Deconstructions and Its Differences.* Albany, NY: State University of New York Press, 1990.
Todorov, Svetan. *The Fantastic.* Trans. Richard Howard. Cleveland: Press of Case Western Reserve University, 1973.
Wimsatt, William K. and Cleanth Brooks. *Literary Criticism: A Short History.* New York: Vintage Books, 1957.
White, Hayden. "The Politics of Historical Interpretation: Discipline and de-Sublimation." *Critical Inquiry* 9 (1982); 113-37.
Wood, Theodore E. B. *The Word 'Sublime' and its Context, 1650-1750.* The Hague: Mouton, 1972.

In Romanticism

Albrecht, W. P. *The Sublime Pleasures of Tragedy: A Study of Critical Theory from Dennis to Keats.* Lawrence: University Press of Kansas, 1975.
Black, Joel. *The Aesthetics of Murder: A Study in Romantic Literature and Contemporary Culture.* The Johns Hopkins University Press, 1992.
Bloom, Harold. *Figures of Capable Imagination.* New York: Seabury Press, 1976.

_____. ed. *Poets of Sensibility and the Sublime*. New York: Chelsea House, 1986.
_____. with Lionel Trilling, eds. *Romantic Poetry and Prose*. New York: Oxford University Press, 1973.
Clarke, Bruce. "Artifice and Oscillation in the Eighteenth-Century Sublime." Review. Knapp, Steven. *Personification and the Sublime: Milton to Coleridge*. *The Eighteenth Century: Theory and Interpretation* 28, no. 2 (Spring, 1987); 271-77.
de Man, Paul. "Aesthetic Formalization: Kleist's *Über das Marionettentheater*." *The Rhetoric of Romanticism*. Columbia University Press, 1984.
_____. "The Rhetoric of Temporality." *Blindness and Insight*.
Gillespie, Gerald. "Romantic Irony and the Grotesque." *Romantic Irony*. Ed. Frederick Garber. Budapest: Akademiai Kiado, 1988.
De Luca, Vincent Arthur. *Words of Eternity: Blake and the Poetics of the Sublime*. Princeton, NJ: Princeton University Press, 1991.
De Quincey, Thomas. "A Brief Appraisal of the Greek Literature" and "System of the Heavens."
Ende, Stuart. *Keats and the Sublime*. New Haven: Yale University Press, 1976.
Ferguson, Frances. *Solitude and the Sublime: Romanticism and the Aesthetics of Individuation*. New York, 1992.
Fry, Paul H. "The Possession of the Sublime." *SiR* 2 (Summer, 1987); 187-209.
_____. *The Reach of Criticism: Method and Perception in Literary Theory*. New Haven: Yale University Press, 1983.
Frye, Northrop. "The Drunken Boat: The Revolutionary Element in Romanticism." *Romanticism: Points of View*. Eds. R. F. Gleckner & Gerald Enscoe. Rpt. 1962; Englewood Cliffs, NJ: Prentice-Hall, 1970.
Guerlac, Suzanne. *The Impersonal Sublime: Hugo, Baudelaire, Lautremont*. Stanford: Stanford University Press, 1990.
Jones, John. *The Egotistical Sublime: A History of Wordsworth's Imagination*. London: Chatto & Windus, 1954.
Kleist, Heinrich von. "On the Puppet Theater." *An Abyss Deep Enough*. Trans. Philip B. Miller. New York: E. P. Dutton, 1982.
McFarland, Thomas. *Romanticism and the Forms of Ruin*. Princeton, 1981.

Modiano, Raimonda. "Humanism and the Comic Sublime." *SiR* 2 (Summer, 1987); 231-245.
Müller, Andreas, ed. *Satiren und Parodien*. Reihe Romantik 9. Darmstadt: Wissenschaftliche Buchgesellschaft, 1970.
Paley, Morton D. *The Apocalyptic Sublime*. New Haven: Yale University Press, 1986.
Praz, Mario. *The Romantic Agony*. Trans. Angus Davidson. London: Oxford University Press, 1970.
Proctor, Sigmund Kluss. "The Sublime." *Thomas De Quincey's Theory of Literature*. Rpt. 1943; New York: Octagon Books, 1966; 78-92.
Read, Herbert. *The True Voice of Feeling: Studies in English Romantic Poetry*. New York: Pantheon Books, 1953.
Reed, Arden. *Romantic Weather: The Climates of Coleridge and Baudelaire*. Hanover: University Press of New England, 1983.
Richter, Jean Paul. *Horn of Oberon: Jean Paul Richter's School for Aesthetics (Vorschule der Aesthetik)*. Trans. Margaret R. Hale. Detroit: Wayne State University Press, 1973.
Ritter, Naomi. *Art as Spectacle: Images of the Entertainer Since Romanticism*. Columbia, MO: University of Missouri Press, 1989.
Schelling, Friedrich W. J. *Heinz Widerporst's Epicurean Confession of Faith*. Reihe Romantik 9. Darmstadt: Wissenschaftliche Buchgesellschaft, 1970.
Schlegel, Friedrich. *Athenaeum Fragments. Lucinde and the Athenaeum Fragments*. Trans. Peter Firchow. Minneapolis: University of Minnesota Press, 1971.
Vischer, Friedrich Theodore. *Über das Erhabene und Komische und Andere Texte zur Aesthetik*. Frankfurt a. M: Suhrkamp, 1967.
Weiskel, Thomas. *The Romantic Sublime: Studies in the Structure and Psychology of Transcendence*. Baltimore: Johns Hopkins Press, 1978.
Wlecke, Albert O. *Wordsworth and the Sublime*. Berkeley: University of California Press, 1973.

The Demonic

In Coleridge

Appleyard, J. *Coleridge's Philosophy of Literature.* Cambridge, MA: Harvard University Press, 1965.

Baker, James Volant. *The Sacred River: Coleridge's Theory of the Imagination.* Baton Rouge: Louisiana State University Press, 1957.

Coburn, Kathleen. "Coleridge and Wordsworth and 'The Supernatural.'" *University of Toronto Quarterly* 25, no. 2 (1955-56).

Haisten, Cherry. *Coleridge's Projected Essay on the Supernatural: An Attempt to Reconstruct its Substance.* Master of Arts Thesis, University of Georgia. Athens, Georgia, 1981.

Hayter, Alethea. "Coleridge, Maturin's *Bertram*, and Drury Lane." *New Approaches to Coleridge: Biographical and Critical Essays.* Ed. Donald Sultana. London: Vision Press Limited, 1981.

Lochhead, Marion. "Coleridge and John Gibson Lockhart." *New Approaches to Coleridge.* London, 1981; 61-80.

Lowes, Jonathan Livingston. *The Road to Xanadu: A Study in the Ways of the Imagination.* Rpt. 1927; Princeton, NJ: Princeton University Press, 1986.

Paley, Morton D. "Coleridge's 'Preternatural Agency.'" *European Romantic Review* (Winter, 1991); 135-47.

Piper, H. W. *The Singing of Mount Abora: Coleridge's Use of Biblical Imagery and Natural Symbolism in Poetry and Philosophy.* Rutherford, NJ: Fairleigh Dickinson University Press, 1987.

Taylor, Anya. *Magic and English Romanticism.* Athens: The University of Georgia Press, 1979.

Tave, Katherine Bruner. *The Demon and the Poet: An Interpretation of "The Rime of the Ancient Mariner" According to Coleridge's Demonological Sources.* Salzburg, Austria: Institut für Anglistik und Amerikanistik, 1983.

In Romanticism

Barth, Robert. *The Symbolic Imagination.* Princeton, NJ: Princeton University Press, 1977.
Beyer, Werner W. *The Enchanted Forest.* Oxford: Basil Blackwell, 1963.
Berkeley, George, Bishop of Cloyne. *Complete Works.* Ed. Alexander Campbell Fraser. 4 vols. Oxford: Clarendon Press, 1901.
Bloom, Harold. *A Map of Misreading.* New York: Oxford University Press, 1975.
_____. *Poetry and Repression: Revisionism from Blake to Stevens.* New Haven and London: Yale University Press, 1976.
Böhme, Jakob. *The Signature of All Things.* Trans. Clifford Bax. New York: E. P. Dutton, 1910.
Burwick, Frederick. *The Haunted Eye: Perception and the Grotesque in English and German Romanticism.* Heidelberg: C. Winter, 1987.
_____. *Madness and the Romantic Imagination.* Pennsylvania State University Press, 1994.
Carnall, Geoffrey. "The Impertinent Barber of Baghdad: Coleridge as Comic Figure in Hazlitt's Essays." *New Approaches to Coleridge.* New York, 1981; 38-48.
Carpenter, Maurice. *The Indifferent Horseman: The Divine Comedy of Samuel Taylor Coleridge.* London: Elek Books, 1954.
Dutt, Sukumar. *The Supernatural in English Romantic Poetry: 1780-1830.* Rpt. 1938; Folcroft Library Editions, 1972.
Frye, Northrop. "The Drunken Boat: The Revolutionary Element in Romanticism." *Romanticism: Points of View.*
Galperin, William H. *The Return of the Visible in British Romanticism.* Baltimore: Johns Hopkins, 1993.
Kayser, Wolfgang. *The Grotesque in Art and Literature.* Trans. Ulrich Weisstein. New York: McGraw-Hill, 1963.
_____. *Das Groteske, seine Gestaltung in Malerei und Dichtung.* Oldenburg und Hamburg: Gerhard Stalling Verlag, 1957.
Koepke, Wulf. "Jean Paul Richter's School for Aesthetics: Humor and the Sublime." *Eighteenth-Century German Authors and Their Aesthetic Theories, Literature and Other Arts.* Ed. Richard Critchfield. Columbia, SC: Camden House, 1988.

———————. "Mephisto and Aesthetic Nihilism." *Subversive Sublimities: Undercurrents of the German Enlightenment.* Ed. Eitel Timm. Columbia, SC: Camden House, 1992; 36-44.

McGann, Jerome. *The Romantic Ideology: A Critical Investigation.* Chicago: University of Chicago Press, 1983.

Ray, William. "Suspended in a Mirror: Language and the Self in Kleist's 'Über das Marionettentheater.'" *SiR* 18, no. 4 (Winter, 1979).

Schneider, Elisabeth. *Coleridge, Opium, and Kubla Khan.* Chicago: University of Chicago Press, 1953.

Shaffer, Elinore S. *"Kubla Khan" and The Fall of Jerusalem: The Mythological School in Biblical Criticism and Secular Literature 1770-1880.* Cambridge: Cambridge University Press, 1975.

Watson, Jeanie. *Risking Enchantment: Coleridge's Symbolic World.* Lincoln: University of Nebraska Press, 1990.

General

Campagnac, E. T. *The Cambridge Platonists.* Oxford: Clarendon Press, 1901.

Clayborough, Arthur. *The Grotesque in English Literature.* Oxford: Clarendon Press, 1965.

Foucault, Michel. *Madness and Civilization: A History of Insanity in the Age of Reason.* Trans. Richard Howard. New York: Random House, 1965.

Frye, Northrop. *Anatomy of Criticism.* Princeton, NJ: Princeton University Press, 1957.

Huet, Marie-Hélène. *Monstrous Imagination.* Cambridge: Harvard University Press, 1993.

Houston, John Porter. *The Demonic Imagination: Style and Theme in French Poetry.* Baton Rouge: University of Louisiana Press, 1969.

Wormhoudt, Arthur. *The Demon Lover: A Psychoanalytical Approach to Literature.* Rpt. 1949; Freeport, NY: Books for Libraries Press, 1968.

Reference

The Compact Edition of the Oxford English Dictionary. 2 vols. Oxford: Oxford University Press, 1971. *OED.*

INDEX

Abgrund
as *buthos* (βυΘσς), bottom or bed, of the sea or an abyss 55; abyss or empty space 150-51; related to metamorphosis 158; ground of unified identity in Kant 161 *See also* Abyss

Abrams, Meyer
theological construct of Kant's philosophy 39 n16; 144

Absence
of order in the sublime 29; of telos in sublime aesthetics 50; 52; of certification as nihilism: 84, 89; of speech in sublime 141, 144; of authorizing godhead in sublime rhetoric cause of bathos 145

Absolute, the
15; as totality in Kant 21-23; 27; as ideal 52; as concepts of self and reason 59; indifference of nature 84, 89; angel in Wallace Stevens 85; raising oneself from limited state to absolute through beauty in Schiller 95; imagination's power of reconciling opposites as 116; being, as God 119-20; identity of principles of mind and nature in Schelling 123; form of Knowledge in Schelling's concept of self-consciousness 125; sole reality of things in 126; as causa sui: father of himself, son of himself 126; in Coleridge's use of Schelling's self-consciousness 125-129; 131, 145

Absolute angel
man as half-dead form of in Coleridge 56n; as Schiller's

figure of the Pure Will (*Reiner Wille*) 85; as figure in Wallace Stevens's "Notes Toward a Supreme Fiction" 85 *See also* Stevens, Pure Will (*Reiner Wille*)
Absolute being
119, 120, 127; as the divine in Coleridge 129
Absolute I AM
in Coleridge as form of transcendental apperception 127
Absolute identity
of the self in Schelling's and Coleridge's transcendental unity of self-consciousness: 123, 126, 128
Absolute selfhood
as source of sacred self-consciousness in Schelling and Coleridge 129
Absolute self-consciousness
as bridge between world-self opposition in Schelling 122
Absolute Whole
only measure recognized by the reason in Kant 21; commanded of subject's intuition by reason in Kant 21
Abyss
as the transcendent, in Kant 10; relation to process of translation 150; unknown, in Coleridge 27 n48; Miltonic 27; infinite fall into bottomless form of in Schiller 34; 103; between subject and desire for meaning 50; as *buthos* ($\beta u\Theta os$) 55; 28, 53; of the sublime 58; terrain of Kant's sublime 74 n29; between soul and body in Christianity 119; 131, 150, 151

Adams, Henry
On self-construction 141
Addison, Joseph
sublime in theories of 11, 35, 56, 73 n19
Adorno, Theodor
on the sublime's revelation of art's inherent conflicts 1 n1
Adyt
third mediating principle given by aesthetic imagination in Coleridge 122; Coleridge's idea for taken from Schelling 122; mediating properties of conflated with those of absolute self 123-127 *See also* Mediation, Tertium Aliquid, Schelling
Aesthetic
negative 11; 132; of inadequacy 29; not of identity but of difference 31; of infinity 56; 5, 10-13, 15, 20, 23, 26-28, 30, 31, 34, 35, 51, 58-60, 62-67, 79-84, 86, 87, 88-104, 113, 114, 116, 119, 120, 131, 142, 154, 161; of the beautiful as basis of the naive in Schiller 3; disinterestedness of in Kant: 63, 65; of infinity 56; fantasies in Schiller 85
Aesthetic configurations
as phenomenal in Schiller 84-87; as properties of external nature in Schiller 86
Aesthetic freedom
touchstone of Schiller's play theory 82 *See also* Freedom in Appearance (*Freiheit in der Erscheinung*)
Aesthetic harmony
as subject-object link in Schiller 90-95; counterfeit nature of in

INDEX

Schiller 92; rejected as delusion in Schiller 102-04; 92, 94; compared to linking project in Coleridge: 120, 113-140
Aesthetic illusion
32, 35, 79; and heautonomy (*Heautonomie*) 80-82; basis of Schiller's play theory 82-86; given objective reality in Schiller 87-89; as response to Kant's divisive philosophy 90-104; 88, 89, 103; in view of words as things in Coleridge 139 n27 *See also Schein*
Aesthetic impulse (Play Drive)
as harmonizer of man's sensuous and rational impulses: 79, 89, 90, 95, 100, 114; as lie in response to sublime in Schiller 83-89; precludes moral code in Goethe 112 11-12 n36; precludes godhead in Goethe 111-12 n36; precludes idea of immortality in Goethe 111-12 n36 *See also* Play Drive
Aesthetic judgment
as link between theoretical and practical in Kant 59-67; of the sublime in Kant reduced to indirect moral experience 62
Ajax
silence of, as example of sublime in Longinus 142
Alembics
in Coleridge's view of associationist philosophy and self's role in sublime 154
Alien
Kant's Reason as 15; 32, 151, 163
Alienation
intrinsic to sublime 33; 28

Alpha and omega
as one and all, combined by self in mediating imagination, in Coleridge 118
Alter-ego
sublime figure of heautonomous *Reiner Wille* in Schiller 84; as ancient sage in Yeats 162; Coleridge's double in Ancient Mariner 161-62; Coleridge's double in "Limbo" 161 *See also* Autoscopy, Metamorphosis, Other
Analogy
as representational process in Schiller 83; taken as fact in Schiller 86; 87-88, 89; basis for judgment of sublime in Kant 61-2; basis of *a priori* principle of the formal purposiveness of nature in Kant 66; 51; radical use of in Schiller 84
Analogical method
problem with in Kant 61; 79-81; as "mere architectonic isomorphism" in Kant 62 *See also* Guyer
Analogical process
as mind's representation of things as being free in Schiller 83
Appearance
80, 83, 85, 87; Schiller's definition of beauty as freedom in 79; of freedom 79; of autonomy as heautonomy in Schiller 82; as aesthetic representation in Schiller 83 *See also* Illusion, *Schein*
Apophrades (metalepsis)
poet's willful raising of the dead in Bloom 31; 27, 28, and

counter-sublime of Schiller and Coleridge 54 *See also* Autoscopy, Counter-sublime, Harold Bloom

Arrest
of movement in the sublime 51; related to action of romantic narrative 52 *See also* Jakobson, Linearity

a priori
principle for aesthetic judgment of harmony of faculties 20; self-given rule of formal unity for aesthetic judgment 26; for judgments of sublimity unstable in Kant 31; bridging function of posited analogically 62; required to make aesthetic judgment a bridge between theoretical and practical in Kant 64-66; merely subjective 80-81; merely regulative 88 *See also* Knowledge, Transcendental Apperception

Art
Schiller's view on origin and progress of likened to Young's *Night Thoughts* 86; emphasis of conflicts in as role of sublime in Adorno 1 n1; not a part of Kant's sublime 2; Kant's peremptory nod toward in the *Critique of Judgment* 27 n36; mediational function of in Schiller 83-89; as free citizen in Schiller 79; inadmissible aspects of inherent in the sublime 84-85

Artistic instinct
as originary forgetting 84; as dissimulative response to conditions of the sublime 85; as compensation for human finitude 84

Ascent
observer's ascent in Burke's sublime 18-19; of the imagination in Burke's sublime 18-19; of the subject in the sublime 19; of the subject caused by imagination in Burke's sublime 19

Asceticism
in Kant: 22, 29, 33

Association of ideas
34, 82, 113; as materialist philosophy in Coleridge 153; lawless law of parallel to sublime's rule of non-regulation: 57, 153; in Hartley 153; French materialist form of 153; deadening nature of in Coleridge 153; affect on the autonomous self compared to chemical sublimation 153; looks death into everything in Coleridge 153; as transforming self into inhuman other 154; 166 n19 *See also* Material Sublime

Autobiographical aesthetic
as major characteristic of romanticism 33; as reflecting or producing oneself in Lacoue-Labarthe: 85, 86, 88; as grand abstraction in Schiller 148; as sublimation in Coleridge 149-64 *See also* Autoscopy, *Heauton*, The Pure Will (*Reiner Wille*)

Autobiographical sublime
27; as romantic form of negative sublime: 27, 33; as skeptical process of self-construction 33; double gesture of 35-36; product of mystified and demystified sensibility 36; forgetting of

INDEX

empirical self in 33 *See also*
Autoscopy, *Heauton*, The Pure
Will (*Reiner Wille*)
Autofiguration
as abstract process in Schiller
85, 148; 33,128, 155, 156, 162
Autonomy (*Autonomie*)
and reason 59; Kant's moral
form of found austere by Schiller
81-83; denies appetitive
inclinations in Kant: 59, 64;
indeterminate in Kant's theory of
aesthetic judgment 81-85;
transformed as heautonomy
(*Heautonomie*) in Schiller: 88,
91 *See also* Heautonomy
Autoscopic transformation
in Coleridge 158-159; in Yeats
160-162; as metamorphosis 150;
to jump over an abyss or
groundless space 150 *See also*
Metamorphosis, Other
Autoscopy
visual hallucination of the
physical self: in Coleridge
158-59; Robert Rogers on 167
n22; Maude Bodkin on 167 n22;
in E.T.A. Hoffmann 167 n22;
Otto Rank on 167 n22; Bryan
Tyson on 167 n22
Aylsworth, Gary
on sublimity and
poststructuralism, 9 n2

Bach, Johann Sebastian
movement of music in compared
to romantic music: 49-50, 69 n2
Baroque music
temporality of compared to
temporality of romantic music:
49, 50, 69 n2

Barthes, Roland
self-representation in compared
to romantic self-construction 52
Bastard prosthesis
finite self as, in Coleridge 128
Bate, Walter Jackson
26, 30 n41, 116, 153, 154
Bathetic
inverse characteristic of sublime
142 *See also* Bathos
Bathos
31; Ferguson on: 37 n2; 48 n54;
in Coleridge 146; as intrinsic to
romantic sublime 145-46 *See*
also Bloom, Ferguson,
McFarland
Baudelaire, Charles
Folie lucide in 55, 132, 139 n6;
on De Quincey's digressiveness
as avoidance of mortality of
linear existence 51-2 *See also*
Folie lucide
Beattie, James
sublime in theories of 11; theory
departed from by Schiller 13
Beautiful, the
10; triumphant aesthetics of 12,
20, 28, 29; as reconciling
aesthetics 32; affinity with
human meaning 32; unity of
vulnerable to sublime 33; 33-35;
object of synthesizing activities:
36; 56, 57, 63, 65, 67, 79, 82,
83, 85-87, 90-97, 99-101, 103
Beautiful Soul (*Schöne Seele*)
prelapsarian inner being in
Schiller 85; alter-ego in Schiller
84-89; Schiller's counter to alien
presence of Reason in Kant
84-89 *See also* Pure Will
(*Reiner Wille*)

Beauty
10, 20, 28, 29, 33-35, 56, 63, 65, 67, 79, 82, 83, 85-87, 90-97, 99-101, 103; as social quality 57; movement of linear and horizontal 57; founded on conformity 57; founded on unity 57; characterized by proportion, order, regularity and rules 57; projection of self outward in 57; characterized by security 57; as object of aesthetic judgment 59, 63; as connection between theoretical and practical in Schiller 84; as object of play in Schiller 85; as symbol of morality in Kant: 63, 65; as freedom in appearance in Schiller: 51, 79, 80, 82, 83, 85, 87; moral form of in Schiller (*Moralische Schönheit*) 85

Beginnings
30, 50-52; as intrinsically unrepresentable: 30, 52; 94, 142, 149 See also Said

Being
in the text 52; absolute form: 119, 120, 127, 129; as principium essendi or absolute principle of in Coleridge 127; substituted in Coleridge with an absolute principium cogniscendi or principle of knowing 127; 121, 125; as sacred self-consciousness 125; "Being who wills" in Schiller, 82; 10, 15-19, 22, 25, 27, 52, 55, 56, 65, 82, 83, 85, 87, 90, 97, 99, 104, 119, 120, 125, 126, 127, 129, 130, 150, 152, 162

Belated
poet as, in Bloom 54; 144 *See also* Bloom

Bernard, J. H.
29, 33 n46; Kant's ignorance of sublime landscape in nature 48 n51

Bible
linear narrative of 51; precritical realistic reading of 51; waning of linear interpretations of: 51, 53 See also, Arrest, De Man, Frei, Jakobson, Linearity

Black, Joel
on murder as logical conclusion of sublime 98; 111 n32

Blake, William
Coleridge's return to sensible language following autoscopic transformation and myopic speaker of Blake's "Divine Image:" 162, 167-68

Blindness
in "Limbo," 161; 51, 53, 55, 161

Bloom, Harold
Blake's Apocalypse: A Study in Poetic Argument: 52, 168 n29
New Perspectives on Coleridge and Wordsworth: 32 n44
Map of Misreading: 54
Anxiety of Influence: 28 n49
romanticism's spatial antinomies of high and low in 53-54; revisionary ratios 53; concept of *Daemonization* related to Coleridge and Schiller 54-5; concept of *Apophrades* related to Schiller and Coleridge 54; and Satan 54; on belated

romantic poet 54; 9, 27, 28, 51, 53-55, 100, 116, 148, 159, 162
Bodkin, Maud
 159, 162, 167 n22, 167 n28
Body
 precluded in Kant's concept of man's destiny 2, 15; sublime provokes unnatural tension of nerves in, in Burke 17; focus on emotions of in Burke: 18, 82; Schiller's "On the Connection between the Animal and Spritual in Man" and *Philosophie der Physiologie* on reciprocal action of body and mind 105 n5; Schiller's studies on body's contributions to work of the soul 105 n5; Christianity as abyss between soul and body in Coleridge: 119, 132; good sense the body of poetic genius, imagination its soul in Coleridge: 158, 162
Boileau-Despréaux, Nicolas
 and Longinus: 11, 42
Bottomless sea of faith
 in Coleridge 132
Brahms, Johannes
 49, 50
Bretall, R. W.
 on tenuousness of Kant's theory of the sublime: 60, 74 n32
Bridge (*Übergang*)
 of aesthetic judgment between theoretical and practical in Kant: 49-77; of aesthetic play between sensuous dependency and moral freedom in Schiller 79-112; of imagination between subject and object in Coleridge, 117-21; of self between subject and object in Coleridge 121-26; likened to strength of lunacy in De Quincey 62; inspired by sublime divisiveness 4; relation to romantic ideas of the self: 141-68; collapsed subject-object bridge in Schelling 122; 4, 5, 49, 58-63, 65-67, 79, 82, 90, 93-97, 99, 100, 102, 103, 109 n24 116-120, 122, 125, 131-133 *See also* Linking Process, Reconciling Aesthetics
Brilliant, Richard
 on modern self in portraiture 187
Brooks, Cleanth
 on relation of Kant's sublime to existentialism 132 *See also* Existentialism
Brooks, Linda Marie
 on relation of sublime to modern ideas of the self 11 n10; on Kant's use of *übersinnliches Substrat* 75 n34
Bruno, Giordano
 concept of Christ as middlepoint (*Mittelpunkt*) in 117
Burke, Edmund
 Philosophical Enquiry into the Origin of Our Ideas of the Sublime and the Beautiful: 11, 13-19, 57; representative of eighteenth-century theories of sublimity 4; 37 n2, 11-22; positive version of the sublime 14-19; compared to Kant's negative version of the sublime 27-30; concept of sublime as aesthetics of transcendence: 29, 32, 34, 54, 56, 57, 98; fate of the self in theory of sublimity 5; positive version of sublime based on imagination's success: 1,

17-19; pleasure in the sublime:
14, 19; pleasant pleasure and
delightful pain in sublime of 20;
physical character of sublime in
18-19; empirical character of
sublime in: 21, 21, n26; in
Weiskel 32
Burnet, Thomas
on duplicity of the sublime: 142,
144, 165 n6

Cadavera rerum
dead bodies of things 153; as
metaphor of self distilled by
sublime in Coleridge 153 *See
also* Caput mortuum
Caput mortuum
death's head: 152, 154, 155; as
residuum after chemical
sublimation and Coleridge
account of self's dissolution in
sublime 153-54; as subject's
death's head identity in sublime
experience
Carlyle, Thomas
on obscurity of Schiller's
theories 110 n28
Carritt, E. F.
on beauty and the sublime 10; on
the sublime as hostile to human
will 10 n7; on incompleteness of
Kant's theory of the sublime: 21
n31, 67, 77 n46
Carthusian
nature of Kant's philosophy: 22,
29 *See also* Asceticism
Cassirer, H. W.
on Kantian reason's command to
discover the conditions of totality
25; on unattainability of
conditions of totality in Kant 25;
on totality as ideal maximum

unattainable in sensible world:
25, 44 n40
Cause and effect
as ground of construction of
personal identity 26; lack of in
Dunciad IV; example of
nonlinearity of romantic
narrative 52; absolute something
as fusion of both 126 *See also*
Arrest, Causa Sui, De Man,
Jakobson, Linearity
Chaos
Milton's 7; 46 n49; of sublime
sought in Kant as foil for order
of Moral Law 34; state of all
things about and in us without
method, in Coleridge 115; of
hyperbolic moment 150 *See also*
Method,
Chopin, Fréderic
music of as example of
romanticism's series of
undirected intensities 50
Christ
idea of as mediator (*Mittelpunkt*)
partial source of Coleridge's
tripartite system 117; chapter 4
of *Biographia* building to
crescendo of Christ and God 132
Christensen, Jerome
on Coleridge's obscure style
tantamount to sublime style 9 n2
Classical music
temporality of compared to
temporality of romantic music
49, 50
Clayborough, Arthur
on Coleridge's belief in
corporeality of thought 113 n2
Closure
precluded by conflict between
representation of actuality and

INDEX

idea of infinity in romantic art 36; lacking in romantic art 49; relinquished in romantic autobiographical project 36
Coadunative
   Coleridge's coinage for process of reknitting subject-object division 3 *See also* Imagination, Linking
Coburn, Kathleen
   10, 114, 135 n3
Coffman, Ralph J.
   on Coleridge's library 136 n5
Coleridge, Ernest Hartley
   2
Coleridge, Henry Nelson
   on Coleridge's inability to pray, 133
Coleridge, Samuel Taylor
   "Limbo:" as instance of negative sublime 27-28 48 n49; old blind man in as Coleridge's double: 1, 4, 54, 114, 161
   "Ne Plus Ultra:" as instance of negative sublime in Bloom 31-2, 48 n49
   "Kubla Khan:" as instance of autoscopy in Coleridge: 158-60, 167 n21
   "Religious Musings:" 147, 148; exclamation points in as instance of hyperbole 166 n13
   "Christabel:" 155
   "Destiny of Nations:" 114, 135 n3
   "Self Knowledge:" 131
   Inquiring Spirit: A Coleridge Reader: 9 n1
   Notebooks of Samuel Taylor Coleridge: 10, 14, 24, 56, 60, 114, 116, 118, 120-124, 129, 132, 140 n29, 146
   Biographia Literaria: 26, 27, 115-119, 121, 124-130, 132, 139 n37, 140 n30, 140 n31, 141, 147, 148, 153, 154, 156, 161, 162
   Inquiring Spirit: A Coleridge Reader: 9
   Rime of the Ancient Mariner: 32, 37, 38, 161; Mariner in: 33, 128, 155, 161, 162
   Logosophia: 132
   Aids to Reflection and the Confessions of an Inquiring Spirit: 146
   Friend: 132, 133, 140 n33, 153
   Stateman's Manual: 117, 118
   S. T. Coleridge's Treatise on Method as Published on the Encyclopaedia Metropolitana: 115
   Table Talk: 84, 113, 119, 128, 133
   Attempted positive constructs of identity in 2; on threat of Kant's sublime to the self 3; and link between sublime and romantic self-construction 3; theory of sublime reflects Kant's theory 11; problems with Kant's sublime 11; recuperative theory of aesthetics subverted by principles of Kant's sublime 12; and Wordsworth 28; as high-jumper of the sublime 31 n44; as strong poet 32 n44; negative sublime in 33; library of 115; writings of: 116, 118; and German Idealism: 26, 115, 116;

dynamic philosophy of 118;
and pantheism 119; poetics
of 123; inabilty to pray 133;
Schelling's bridge of
self-consciousness in 133; as
mad 152; confronts madness
of sublime in *Ancient
Mariner* and *Christabel* 155;
as gray-haired passenger
161; and John Gibson
Lockhart 152; and the
disjunctive personality
113-140 *See also*
Autoscopy, Pantheism, Self,
Sublime, Bloom,
McFarland, Schelling
Conformity
fundamental to beautiful 57 *See
also* Beautiful
Constable, John
49
Contemplative sublime
in Schiller's "Of the Sublime"
98-100; 111 n31 *See also*
Death, Negative Sublime,
Sublime
Continuity
element of the beautiful 51, 54
See also Beautiful
Contranatural
in Coleridge's system of
philosophy 14; and defeat of
natural in the sublime 33; state
of sentimental and romantic
subject in experience of sublime
151; hyperbolic moment as:
148-151, 163; in Wordsworth's
description of Coleridge as
"debarred from Nature's living
images / Compelled to be a life
unto itself:" 149, 159, 162

Cottle, Joseph
117, 132
Counter-identity
85, 28, 54, 55; Wallace Stevens'
The Rock as instance of 47 n49;
as instance of in Coleridge's
Mariner, "Kubla Kahn" poet and
Biographia speaker 154-64;
Yeats' Ancient Sage as instance
of 159-61 *See also* The Pure
Will (*Reiner Wille*) and The
Death's Head
Crawford, Donald
60, 63-65, 77 n40, 77 n42
Crisis
51, 98; of romantic self related
to Jakobson's
metaphor-metonymy distinction
70n
Croce, Benedetto
rejection of "sublime" as
aesthetic term 10
Crowther, Paul
19, 25; 44 n40; on Kant and art,
27 n36; 41 n24, 60, 62, 77 n39

Daemonization (Hyperbole/Litotes)
54, 159 *See also* Bloom,
Hyperbole
Danger
15, in Burke's sublime 16;
before which one can never be
secure: 98-100; 18; of going
beyond possibility in Schiller's
sentimental subject 146; of
sublimity to the romantic or
modern sensibiilty 146; 145, 163
See also Contemplative Sublime
Darkness
property of Burke's sublime 14;
32

INDEX

Davies, Sir John
  concept of the soul's sublimation of the poet used by Coleridge for imagination's sublimation of self: 157-159; meaning misinterpreted by Coleridge: 161, 162
Dead
  return of in Bloom's *Apophrades* 27; 28; sublime bridge between living and 49; raising of in romantic sublime 54; 56, 132
Death
  solitude as living form of in Coleridge 32; 37, 50, 52; as self's moral suicide in Schiller's sublime 98; basis of Schiller's contemplative sublime 98-100; as *Abgrund* of the sublime 98-100; not aesthetic in Schiller 100n; question of central to sublime in Deguy 152n; 104, 133, 145-46, 152-155, 159-161, 163
Death's Head, The
  152-54; 159-61
Death-in-life
  in Coleridge 160
Dédoublement (Doubling)
  52, 55 See also Autoscopy, Baudelaire, De Man, Other
Deguy, Michel
  on centrality of death in sublime: 152n; 152-154, 159
Dejection
  component of Kant's sublime 3; result of the sublime: 14, 55 See also Pain
De Luca, Vincent
  9 n2
Delusion
  in Schiller: 86, 89
De Man, Paul
  arrest of linear narrative and Jakobson's metaphor-metonymy distinction compared to crisis of romanticism 70n; on spatial antinomies of high and low in romanticism 53; concept of demystification and romantic alternative identity: 55, 71-2 n17; concept of ironic duality compared to romantic self, 55; on literal and theological sense of the Fall, 71-2 n17; on Baudelaire's *Folie lucide* compared to romantic sensibility 132 See also *Folie lucide*, Jakobson
Demystification
  33, 55
Dennis, John
  on lack of authorizing godhead as source of sublime bombast: 11, 143-146
De Quincey, Thomas
  Hillis Miller on 51; digressiveness in 51-52; Baudelaire on 51-53; lack of tight cause and effect in as avoidance of mortality 52; *thyrsus* in 52; bridge compared to strength of lunacy in 62; 53 n11, 71 n11, 76 n37
Derrida, Jacques
  on apocalyptic tone of Kant's philosophy 74 n32; on Schiller's path as fracta or broken 73 n24; on the nature of pleasure in Kant 112 n41
Descartes, René
  117, 123, 124
Desire
  abandoned in Kant's sublime 1; 32, 50, 51, 61, 62, 64; expression in Schiller conflated

with dissimulation and
forgetting: 89; 160
Dialectic
intellect, 119; 129; 63, 81, 116
Dichotomy
between sense and reason in
Kant: 82, 91, 94 See also
Duality
Dignity
man's state in the sublime: 18,
19, 90, 92-94, 103, 116
Digression
in De Quincey 163
Dilemma of the self
2, 147
Ding an sich
31, 87 See also Thing in Itself
Disappearance of God
in romanticism: 52, 58 See also
Miller
Discontinuity
in *Apophrades*: 51, 54 See also
Bloom
Disinterestedness
in aesthetic judgment, 63, 65
Disjunction
fundamental to sublime: 4, 113,
132
Disjunctive personality
as subject of the sublime 92; in
Schiller's concept of the
Sentimental 90-95; in Coleridge
113-140
Dissimulation
double indeterminacy of
Schiller's theory a dramatization
of 83; process by which one
supplements one's mortality 84;
element of romantic
self-construction in the sublime
83; unconscious artistic instinct
83; originary power of 83; art of

83; as perversion of *Vorstellung*
or representation 84; Schiller's
figure of The Pure Will
constituted by 84; as explanation
of Schiller's use of *Schein* 89;
and Kerry's explanation of
Schiller's use of *Schein* 89; as
lie that passes itself off for truth
in the sublime 89; as way of
overcoming uncertainty of
sublime in Coleridge 151
Divided self
romantic form of basis of
modern identity 3; bridge model
of in Schiller 82 93-96; path
model of in Schiller 100-104
Divine, the
in Burke's sublime: 11, 17;
Almighty power of in Burke's
sublime 19; reason equivalent to
and substitute for in Kant: 25,
31, 56, 101, 116, 125;
metaphysics carried into in
Coleridge's system: 127-29; 128,
131; metaphysics as nothing but
divinity in Coleridge 132; 162
See also Abrams
Divisiveness
in sublime subversive of
coherent concept of identity 3-5;
of Kant's sublime 3; and sublime
as aesthetics not of identity but
of difference 31; 35, 65, 66, 95,
97, 101 See also Disjunction
Donato, Eugenio Umberto
on *Abgrund*, 151; on translation
150-51; on hyperbole 150-51; on
relation of hyperbole to
metamorphosis: 158, 166 n16
Double (*Doppelgäanger*)
Coleridge's double in Ancient
Mariner 161-62; Coleridge's

INDEX

double in "Limbo" 161: old
blind man as Coleridge's double:
1, 4, 33, 54, 83, 147, 159, 162
See also Autoscopy,
Dédoublement, Other
Dunstan, A. C.
on Coleridge's knowledge of
German writers 136 n5

Ecstasis
absent in eighteenth-century
sublime 12
Ellis, J. M.
on Schiller's *Kallias* letters 82
Emptiness
result of sublime's isolation 32;
related to sublime insularity, 32;
56 *See also* Solitude, Vacuity
Ende, Stuart
on Keats and the sublime 37 n2
Engell, James
26, 30 n41, 116-121, 153, 154
Entelechy
36 *See also* Closure
Esemplastic
1, 2; as coadunative 3; as linking
power characteristic of
imagination in Coleridge 117-21
See also Bridge, Linking
Eternity
9; Mariner's autobiographical
project as 33; circular snake as
symbol for used by Coleridge for
imagination 132; 160
Evil
inevitability of as province of the
sublime in Schiller 102;
swellings of sublime as, in
Longinus 141
Ewen, Frederic
on knowledge of Schiller in
England 136 n5

Exaggeration
143, 145, 150 *See also*
Hyperbole
Exaltation
of the self in Kant 15; 17-19; of
the self as affective
representation in art in Burke 20;
disappearance of affective
representation of in art in Kant's
sublime 20; compared to respect
(*Achtung*) in Kant's sublime 21
Existentialism
alienation in prefigured in
romantic sublime 28; resignation
of prefigured in romantic
sublime 28; resignation of
contrasted to Bloom's concept of
Oedipal revolt 32 n44; 33;
tendencies of in romanticism
132; stance of in romanticism:
141, 145, 164
Extravagance
54, 129, 141, 144 *See also*
Hyperbole
Extremes
60, 122, 131

Fall
22; infinite into bottomless abyss
in Schiller: 34, 103; as
fundamental to romantic
dynamic 53; and rise of romantic
sensibility 55; in literal and
theological sense in de Man 71
n17; man unintelligible without
Christian version of in Coleridge
119
Farrago
and associative thought in De
Quincey 51
Fear
20, 21; private form of in

romantic sublime 32; 37; of
dynamic sublime conflated with
respect for mathematical sublime
43 n33; permanent state of
regarding sublime objects about
which we cannot feel secure
98-99; 102, 122, 161
Ferguson, Frances
9 n2; 31-32; on tendency of
sublime's isolation to lift subject
above relations with others 31;
48 n54
Fichte, J. G.
115, 116, 136 n5
Finitude
84, 89
Folie lucide
55, 132; as conscious madness
139 n6
See also Baudelaire, de Man
Forgetting
of empirical self in the sublime:
33, 38; original form of as
reponse to sublime 84; as
aesthetic response to terror 84;
as dissimulation 84; in Schiller's
fusion of subjective vision and
objective reality 87-89; of
empirical self and substitution of
contranatural self in the sublime
151
Formlessness
14, 34, 65, 66
Freedom (*Freiheit*)
23, 49, 50, 60, 62, 79-83;
supersensible in Kant 80; play as
aesthetic representation of in
Schiller 83; analogical basis of
in Schiller 83; intentionally
illusory in Schiller's concept of
heautonomy: 83-85, 86, 88-89;
91, 95, 93-96, 99, 101-103

Freedom in appearance (*Freiheit in
der Erscheinung*)
79; Kant's subjective concept of
heautonomy objectified as
aesthetic play in Schiller 83; as
imaginative representation of
freedom (*Darstellung der
Freiheit*) in Schiller 83; double
indeterminacy of 83; given by
illusion of the harmony of man's
faculties in art 85; 87, 91, 93,
95
Frei, Hans W.
on waning of linearity in
biblical narrative: 51, 70 n6
Freud, Sigmund
73 n24; sublimation in 152
Frye, Northrop
on vertical character of
romantics' spatial projection of
reality 53, 141; on Recognition
Poems of Collins, Coleridge and
Yeats 159-60

Genius
2; Kantian imagination creative
in case of 8; 100, 143, 145, 150,
158, 162, 163
God
sundered from subject in
romantic sublime 4; subject's
union with in Burke's sublime
17; reason as equivalent and
substitute for in Kant 22;
Leibniz's mirror of the mind of
contrasted to romanticism: 50,
69 n2; disappearance of: 58, 70
n8; 117, 119, 127; as the sole
identity in Coleridge 128;
subject's self lost in, in
Coleridge 131-133

INDEX

Goethe, Johann Wolfgang von
90, 100; 112 n37; 112 n40; 122;
Coleridge's familiarity with the
Farbenlehre 136 n5; Coleridge
apparently translating *Faust* of
136 n5; on preclusion of
godhead, immortality, law, and
moral code in Schiller's play
drive 111-12 n37; 112 n39
Gray-haired passenger
as alter-ego of Coleridge 161
See also Mariner
Greatness
necessarily connected with
godhead in Burke's sublime
17-18
Greene, David
on romantic music as undirected
series of peaks of intensity 49
n2, 69 n2
Grotesque
in art 113; 149
Guerlac, Suzanne
9, 119, 132, 137 n13; on
relation of representation to
interaction between subject and
object in the sublime, 139 n7
Guyer, Paul
26; 59-65; 74 n31; on damage of
analogical method to Kant's
theory of sublime: 61, 80-81; on
the architectonic isomorphism of
Kant's *a priori* principle for
aesthetic judgment, 77 n38; 77
n42; on moral nature of Kant's
aesthetics 77 n43; 80, 81, 87

Hamann, J. G.
as partial source of Coleridge's
mediating system 117
Hamilton, Paul
123, 130, 131, 138 n21, 144

Haney, J. L.
on Coleridge's knowledge of
German writers 135 n5
Harmony
of the faculties created by
judgment in Kant 63-66; of sense
and reason created by play in
Schiller 80-86; of subject and
object created by imagination
and poet's self in Coleridge:
90-97; 100, 101, 113, 115, 119,
120, 128; precludes feeling of
the sublime 64; concept of in
Kant 63-66; concept of in
Schiller 80-86, 90-97; in
Coleridge's concept of third
mediating principle 113-140
Harmony of the faculties
64, 80-85, 90; ontological
ground in supersensible in Kant
64; required supersensible
ground in Kant 65; discovered as
impossible in Schiller 103-04
Hartley, David
113, 153
Hartman, Geoffrey
32 n44
Heauton
85, 86, 88
Heautonomy (*Heautonomie*)
principle of in Kant 63-4; not in
external phenomena in Kant 64;
as only subjective and regulative
in Kant 64; purpose of in Kant
to regulate way we reflect on
obejcts of nature 64; not in
external nature in Kant 81; as
aesthetic illusion in Schiller 83;
as appearance or semblance of
autonomy (*Autonomie in der
Erscheinung*) in Schiller 83; as
freedom in appearance in

Schiller 83; touchstone of
Schiller's theory of unified self
83-85; projected onto external
phenomena in Schiller 88;
objective freedom of in Schiller
88; as self-delusion in Schiller
89; undermined by Kantian
principles 90-104
Hegel, Georg Wilhelm Friedrich
on sublime unrepresentability as
the waning of romantic art 13;
on night-like mine or pit of the
self 57; 73 n23
Herder, Johann Gottfried von
partial source of Coleridge's
tripartite system 117;
Coleridge's familiarity with
Kalligone 136 n5
Hertz, Neil
on sublimity and problems of
quotation and representation 9 n2
Hillis Miller, J.
51, 52, 58, 148
Hipple, Walter
34, 35, 37 n2, 57
Hoffmann, E. T. A.
the double in 167 n22
Hugo, Victor
119, 137 n13
Human being
phenomenal form of forgotten in
Kant's sublime: 9, 15, 36; fate
of in Burke's sublime 19; Kant
on corporeal character of
pleasure in Burke's sublime: 21;
21 n26; eschewed in Kant's
sublime 24; 30 n42; unaided by
imagination, understanding or
reason in Kant's sublime 25-6
Hutcheson, Francis
37, 37, 73 n20

Hyperbole
in Burke: 16, 18-20; as
self-construction 5; and failure
of romantic linking theories 5;
flat-footedness of in Wordsworth
148; sign of self-constructive
nature of romanticism 148;
stance of: 145, 148, 149;
intrinsic to romantic project 145;
movement by which thought
ravishes itself: 152n, 154;
metamorphic power of 150-51;
swellings of as evil in Longinus
141; potential weakness of 142;
Baudelaireian form of: 55, 132,
139 n26; 54, 132, 141-148, 150,
151; autoscopic form of peculiar
to *übersetzen* or translation 154;
movement by which thought
ravishes itself 154; 158, 163
See also Verticality,
Daemonization, Bloom, Donato,
Autoscopy, Metamorphosis,
Other
Hyperbolic moment
148-151, 163, subject's
transformation during 149; the
subject sublimed in 149-64, 152;
wavering of poet's conventional
posture in 149; loss of balance in
149; subject's metamorphosis in
150-51; *imposteur absolu* in 151;
superhuman in 150; uncanny in
150; alternative identity in 36,
151; forgetting in 151;
dissimulation in 151;
metamorphosis of subject in as
integral to romantic aesthetics
161; subject's becoming other in
152, 158; subject's conventional
self displaced by other then self
in 159; subject alien in 162;

subject contranatural in 162; and
"Kubla Khan" 158-60; subject's
transformation in deliberate
159-61 *See also* Verticality,
Daemonization, Bloom, Donato,
Autoscopy, Metamorphosis,
Other
Hypsous
of sublime as leap of faith or
uncanny fall 55

I AM
as active verb in Coleridge 24;
as infinite 116; as self and
self-consciousness in Coleridge
121; as absolute in Coleridge
127
I Know myself
127
'I' and 'Not I' (*Ich und nicht-Ich*)
115, 116
Idealism
26, 27; heautonomy source of in
Schiller 81; 115, 116, 124, 132;
radical form of in Coleridge
138-39 n26
Identity
of the romantic poet, 2, 35;
modern form of grounded in
Schiller's Sentimental 3;
coherent sense of denied in
sublime 5; versus difference in
the negative sublime, 36; illusion
of 84-85; finite form a bastard
prosthesis in Coleridge 128; as
quasi-identity 128;
sentimental/modern form of 2;
third and higher form of 115; In
Coleridge, no real and absolute
form of in finite existence 128;
God alone as, in Coleridge 128;
poet's identity: 3, 31, 116, 121;

finite form of a quasi-identity,
128; 2-4, 12, 15, 26, 30, 31, 33,
34, 36, 49, 54, 55, 59, 63, 66,
67, 79, 82, 85, 90, 100,
101-103, 113-117, 121-123, 126,
128, 131, 132, 147, 151, 152,
160, 161, 164 *See also* Self
Illusion
32, 35, 79; basis of Schiller's
theory of unified subject 82-86;
88, 89, 103 *See also*
Appearance, *Schein*
Illusory
28, 33, 83, 85, 86, 95, 97 *See
also* Appearance, *Schein*
Imagination (*Einbildungskraft*)
inadequacy of as basis of Kant's
sublime: 2, 3, 10, 12, 13, 21;
creativity of in genius irrelevant
to failure of in Kant: 2, n2;
18-23; bridging role of 119; as
tertium aliquid in Coleridge 128;
blind but powerful function of
the soul in Kant 26; faculty
required for subject's knowledge
in Kant 26; powerlessness of in
Kant's theory of the sublime 2;
"nothing" compared to reason in
Kant's sublime 3; coadunative or
linking ability of in Coleridge 3;
underwrites self in Coleridge 3;
success in Burke's theory of the
sublime 18; rising to idea of
infinity in Burke's sublime 19;
primary source of self's
exaltation in Burke's sublime 19;
role active, positive, and
effective in Burke's sublime 19;
no positive role in Kant's
sublime 20; interplay with
reason in Kant's sublime 21 n26;
higher function in Kant's

sublime 21 n26; inadequacy of a type of negative representation in Kant 23; produces obedient respect in Kant's sublime 23; might and extension gained in Kant's sublime 25; basis of cause/effect relationship in Kant 28; ground of human knowledge 25-6; the forming force (*die bildende Kraft*) of reason or transcendental imagination in Kant 84; free play of in Schiller 85; analogical and representational response to phenomena of in Schiller 83; transcendental form of as forming force in Kant 107 n10; capacity of to sublimate the romantic subject 149-64; subliming force of in Coleridge 157-60; spectre of 156; as synthetic 156; 159; as magic 156; 18-23, 25-26, 29, 36, 53, 56, 58, 61, 63-65, 83-87, 91, 95, 97, 101, 102, 115-121, 128, 129, 131-133, 145, 148, 155-159, 161, 162

Inadequacy
feeling of equivalent to respect in Kant's sublime 23; inability to give anthropomorphic order to phenomena 33

Incomprehensibility
reminder in Kant of human reason: 1, 25; effect on self in sublime 1; evidence of an ordering divinity in Burke's sublime 11; contained by reason in Kant 23; and cognitive meaninglessness in Kant's sublime 26; in Kant's sublime 28

Indeterminacy
in phase two of sublime, 34; as character of sublime, 38; 29, 33, 34, 80, 81, 83, 103

Infinite, the
in Burke's sublime 16- 17; 22, 34, 35, 84, 89, 96, 102, 103, 116, 118, 126

Infinity
in Burke's sublime 17; 19; fills mind with horror in Burke, 17; dilates the soul in Burke 18; imagination commanded by reason to embody in Kant 20-22; contained by reason as a unit in Kant's sublime 22; romanticism as aesthetics of 56; 117, 120 *See also* The Absolute

Intellect (*Verstand*)
9, 13, 14, 56, 84, 89, 95, 119, 129, 130, 132; subordinated to reason in Kant's philosophy 13; dialectic form of in Coleridge: 119, 129

Jakobson, Roman
related to romantic crisis by de Man 70 n7; and arrest of linearity in romanticism 70 n7; distinction between disruption of romantic crisis literature, expressed in metaphor, and metonymic dominance of linear history 70 n7 *See also* de Man, Linearity, Arrest, Cause and Effect

Jay, Paul
on Wordsworth's *Prelude* as tale of possibility of representation 52; on self-representation 52;

INDEX

John, St.
   compared with Spinoza in Coleridge 117

Job, Book of
   Burke's example of God in the sublime 17; and God's commandment against graven images in Kant 43 n35

Judgment
   as middle term 61; transition from understanding to reason 58-62; egoistic when based on pleasure in Kant 20; pure form of dependent on universality in Kant 20-2; dependent on *a priori* principle in Kant 22

Kallias letters
   61, 82, 83, 86, 88, 90-97, 99-103 *See also* Schiller

Kant
   "Analytic of the Sublime" 2; as model of romantic sublime 13
   Critique of Judgment: Introduction 4; as failed bridge between Kant's first two *Critiques* 5; 14, n18; 20-28; authorial fiat in 60-61; use of mystical oxymorons in 61; mediating strategy of 61; 2, 3, 10, 19-23, 29, 57, 59-64, 66; 2, 13, 14, 19, 25, 59, 61-64, 80, 91, 161
   Critique of Practical Reason: 3, 59, 62
   Critique of Pure Reason: 4, 24, 25, 26, 29, 59, 66
   Observations on the Feeling of the Beautiful and the Sublime: influenced by Burke's *Enquiry* 14, n18; "splendid sublime" and "noble sublime" in 14 n18
   Dreams of a Spirit-Seer, Illustrated by Dreams of Metaphysics: 15 n19
   The Contest of the Faculties: 26
   Groundwork of the Metaphysics of Morals: 108 n19
   Disunity between ideas of first and second *Critiques* in 4; self-fashioning in 5; theory of sublime model of romantic sublimity 11; gives sublime epistemological concern: 15, 23-24; transcendental theory of sublime compared to Burke's empirical theory 15; pleasure in the sublime based on noumenal principles 21; unfamiliar with sublime landscape 34 n46; architectonic isomorphism in theory of sublime 76 n38; Draco in Schiller 103; unintended equivocation in 81; tenuousness of his system 81; dismissal of sublimity as mere appendix to aesthetic judgment: 2, 3, 29, 62, 66, 81, 116; divorce of sense and reason in, 15, 19-26; as third or synthesizing factor in Coleridge's concept of self 123; as complement to Schelling in Coleridge's concept of self-consciousness 124; opposition to Schelling concept of absolute self-consciousness 124;

Keats, John 9
Kemp Smith, Norman 44, n42, 46 n47
Kenosis
in Jakobson 70 n7; fragmentation of totality in 70 n7
Kernan, Alvin
on repetition in Pope's *Dunciad* 52; and preromantic satire 52
Kerry, S. S.
on Schiller 82, 84-89
Keynes, Geoffrey 169, 171
Kierkegaard, Sören
as heir to romantic sublime: 132, 164 *See also* Louis Mackey
Kleist, Heinrich von
in de Man, 132; *Marionettentheater* 136 n5
Knapp, Steven
on personification and the sublime in Coleridge 9
Knowledge
limits of as topic in Kant's sublime: 2, 24-25, 35; ultimate form of not sensible but intelligible in Kant 26; only negative form of accessible to man in Kant 26; as negative wisdom 26; grounded in imagination in Kant 28; certain impossibility of in Kant's sublime 29; ground of objective form of denied in Kant's philosophy 30; synthetic *a priori* nature of denied to corporeal subject in Kant 30 n42; higher irreconcilability with Descartes' phenomenological definition of truth in Coleridge 124

form of in Schelling's mediating self capable of unifying world-self opposition: 122, 137 n18; higher form of in Schelling's mediating self abstractly opposed to understanding 122; as absolute in Schelling and Coleridge 125; absolute form of given by sacred self-consciousness in Coleridge 126; human form of based on principle of act of self-consciousness 127; absolute form of displaced by human form of in Coleridge's later writings 127
Körner, Gottfried 82, 83, 86, 93, 97
Kroeber, Karl
on romantic narrative, 70 n3

Lacoue-Labarthe, Philippe 81; on originary dissimulation 83-85; on self-construction as a *heauton* 85; compared to Kerry 88; notion of dissimulation and Schiller's deliberate conceptual blurrings 89, 105 n3; on the process of the unsure initiated by the sublime 151
Law
in Kant's sublime 21, 23; absence of in sublime 38; 60; rule of non-regulation in sublime: 57; 153
Leap (Sublime Vaulting)
as vault into the sublime in Bloom 48 n48; 53, 55; romantic form of compared to eighteenth-century form 56; deathly 120, 126, 151 *See also Salto Mortale*

INDEX

Leibniz, Gottfried Wilhelm von
  69 n2
Lessing, Gotthold Ephraim
  as formidable heretic in
  Coleridge 136 n5
Librett, Jeffrey
  on poststructuralism and the
  sublime 37 n2
"Limbo"
  Coleridge's comment on as
  articulation of negative sublime
  1; irrationality and violence in 1;
  167 n27 *See also* Coleridge
Linearity
  25, 35, 36; in narrative: 51,
  50-53, 55, 57, 58, 132, 141;
  meaning given by as ground of
  conventional selfhood 147 *See
  also* Arrest, Cause and Effect,
  De Man, Jakobson, Bible,
Linking process
  2; aesthetic theories of in
  Schiller and Coleridge, Intro 3;
  abandonment of linking theory
  germinal to modern self 3; 4,
  49, 52, 55, 58, 59, 62, 64, 65,
  66, 116, 121, 122, 128, 131,
  132, 150
Lochhead, Marion
  166 n17
Locke, John
  21 n26; 31-2
Lockhart, John Gibson
  152, 136, n5
Longinus
  9, 11, 18, 141-143, 163
Lunacy
  62 *See also* Madness
Lyotard, Jean-François
  "Philosophy of Phrases" 37 n2;
  anti-social character of sublime
  as model of postmodernism 37

n2; lawlessness of sublime, 37
n2; *Begebenheit* (occurrence) of
sublime marking the postmodern
38-39, 39 n10; 73 n22; 11, 57,
153

Mackey, Louis
  on nonreferentiality of
  existentialism 164
Madness
  of specularity of negative
  sublime 32; and the imagination
  158; conscious form as *folie
  lucide* in romantic sublime 139
  n26 *See also* De Man, *Folie
  lucide*
Magic
  related to the senses in Coleridge
  135, n3; related to human
  understanding through the senses
  in Coleridge 135 n3;
  characteristic of the imagination
  in Coleridge 157-58; Coleridge's
  state in the *Biographia*, 159
Makkreel, Rudolf
  on Kant's use of *übersinnliches
  Substrat* 75 n34 *See also* Linda
  Marie Brooks, "Sublimity and
  Theatricality"
Mariner, the
  and Yeats's ancient sage 162; as
  Coleridge's double in *Rime of
  the Ancient Mariner* 161-62; 32;
  endless autofiguration of 33;
  128, 155, 161, 162
Material sublime
  in Schiller 113n *See also*
  Association of Ideas, Sublime:
  Kant's theory
Mathematical sublime
  20, 22, 45 n4 *See also* Sublime:
  Kant's theory

McFarland, Thomas
    on Coleridge's aversion to pantheism in Wordsworth and Schelling 137 n14; on bombast in Coleridge's aspiration to sublime poetry: 146-147, 166 n11
Meaning
    of sublime dependent on self's role in sublime experience 12; human 28; as alien 32; veil of in Schiller 33; despair of as sentimental-modern dilemma 33; telic 50; as relinquishing telos 50-51; informed by myth of totality 55; demystified dual form given by *folie lucide* 55; telic form of assured by beauty 57; 58, 88, 132, 142-144; linear form of as basis for conventional selfhood 147; 150, 153, 154, 158, 162
Mellers, Wilfred
    49, 50, 69 n2
Meredith, J. C.
    7 n2
Metamorphosis
    of poet's self as deliberate in Coleridge 159; of the self integral to romantic aesthetics 150; subject resulting from, contranatural 151; romantic form of entails forgetting of conventional self 151; entails dissimulation 151; of romantic poet resulting in *imposteur absolu* 151; 161, 162 *See also* Autoscopy, Frye, Other, Recognition Poems
Metaphor
    passed off as concept in Schiller's theory 84 *See also*
Lacoue-Labarthe, Dissimulation, Jakobson
Metaphysics
    carried by Coleridge into divinity 125; only religion in Coleridge 132
Method
    Kant's negative form of 30, 61-62; analogical in Kant 80; of compromise in Schiller, 95; 115, 118; trichotomous in Coleridge 123-4
Miller, J. Hillis
    51, 52, 70 n8; and the disappearance of God 73 n25; on orgasmic hyperbole in Shelley 148
Milton, John
    chaos in 27; Miltonic abyss 27-28; *Paradise Lost* 29n
Modiano, Raimonda
    on self's central role in the sublime 12; 70 n13
Monk, Samuel
    37 n2, on Addison as first to establish the sublime as distinct aesthetic category 39 n12; Coleridge's introduction of Kant's third *Critique* to English readers 40 n19
Moral law
    humiliates self-conceit: 19, 41 n24; threat to exaltation of self in Burke's sublime: 20, 19, 20, 34, 91
Morality
    symbolized by beauty in Kant 63; as denial of the senses in Kant 24-37; 15, 19, 25, 35; focus on primary theoretical problem in Kant's sublime 62; 63, 65; bridge model of a major

compromise of Schiller's *Kallias* theory of unified self 94; 100, 103, 114; 33, 55; postulates of 130
Mortal flux
implied by sublimity: 84, 85, 89
Mozart, Wolfgang Amadeus 49
Mysticism
in Wordsworth 119; Coleridge's view of Wordsworth's as sickly -- mere fog and dimness 119; Schiller' view of Schelling's as ignoring experience 122; 137 n14
Mystification
33, 55, 72 n2 *See also* de Man

Nature
opposed to contranatural in Coleridge 14n; excites ideas of the sublime 20; omnipotence of in Kant 24; 33, 55, 56, 58; realm of the concept of 60; formal purposiveness of: 63, 64, 66, 81; 71 n17 absolute indifference of 84; infinite, repetitive mortal flux of 84; subjective ideas in Schiller projected onto 87-89; heautonomy projected onto in Schiller 89
Negative sublime
nontranscendent 9; in Bloom: 9; as perverse zeal in 47 n49; in Weiskel: 8, 9, 28, 29, 31, 32, 56, 92, 98, 99, 132; inability of romantics to come to terms with 12; questioning art's representational function 11; disintegration of self in 12-13; irresolvable 13; Kant's "Analytic of the Sublime" a model of 13; compared to Burke's theory 15; in Kant 19-31; as romantic autofiguration 31-33; defeatist aesthetic 28; defeatist ethic 28; leads to existential alienation: 28, 36; transcendent dead-end 28; leads to suicide 28; pure expression found only in the Germans in Weiskel 28; missing phase three of sublime progress 29; isolating tendency in 31-2 *See also* Sublime
New Literary History
8 n2
Nicolson, Marjorie Hope
9, 56, 57, 143, 144, 149
Nihilism
absence of certification in the sublime a form of: 84, 89
Novalis (Friedrich, Freiherr von Hardenberg)
Coleridge's familiarity with 136 n5; *Heinrich von Ofterdingen* 136 n5

Oedipal revolt
in Bloom 32 n44; contrasted to existential resignation 32 n44
Oliphant, M.
166 n17
Origin
11, 30, 52, 54, 83, 86
Orsini, G. N. G.
on Kant's concept of the unity of transcendental apperception 44-45 n 43; 136 n5
Other
and metamorphosis 150; as subject debarred from natural 151; as subject that is a life unto itself 151; as alien 151; as

contranatural 151; as product of transformation, 151; as product of sublime's hyperbolic assault 151; as poet's alternative identity 151; poet's deliberate act of becoming 151; as mode of *übersetzen* 151; as displacement of annihilated self 151; process of becoming as leap over abyss or groundless space 151; as product of willful forgetting of annihilated self 151; as product of artistic dissimulation 151; as *imposteur absolu* 151; as death's head identity 152-53; as product of sublime 151-52; as product of sublimation of conventional self 152-53; as entailing death of conventional self 152-53; contrasted to exaltation of self in positive sublime 152-53; product of sublime's lawless law 153; as caput mortuum 153; as product of sublime's incomprehensibility 154; in Coleridge 155-60; the "Kubla Khan" poet as Coleridge 159; as Coleridge's alter-ego in the Mariner 159; romantic poet's other as subject of Recognition Poems 159-60; as Yeats's Ancient Sage: 160, 162; as "Limbo" blind man in Coleridge 161; Coleridge as the gray-haired passenger 161 *See also* Autoscopy, Mariner, Metamorphosis, The Pure Will (*Reiner Wille*)

Pain (*Unlust*)
of sublime as menace to self: 3, 7 n4; as delight in Burke 15; 17, 20, 61, 62, 64; component of Kant's sublime 3 n4; tinged with tranquility in Burke 18; "delightful" in Burke
Pater, Walter
recanting in favor of religion and morality 111 n37; compared to Schiller 111 n37; "Coleridge's Writings" 136 n7
Path
to Schiller's ideal self blocked by sublime 50; 58; endless form of toward ideal unified self in Schiller 100-103; 132, 157 *See also* Bridge, Linking Process
Paul, St.
contrasted to Spinoza in Coleridge 117 *See also* Spinoza
Peacock, Thomas Love
"Newark Abbey, August, 1842: With a Reminiscence of 1807" 69 n1
Piranesi, Giovanni Battista
ruins of 49; exemplary of romantic sublime art 49
Plato
11, 141
Play
as bridge model 36; beauty as sole object of in Schiller 85; as process of illusion 85; freedom of as delusion which Schiller projects onto phenomena 86; projected harmony of impossible 90; 95, 102, 103, 114, 115
Play drive (*Spieltrieb*)
as poet's shift to hyperbolic level 36; as process capable of fusing sense and reason 90; conflicting accounts of between actual harmonizer and mere mediator 95; abandoned in *Naive and Sentimental Poetry*: 102, 114;

INDEX

compared to Kant 83-85; man only fully man when he plays 85
Pleasure
  15; pleasant pleasure in Burke, 20; 20, 22, 23, 61-64, 92, 93, 104; negative form of in Kant 64; 112 n40
Poet
  2, 3, 20, 27, 28, 30-36; defiant 54; belated 54; begetting own perverse counter sublime 54; 55; self-delusion of in the sublime 89; 100-102, 116, 121, 122, 125; extremes meet in apperceptive identity of: 131, 132; sentimental-modern type avoids exaggeration only by ceasing to be a poet, 143; 144, 145, 149-151; sublimation and metamorphosis of: 149-64; 156, 157, 159, 161-163
Poole, Roger
  on Kierkegaard, 168 n30
Pope, Alexander
  waning of romantic linearity and abortive movement of *Dunciad* IV 52; absence of corrective stance in *Dunciad* IV 52
Positive sublime
  affirms and heightens subject's sense of self 12, 16-17; requires subject's self-consciousness 12; raises subject's self-estimation 18; 14 *See also* Sublime
Power
  2, 12; component of sublime in Burke 16; terror of consists in ability to hurt in Burke 16; effectiveness of in sublime dependent on danger 16; 14-17; observer participates in 18; almighty power of divine in Burke's sublime, 19; 19-23; imagination as blind but powerful function of the soul in Kant 26; 29, 54, 56, 83; originary power of dissimulation 84; 91, 114; imagination's power of reconciling opposites as 116; linking power of the imagination in Coleridge 117-21; 118, 119, 121, 124, 126, 129, 130, 132; metamorphic power of hyperbole 150-51; 156-159, 162
Process of the unsure
  as element of the sublime 83-89, 151 *See also* Uncertainty, Dissimulation
Pure will (*Reiner Wille*)
  as sublime figure of man's heautonomous pure will in Schiller 84; unfallen unity of 84; correlate to Freedom in Appearance 84; exists prior to aesthetic or ethical differentiation 84; harmonizes subject and obect 84; as myth taken for science in Schiller 84; as perversion of representation 84; product of *Verstellen*, 84; perversion of *Vorstellung* 84; foreshadows counter-identity of romantic sublime 85; as autofigurational abstraction in Schiller 85; compared to Wallace Stevens' Absolute Angel 85; as presence or thing in Schiller's system 85; as prelapsarian inner being 85; outstrips Kant dissimulation as philosophy of self 85; as primordial aspect of man's objective identity in Schiller 85; as prelapsarian alter-ego 90

See also The Beautiful soul
(*Schöne Seele*)
Purposiveness without purpose
(*Zweckmässigkeit ohne Zweck*)
63, 64, 66, 81

Rank, Otto
on the double (*Doppelgänger*)
167 n22 *See also* Autoscopy
Read, Sir Herbert
28, 104, 115, 128; *The True Voice of Feeling*; 132-33
Reason (*Vernunft*)
underscored by experience of incomprehensible 1; subordinates intellect (understanding) and imagination 13; as "foreign will" in Kant 15; as "secret power" in Kant 15; foreign to the subject in Kant 15; as internal sublimity 21; vast and supersensible power in Kant 21; comprehends infinity 21; concerned with the independence of the absolute totality 21
Recognition poems
158-59
Reconciling aesthetics
Schiller's and Coleridge's abandonment of germinal to romantic poetics 3; subverted by sublime 3; abandoned by Schiller 2: 79-112; abandoned by Coleridge: 2, 113-140
Reflection
19, 25, 50, 64, 81, 118, 130, 132, 146 *See also* Self-reflexive
Reiman, Donald
132; sublime's relation to existentialism 140 n32
Religion
as bridge 111 n36; 111 n37; as displacement of Schiller's model of aesthetic harmony, 98-100; displaces mediating imagination in Coleridge 119
Representation
dissimulation perverted form of 84; linear form of in bible: 51, 60 n6; relation to interaction between subject and object in the sublime, 139 n7
Representation of freedom
in Schiller 83 *See also* Illusion
Respect (*Achtung*)
in Kant's sublime: 21, 23, 45 n32; conflated with concept of fear 45 n33
Revulsion
component of Kant's sublime 3
Rogers, Robert
on visual hallucination of the physical self 167 n22; on the double 167, n28
Romantic poetics
dark side in negative sublime 11
Rousseau, G. S.
on pain in Burke 45 n22
Rule
26, 57, 64-66, 153
Rule of non-regulation
of the sublime: 57, 153
Ruskin, John
on subjects which ought to upset subject's balance and cause her to use hyperbole, 149

Sachs, Hans
Coleridge's knowledge of 136 n5
Said, Edward
30 n52 *See also* Beginnings
Salto mortale
as signal of imagination's limits in Coleridge 120; relation of to

INDEX

"*übersetzen*" 150; relation of to metamorphosis 170 *See also* Leap, Religion, Verticality

Satan
  Milton's version of 54; counter-sublime of compared to Schiller and Coleridge 54-55

Satire
  Pope's *Dunciad* IV as preromantic form of 52; absence of corrective stance in 52; lack of cause and effect progression in 52 *See also* Cause and Effect, Jakobson, Linearity

Schein
  82, 83, 86, 90, 95 *See also* Appearance

Schelling, F. W. J.
  26n; identifies necessity with freedom of deepest self 69 n2; on unity of apperception as transcendental reality or act of will 45 n46; recanting in favor of religion and morality contrasted to Schiller 111 n37; recanting in favor of religion and morality paralleled with Pater 111 n37; source of Coleridge's definition of the imagination 115; fusing imagination in 117; Coleridge's view of pantheism in 119; as source of Coleridge's fusion of subject and object 121; version of Kant's transcendental apperception in 121; transcendental apperception as absolute self-consciousness in 122; problems with Coleridge's application of 122; source of Coleridge's idea of dark adyt as mediating principle 122; source of Coleridge's idea of tertium aliquid as mediating principle; 122; higher form of knowledge of mediating self in 122; knowledge of mediating self capable of unifying world-self opposition in 122, 127; knowledge of mediating self abstractly opposed to understanding 122; problematic idealism of 122, 126-133; subject-object bridge in 122, 133; principles of unsuccessfully combined with Kant's in Coleridge 123-36; unsuccessfully used by Coleridge as base from which to appeal to Kant's negative qualities 123; irreconcilability with Descartes' phenomenological definition of truth in Coleridge 124; verbatim source of bulk of Coleridge's Ten Theses *Biographia* chapter 124; idealism of in Coleridge 124; need for firmer ground than, in Coleridge 125; absolute self in as finite and infinite 126; system in Coleridge aborted by Kantian principles 128-133; 136 n5

Schiller, J. C. Friedrich von
  "Detached Reflections on Different Questions of Aesthetics:" 13, 13 n14
  "Grace and Dignity:" 90, 92-94, 109 n23, 116
  "The Moral Utility of Aesthetic Manners:" 93
  "On the Necessary Limits of Beautiful Form:" 93
  "On the Pleasure We Derive from Tragic Objects:" 92, 93

"On the Vulgar and Low in Art:" 93
"Of the Sublime:" 9-11, 21, 53, 81, 101, 111 n34; 111 n35; 111 n36, 146
"On the Sublime:" 9, 11, 61, 99, 100, 102, 103, 141, 147, 163
"The Poetry of Life:" 35 n48
Naive and Sentimental Poetry: 38, 100-104; 112 n39
"The Stage as a Moral Institution:" 93
"*Philosophie der physiologie*:" 105 n5
"On the Connection between the Animal and Spiritual Nature in Man:" 105 n5
On the Aesthetic Education of Man: 82, 95, 96, 100-102;
"On the Pathetic:" 92
"The Homeric Hexameter:" translated by Coleridge 135 n3
"The Ovidian Hexameter:" translated by Coleridge 135 n3
"The Visit of the Gods:" translated by Coleridge 135 n3
"Genius with the Inverted Torch:" 100, 112 n38
Briefwechsel zwischen Schiller und Körner: 83
Wallenstein: translated by Coleridge 135 n3
Kallias Briefe (Kallias Letters): 82-86; divided into logical and empirical: divided into harmony versus bridge model 90
Attempted positive constructs of identity in 2; reconciling aesthetics in 3; on threat to the self in Kant 3; and link between sublime and romantic self-construction 3; theory of reconciling aesthetics basis of "sentimental" or "modern" identity 3; theory of sublime reflective of Kant's theory 11; problems with Kant's sublime: 11, 35; recuperative theory of aesthetics subverted by principles of Kant's sublime 12; as "Bard tremendous in sublimity" in Coleridge 84; aesthetic fantasies in 87; 84-88

Schlegel, A. W.
136 n5

Schlegel, Friedrich von
Coleridge's marginalia on *The Athenaeum* 136, n5

Schumann, Robert
49

Scott, Sir Walter
on Coleridge's translation of Schiller's *Wallenstein* as superior to Schiller's original 136 n5

Self
dependent on meaning 1; dilemma of related to the sublime 1; effect of incomprehensibility on 1; based on imaginative connections to empirical phenomena 2; overweening selfhood of romantic poet 2; dilemma of in romanticism 2; in Kant's sublime: 20, n23; disintegration of 12;

INDEX

fate of in Burke's positive sublime: 4; 17-19; exaltation of caused by imagination in Burke's sublime 19; fate of in positive and negative sublime contrasted 5; as romantic quest for unity with external world 7; exaltation of as affective representation in art 20; relation to objective world restored in phase three of positive sublime 33; poet's "conscious self" becomes "an intermediary 121; ironic two-fold 55; phenomenal 56; empirical alienated 71-2 n17; outward projection of in beauty 57; disenfranchised 57; night-like mine or pit of 57; as death's head: 152, 154, 155; metamorphosis of in hyperbolic moment 152-64; contranatural 151; sublimated by the imagination 154-60; as other: 151, 152, 154, 156, 159, 161, 162

In Kant: negative fate of in sublime 4; corporeal aspect "humiliated" in theory of sublime 15; humiliated as self-conceit by moral law 20 n23; 20; intellectual sacrifice of in sublime 25; subject a mere trifle in comparison to nature 26; abnegation of basis of morality in 27; no comprehensible relation to objective world 30; as act of unity of apperception: 26, 114, 121, 130, 132

In Coleridge: as one object in 9 n4; loss of in Coleridge's concept of the sublime 9 n4; as active, intransitive, sui generis verb 'I Am' 26 n33; effect on of associationist philosophy 152-53; as principium essendi (principle of being) 127; absolute form as self-conscious will 122; finite form of as absolute a bastard prosthesis 128

In Schiller: as dissimulated *Ich* 83-90; self-production of as *heauton*: 85, 86, 88; self-delusion 89; defined as "Being that wills" 82; unified identity of 82-86; fragmented 90-97 See also The Pure Will (*Reiner Wille*)

Self-conceit
and Kant's moral law 20 n 23; 20; 21-2; and egoistic judgments 22; and Kant 26-30;

Self-consciousness
26, 33, 121, 122, 125-127, 130, 131, 133; as transcendental apperception in Kant 26; as transcendental unity of apperception or 'I think' 121; basis of knowledge in Kant 26; 26 n38; *a priori* condition of all experience in Kant 26 n38; subverted in Kant's "Analytic of the Sublime" 27; given only subjective validity in Kant, 29, 29 n40; sacred form of identified as Being, not knowing, in early sections of Coleridge's Ten Theses 125; changed from absolute Being to human knowing in later sections of

Coleridge's Ten Theses 125;
knowledge of in Schelling's and
Coleridge's version as absolute
125; Schelling's form of both
finite and infinite 126; as causa
sui: father of himself, son of
himself 126
Self-construction
   3, 5, 27, 29
Self-delusion
   response to menace of sublime
   89
Self-loss
   in Coleridge's concept of the
   sublime 9 n4; a form of *ecstasis*
   in sublime 12-13
Self-reflexiveness
   32, 33, 131
Self-reflexive bridge
   131
Self-reflexive circle
   32
Senses
   as having an essential
   constructive part in the
   construction of the understanding
   in Coleridge 135 n3; essential
   nature to understanding related
   to magic in Coleridge, 13, 56 n3
   See also Body
Sentimental
   3, 13, 33-35, 94, 100-103, 116,
   145, 146, 150, 151, 161, 163
Sentimental identity
   subverted by the Kant's sublime
   3 *See also* Schiller
Shaftsbury, Anthony Ashley, third
Earl of
   sublime as a higher and more
   majestic beauty 72 n19
Shelley, Percy Bysshe
   narrative linearity disrupted in
"Triumph of Life" 52; orgasmic
hyperbole in "Epipsychidion"
148; bombast in "Ode to the
West Wind" 148
Shawcross, John
   121, 132, 140 n30
Silence
   Ajax as instance of sublime form
   of in Longinus 142; as affect of
   sublime specularity 32; 37
Silverman, Hugh
   42 n2
Smith, Joseph H.
   26, 27, 164
Snyder, Alice D.
   115, 135 n4
Solger, Karl Wilhelm Ferdinand
   136 n5
Solitude
   as living death in Coleridge 32;
   Ferguson on 37
Sparshott, F. E.
   on sublime as important aspect
   of the most outstanding
   encounters with the arts 9
Spatial projection of reality
   in romanticism 49-58
Specularity
   maddening 32; self-reflexive
   circle of 37; characteristic of the
   sublime 37; in Schiller 37-8; in
   Coleridge 38
Spinoza, Benedict de (Baruch)
   117; atheism of in Coleridge 136
   n8
Stevens, Wallace
   The Rock, as example of the
   counter-sublime 49 n49; "Notes
   Toward a Supreme Fiction" 85
Strong poet
   Bloom's definition discussed 32
   n44; Coleridge as 32 n44

INDEX

Sublimation
  as devastation of subject 152-155; metaphor of chemical reduction and associationist philosophy 152-54; 158, 159; of self intrinsic to romantic project in general 159-63; of subject in sublime moment unrelated to self's exaltation in Burke 162

Sublime
  As aesthetic term
    as "boundless or endless allness" in Coleridge 7; impossibility of rigorous definition 9 n6; excluded from aesthetics 9 n6; rejected as loosely descriptive adjective 9; as part of psychology 9 n6
  Negative aspects of
    menace of: 1, 3, 89; as signal of art's inherent conflict in Adorno 1n; related to irrationality and violence 1; threat to romantic poetics 1; lawlessness of 1; mytaphysical relationships sundered in 4; hostile relation to human will 9; aesthetic expression of skepticism 11; unrepresentability 12-13; hostile to human physical and cognitive capacity: 16, 27; positive and negative versions contrasted 11; alienation of 33; subversive of meaning 39; subversive of the beautiful 39; purpose to subvert reconciling aesthetics 33; abyssal incoherence of 38; secondary discourse of built on failure of reconciling aspects of beautiful 93; *Abgrund* or groundless space intrinsic to 10, 150, 161; as question of death: 152-54, 159; as transcendent dead-end 28
  And the self
    affect of incomprehensibility on 1; threat to arguments for ordering form of in subject ordering self 1; violence toward the self in Kant: 1, 3 n4, 20; link to romantic strategies of self-construction 4, 3, 5, 27, 29; the romantic self in 5; sublime's meaningless without relation of self to sublime object 12; pain of self-abnegation in Kant's theory 24; alienation in 33; Weiskel's three-phase progress of n33-4; at expense of empirical self 35-6; self's metamorphosis in hyperbolic moment of 152-64; romantic subject reduced in 152-54
  Burke's theory of
    and the divine 11; as thrilling 14; as "delightful horror" of 14; empirical character of: 15, 20, 20 n26
  Kant's theory of
    divisive 3; as "mere appendix to aesthetic judging:" 2, 3, 29, 34 n46, 62, 66, 81, 116; pain in: 3, 15, 17, 20, 61, 62, 64; "splendid sublime," and "noble sublime" in 14 n18;

impossibility of knowledge
in 15; moral resonance of
20; 20 n25; not a property
of the object in 21 n26;
"negative pleasure" of 20
n26, 24; pleasure of
compared to Burke's painful
delight 24-5; transcendental
character of 22;
mathematical and dynamic
sublime in: 20; 42 n30;
conflated in discussions of
Kant's sublime 43 n33;
incompleteness of 43 n33;
epistemological concern of
26; paradigm of self-denial
27; as appendix to The
Critique of Practical Reason
76 n39; as afterthought in
Kant's aesthetic theory;
moral focus of primary
cause of theory's failure 62

General
ascendance of as articulation
of conflict in art 1;
apocalyptic experience of as
construction of missing
ending and romantic poetics
36; romantic art 12; as
artistic representation:
16-17; in architectural
structures, 16; in natural
scenes 16; 21, 24, and
disappearance of linear
thought 5; anti-social
character as model of
postmodernism in Lyotard
37 n2; and representation
35; and poststructuralism 37
n2;. power in: 16, 22;
romantic form of: 31-35;
egotistical form 32;
three-phase process of: 33-4;
aesthetics not of identity but
of difference 36; as
precluding harmony 64;
initiated by process of
unsure 84-89; *salto mortale*
intrinsic to: 120, 150; as
abyss between Schelling and
Kant 130

Subreption
5; 28, 32; nature of beauty's
harmony 28

Suicide
28; in Schiller 33; 54, 98, 99,
103, 120 *See also* Negative
sublime

Superhuman
20-23, 31, 59-61, 63, 65, 66,
80, 81, 83-85, 87, 127;
unrepresentable 150; state of
sentimental existence 150-51

Supernatural
28, 128, 129

Supersensible
20-23, 31; determination of the
imagination 45 n34; 59-61, 63,
65, 66, 80, 81, 83-85, 87, 127

Supersensible substrate
(*übersinnliches Substrat*)
61 *See also* Makkreel, Wolff

Sussman, Henry
Psyche and Text 9 n2

Synesius
appealed to by Coleridge 117;
119, 127

Synthesis
blind but powerful function of
imagination in Kant 26

Telos
36, 57-59

INDEX

Temporality
29, 49, 50, 55, 61, 132
Terror
in Burke's sublime 14-15, 16, 19; external source in 22; in Kant's sublime 15, 21; internal source in 22, 23 n31; as awe in Kant 23 n31; 11, 14-18, 20, 21, 29; dissimulation as aesthetic response to: 84, 89; of human finitude as province of negative sublime 84; 11, 14-18, 20, 21, 29, 84, 89, 99
Tertium aliquid
third mediating principle: 139 n26; of imagination 128; of the self; 115, 122, 124, 128, 131, 132
Thing in itself (*Ding an sich*)
31, 87; as Noumenon in Coleridge 129
Thomas, Calvin
The Life and Works of Schiller 95, 180
Three-phase progress of sublimity 33; third phase missing in negative sublime 33-4;
Thyrsus
51, 52
Tieck, Ludwig
Coleridge's familiarity with *Phantasien* 136 n5
Totality
as "boundless or endless allness" in Coleridge" 1; recognized by reason in Kant: 2 n30, 21; 25; as idea of reason in Kant 27; command given by reason to discover the conditions of in Kant 25; undiscoverability of conditions of in Kant 25; as ideal maximum unattainable in

sensible world: 25, 45 n34; falling into myth of organic form of in de Man 55
Transcendental apperception
in Kant as original unchangeable consciousness 26; as self's consciousness of the identity of itself 26; 114, 121, 130, 132; entails absence of any means for verifying claims of knowledge 27 n40; given only subjective validity in Kant: 26-27, 27 n47; projected as a conscious act of will in Coleridge and Schelling 30 n41
Tyson, Bryan
on autoscopy, visual hallucination of the physical self 167 n22

Uncanny (*unheimlich*)
55, 85, 150, 151, 162 *See also* The Pure Will (*Reiner Wille*)
Unity
idea of in Kant 4; subverted by sublime: 4, 64; as logical 4; as imaginative 4; merely subjective in Kant 125; man's original natural form of in Schiller 100; as unfallen or prelapsarian nature in Schiller's figure of the Pure Will (*Reiner Wille*), 84; 3, 4, 9, 26, 52, 57, 60, 64, 66, 79, 84, 85, 89, 95, 96, 100-102, 113, 114, 118, 119, 120-122, 125, 130, 132, 156
Universality
as pluralistic validity in Kant 34; loses basis in the sublime 64-66
Unrepresentability
11, 13, 34, 147

Unsure
  81; process of: 84, 89; 151
Vacuity
  32, 56 See also Emptiness
Vastness
  in Burke's sublime 16; 18, 20,
  56
Verticality
  in romanticism: 5, 49-60; role in
  romantic self-construction 5;
  and hyperbolic self-construction
  5; 53, 54, 56, 57, 58, 141, 142;
  as aesthetics 148 See also
  Hyperbole
Violence
  in "Limbo" 1; possible
  characteristic of original imagery
  1; toward the self in Kant's
  sublime 3; toward the self as
  purposive in regarding the whole
  mind 7 n4, 20

Wackenroder, W. H.
  Coleridge's familiarity with the
  Phantasien 136 n5
Ware, Malcome
  on sublime as loosely descriptive
  adjective 38 n6
Warfare
  imagery of in Schiller's account
  of sublime 110 n28; battle
  imagery in Schiller's challenge
  of Kant's sublime 111 n28
Wasserman, Earl
  de Man on Wasserman's claim
  for Coleridge as reconciler of
  subject and object 138 n26
Weiskel, Thomas
  systematic focus on sublime
  transcendence in 9; on negative
  sublime: 28; theory of compared
  to Burke 29; three-phase
  progress of the sublime 29;
  compared to Kant 31; 38 n3; on
  sublime soarings 56; beauty's
  failure as secondary discourse of
  sublime 92; suicide in the
  sublime 98; underestimates
  self-annihilative character of
  Schiller's sublime 99
Wheeler, Kathleen
  122-127, 131, 132, 138 n19
Wieland, Christoph Martin
  and Schiller's poetry: 86, 136 n5
Wilkinson, Elizabeth
  105 n5, 109 n27, 111 n37, 136
  n6
Wimsatt, William
  on the sublime as forerunner of
  existentialism 132
Wlecke, Albert
  9 n2
Wolff, Robert Paul
  59-61, 74 n31; on Kant's mixed
  metaphor "*übersinnliches
  Substrat*" 75 n34
Wordsworth, William
  The Prelude: linear progression
  disrupted in 52; 145, 148
  "Tintern Abbey:" 119
  Immortality Ode: 119
  Lyrical Ballads: 145, 156
  Egotistical sublime in 28; 46
  n49; self-representation in: 52,
  70 n10; pantheism in 119 *See
  also* Albert Wlecke, Paul Jay

Yaeger, Patricia
  on female version of sublime 1
  n2
Yeats, William Butler
  "Sailing to Byzantium:" 160,
  162 "Byzantium:" 160, 162

Sublime in Last Poems of and romantic sublime 32 n44; alter-ego of ancient sage in and Coleridge's Mariner 115, 162; autoscopic transformation in compared to Coleridge 160-62.

Young, Edward
Night Thoughts compared by Wieland to Schiller's poem on origin and progress of art 86